מסורה

ArtScroll Judaiscope Series

Rabbi Nosson Scherman / Rabbi Meir Zlotowitz

General Editors

SHIDDUCHIM

Published by

Mesorah Publications, ltd

in conjunction with

Agudath Israel of America

SHALOM BAYIS AND BEYOND

BUILDING A BAYIS NE'EMAN B'YISROEL

Collected from the pages of
The Jewish Observer

by Rabbi Nisson Wolpin
Editor

FIRST EDITION
First Impression … November 2005

Published and Distributed by
MESORAH PUBLICATIONS, LTD.
4401 Second Avenue / Brooklyn, N.Y 11232

Distributed in Europe by
LEHMANNS
Unit E, Viking Business Park
Rolling Mill Road NE32 3DP
Jarow, Tyne & Wear,
England

Distributed in Israel by
SIFRIATI / A. GITLER
6 Hayarkon Street
Bnei Brak 51127

Distributed in Australia and New Zealand by
GOLDS WORLD OF JUDAICA
3-13 William Street
Balaclava 3183, Vic., Australia

Distributed in South Africa by
KOLLEL BOOKSHOP
Shop 8A Norwood Hypermarket
Norwood 2196, Johannesburg, South Africa

ISBN:
1-4226-0025-4 (hard cover)

Typography by CompuScribe at ArtScroll Studios, Ltd.
Printed in the United States of America by Noble Book Press Corp.
Bound by Sefercraft, Quality Bookbinders, Ltd., Brooklyn N.Y. 11232

Table of Contents

III. Preparing for Marriage

IV. The Wedding Celebration

CONTRIBUTORS
TO THIS VOLUME

Rabbi Yitzchok Berkowitz heads the Jerusalem Kollel in Sanhedria Murchevet, as well as the network of Linas Hatzeddek Night Kollelim in *Eretz Yisroel*. He is co-author of *Chofetz Chaim: A Lesson A Day*.

Rabbi Avrohom Birnbaum is an educator in Lakewood, NJ, a regular columnist for *Hamodia*, and a frequent contributor to *The Jewish Observer*.

Rabbi Mordechai Biser, an alumnus of Yeshiva Rabbi Chaim Berlin, is Associate General Counsel of Agudath Israel of America, and gives occasional *shiurim* to *chassanim* and older singles on marriage and *shalom bayis*.

Rabbi Matis Blum compiles and edits *Torah Lodaas,* a weekly compendium of commentaries on the *Parsha*, which has been appearing regularly for the past twenty three years. He also lectures in various Bais Yaakov high schools in the New York area.

Zelda Cutler is a writer and photographer who lives in Spring Valley, NY.

Ariella Davidson is a freelance writer living in the New York area.

Rabbi Shimon Finkelman, a *rebbe* in Yeshiva Darchei Torah, Far Rockaway, NY, is the author of several biographies published by ArtScroll Mesorah Publications, as well as the recent *More Shabbos Stories.*

Rabbi Jeff Forsythe is a specialist in human relations and self-development. He writes for Jewish publications on interpersonal relations.

Rabbi Shlomo Furst, who was a *talmid* of Rabbi Chaim Pinchos Scheinberg of Yeshiva Torah Ore for fifteen years, serves as *Mashgiach* of Kollel Ruach Chaim in Jerusalem.

Rabbi Shmuel Gluck is director of Areivim, an organization that offers Jewish youth advice and assistance with a wide array of support systems. He lives in Monsey, NY.

Rabbi David Gottlieb, a member of the faculty of Yeshiva Ohr Somayach in Jerusalem, lectures on Torah topics in Israel as well as virtually in every English-speaking country on the globe.

Mrs. Faiga Koenig lives in Jerusalem

Mrs. Chana Levin lives in Jerusalem.

Rabbi Aaron Lopiansky, author of *Time Pieces*, a collection of essays on the Festivals, is *Rosh Beis Midrash* in the Yeshiva of Greater Washington.

Shia Markowitz of Monsey, NY, a partner of The Goldmark Group, which has been designing *The Jewish Observer* and preparing it for publication for close to thirty years, is active in communal affairs.

Sara Medwed counsels and lectures on Jewish marriage and family. She assisted her husband in writing *Together We Are One — Making Marriage Work* (Feldheim Publishers), and they have jointly created the Together We Are One Center for Marital and Family *Hadracha*.

Dr. Judith Mishell Ph.D. is on the faculty of the Moreshet Institute at the Neve Yerushalayim and maintains a private practice in Yerushalayim.

Mr. Shaya Ostrov is a trained marital and family therapist. He is the author of *The Inner Circle, Seven Gates to Marriage* (Feldheim), and voluntarily serves as the Director of Training for Invei Hagefen.

Rabbi Avrohom Pam זצ"ל, a *rebbi* in Mesivta Torah Vodaath for over 65 years, most recently as *Rosh Hayeshiva*, was a member of the *Moetzes Gedolei Hatorah* (Council of Torah Sages) of Agudath Israel of America.

Rabbi Yaakov Perlow שליט"א, the Novominkser Rebbe, heads Yeshivas Novominsk Kol Yehuda in Brooklyn, is a member of the *Moetzes Gedolei Hatorah* (Council of Torah Sages) of Agudath Israel of America and serves as Rosh Agudas Yisroel.

Pnuel Peri is a writer and translator living in Jerusalem, and a frequent contributor to *The Jewish Observer*.

Rabbi Yisroel Reisman serves as *Rav* of Agudath Israel of Madison in the Flatbush section of Brooklyn, says a *shiur* in the *beis midrash* of Mesivta Torah Vodaath, and delivers a highly popular weekly *shiur* on *Navi*.

Dr. Yosef S. Rosenshein Ph.D. is in private practice of child and family counseling. He is Director Emeritus of the Jewish Board of Family and Children's Services in Mishkon, Chairman of the Professional Committee of P'tach, consultant for Rofeh Cholim Cancer Society, and Community Therapies.

Rabbi Matisyahu Salomon שליט״א, formerly *Mashgiach* of the Yeshiva in Gateshead, is currently *Mashgiach* of Beth Medrash Govoha in Lakewood, NJ.

Dr. Yaakov Salomon CSW, a psychotherapist in private practice in Brooklyn, is a frequent contributor to *The Jewish Observer*, and co-authored *What the Angel Taught You* (Shaar Press).

Rabbi Zvi Schachtel, originally from Melbourne, Australia, lived in Yerushalayim, studying in the Mir Yeshiva and teaching at several schools, in particular at Neve Yerushalayim. He has been residing in Monsey, NY, for the last fifteen years, and at this writing (2001) had completed sixty-four *shidduchim.*

Dr. Sylvan Schaffer J.D., Ph.D. is an attorney and clinical psychologist, who practices both law and psychology, and is affiliated with NYU, Einstein Medical School, and Hofstra Law School.

Rabbi Chaim Pinchas Scheinberg שליט״א is founder and *Rosh Yeshiva* of Yeshiva Torah Ore in Jerusalem, and a senior member of the *Moetzes Gedolei Hatorah* (Council of Torah Sages) in Israel.

Chaim Shapiro ז״ל, of Baltimore, who wrote about life in pre-War Europe, often focusing on great Torah personalities of the time, was a frequent contributor to *The Jewish Observer*. Two books of his reminiscences have been published, *Go My Son* (Feldheim) and *Once Upon a Shtetl* (ArtScroll/Mesorah).

Rabbi/Professor Aaron D. Twerski, a member of the Editorial Board of *The Jewish Observer*, is Dean of the Law School of Hofstra University, and serves as chairman of the board of Agudath Israel of America's Commission on Legislation and Civic Action.

Rabbi Ephraim Wachsman serves as *Rosh Hayeshiva* of Yeshivas Meor Yitzchok and *Rav* of Congregation Ahavas Torah in Monsey, NY.

Dr. Meir Wikler, A.C.S.W./ D.S.W. is a psychotherapist in private practice of individual, marital and family counseling. Many of Dr. Wikler's articles that are featured in this volume appeared in varying formats in his books: *Bayis Ne'eman B'Yisroel: Practical Steps to Success in Marriage* (Feldheim, 1988), *Partners with Hashem: Effective Guidelines for Successful Parenting* (ArtScroll 2000), and *Ten Minutes A Day to a Better Marriage: Getting Your Spouse to Understand You* (ArtScroll, 2003).

Rabbi Shlomo Wolbe זצ"ל, author of *Alei Shur* and other works, was one of the leading *Mussar* figures of the past generation. Founder of Yeshivas Be'er Yaakov in *Eretz Yisroel*, which he headed with Rabbi Moshe Shmuel Shapiro for over thirty years, he more recently was the *menahel ruchani* of Yeshivas Givat Shaul and of Jamie Lehmann Bais Hamussar in Jerusalem.

Shidduchim Shalom Bayis and Beyond

Please allow light and gladness, peace and companionship to dwell in this home, and bestow abundant blessing and holiness in all of its rooms and corners, and may the illumination of your holy Torah and your commandments shine there always, amen.

OVERVIEW

E very person is created *betzellem Elokim* — in G-d's image. Yet one does not fully realize this noble design until he or she marries. In fact, before *Hashem* created Chava, He described Adam's status as "*Lo tov* — It is not good for man to be alone" (*Bereishis* 2,18). This sense of incompletion flows from a source deeper than unmet emotional or biological needs. It reflects a spiritual vacuum, something essential that is lacking in one's *neshama* — a longing that finds expression on many levels. Only through marrying did Adam and Chava attain the status of "good." And the same prevails for all their progeny.

This crucial subject must be viewed from a Torah perspective, for how else can one build a *Bayis Ne'eman BeYisroel* — a Jewish home that is true to its sacred calling, one that reflects its holy sources, and will bear fruit in a way that brings pride and hope to our people?

In the past, one studied sacred texts and absorbed relevant guidance and values from the very air breathed in the classic Jewish home. Today, however, we are faced with a growing number of singles who are searching unsuccessfully for their predestined *zivug* (mate). In addition, the number of homes beset with *shalom bayis* problems (lack of harmony) is also rising. How can we reduce these problems, and enhance the *shalom* of our homes?

Thus this book, culled from the pages of *The Jewish Observer*, is dedicated to promoting *shidduchim* and improving *shalom bayis*, based on guidance from Torah personalities who draw their insights from the words of *Chazal*, and the observed actions and attitudes expressed by their *Rebbe'im* — their mentors, whose every gesture and remark reflected Torah values. Many of the articles in this issue are based completely or in part on their own words — including those of Rabbi Avraham Pam, Rabbi Shlomo Wolbe, and Rabbi Chaim Friedlander זצ"ל, as well as יבדל"ח Rabbi Chaim Pinchas Scheinberg and Rabbi Matisyahu Salomon, שליט"א. In addition, others with years of experience in the field were also invited to contribute to this issue.

We are told that a *Bas Kol* (Heavenly Voice) proclaims who will marry whom forty days before a child is formed in the womb. Destiny is proclaimed, but unfortunately the road to finding that preordained mate is often long and rocky. In addition to wise guidance from Torah mentors — for both men and women — *halacha* directives for how to search for information about *shidduch* prospects, and how to provide it to those who require it, must be scrupulously honored. Irrelevant, subjective, distorted, or gratuitously harmful data must be avoided at all costs. And at the same time, some facts must be shared. Guidelines are offered in several of the articles in these pages.

And the principals need encouragement, compassion and counsel … from parents, peers, mentors, and, on occasion, professionals … guided, to be sure, in concept and practice by Torah values.

We should all bear in mind that when we face the Heavenly Tribunal after our years on this world are completed, one of the questions we must answer is, "*Osakta be'friya u'reviya?* Did you fulfill your obligation to be fruitful and multiply?" (*Shabbos* 31a) The *Maharsha* (ad loc.) explains this to mean: "Were you involved in matching up couples? Were you sympathetic to single people, helpful in setting up *shidduchim* for them, supporting them in making their crucial decisions?"

In preparing this volume, we endeavored to consult seasoned and successful practitioners who have been involved in what we call The *Shidduch* Process, to shed light on the needs of our singles, and how best to meet them.

Similarly, in projecting the goal of establishing and maintaining the much glorified — and much envied — classic Jewish home, we are presenting selected writings and lectures from leaders and teachers of Torah, as well as from mentors and professionals in marriage counseling — the better to help the reader to envision, promote and achieve *shalom bayis*.

May the thoughts expressed in this book be an impetus for all who read them to engage in a positive response to our calling, bringing all our people's children to fulfillment in building a *Bayis Ne'eman BeYisroel*.

Rabbi Nisson Wolpin
Editor, *The Jewish Observer*

APPROACHING SHIDDUCHIM

The Talmud teaches that Hashem decrees "The daughter of So-and-So is destined to marry So-and-So." How does one properly reach out to this Hashgacha? What are one's priorities in seeking one's zivug (partner in life)? What are one's obligations? And what may one say – and not say – when it comes to shidduchim?

Shidduchim
Where Heaven and Earth Meet
Based On A Lecture Delivered
By Rabbi Matisyahu Salomon שליט״א
Mashgiach Of Bais Medrash
Govoha, In Lakewood, NJ

❊ In the Path of the Patriarchs

The Torah describes in great detail *Avraham Avinu*'s approach to finding a match for his son Yitzchak. Many relevant lessons can be learned from this entire episode.

The Torah relates how Avraham summoned Eliezer and made him swear by "the G-d of Heaven and Earth" that he would only take a wife for Yitzchak from Avraham's own family in Charan. (See *Bereishis* 24,3.) In his commentary on this *pasuk*, Rabbeinu Bachya asks why Avraham insisted that Eliezer take an oath, particularly in light of the fact that Eliezer was Avraham's most trusted servant – he administered Avraham's entire fortune and was in charge of all of his master's affairs. Moreover, Eliezer was the main transmitter of Avraham's teachings to the world. In fact, *Chazal* explain the words of the Torah, "*mosheil bechol asher lo* – he [Eliezer] ruled over all that was his" (*ibid.*, v. 2) in the sense that Eliezer had the same complete control over his own *yeitzer hara* (inclinations) as did *Avraham Avinu*. Why then would Avraham find it necessary to make him swear? Surely, he could trust him to follow his instructions and find the proper *shidduch* for Yitzchak!

This story raises even more questions. Why did *Avraham Avinu* choose to seek a wife for Yitzchak in Charan, his birthplace? *Ramban* states that Avraham had attracted tens of thousands of students whom he had inculcated with belief in *Hashem*. He painstakingly built an entire community dedicated to the service of *Hashem*; indeed, the *pasuk* refers to him, *"N'si Elokim* – a Prince of G-d." Yet, he did not choose a wife for Yitzchak from this exemplary *kehilla*. Rather, he chose to send his servant to seek out a match in Charan from his own family, who were outright idol-worshippers. From the wording of the Torah, *Chazal* deduce that, upon Eliezer's arrival at the home of Lavan, Lavan had to reassure him that he had removed all idols from the house so he could enter. Why then did *Avraham Avinu* not seek a *shidduch* from among his pious students, his *kehilla*, all of whom had become monotheists?

❧ The Power of *Middos Tovos*

Abarbanel explains that although Avraham's family were idol worshippers, they inherently possessed *middos tovos*, positive character traits in their very blood. It was these traits that Avraham had wanted his own descendants to possess. His *talmidim*, on the other hand, were descendants of Canaan, whom the Torah refers to as cursed. Despite their belief in *Hashem*, their inherent character traits were deficient and Avraham knew that his progeny would not be suitable for being the forebears of the Jewish nation (*Klal Yisroel*) if they were to have the *middos* of Canaan in their genes.

We can thus understand the common aphorism often cited in regard to *shidduchim*, "If the choice is between *'frumkeit'* and *middos*, *middos* take precedence." At risk of being misunderstood, let me explain: *Emuna* is certainly the foundation of *Yiddishkeit*. Without *emuna* – without being *frum*, which is a by-product of *emuna* – a person possessing the finest *middos* is still a "lost soul" in a religious sense. That aphorism about *frumkeit* and *middos* refers to a person in possession of sterling traits who enters the "House of *Avraham Avinu*," a house permeated with *emuna*. He will eventually become a *maa-*

min, a believer. Somebody who has *emuna*, however, but lacks the requisite positive character traits, will have a much more difficult time changing his inherent negative *middos*, even when exposed to an atmosphere where *middos tovos* are the norm. For unlike *emuna* or *frumkeit*, which can be more easily acquired on their own, *middos* are largely inborn and are therefore difficult to learn and acquire later in life. It is for this reason that when choosing a *shidduch*, *middos* is stressed over *frumkeit*.

Rabbeinu Bachya explains *Avraham Avinu*'s concern over *middos* in a similar manner, and concludes his discussion by mentioning the Sephardic custom of taking out the Torah and reading the *Parsha* of *Chayei Sarah* to a groom on his wedding day. This is to remind the groom to contemplate *Avraham Avinu*'s approach to finding a partner for his son Yitzchak: He too should not marry for beauty, money or honor, but rather for the sake of Heaven, and take pains to choose a wife from a worthy family. This, he explains, is why the Torah relates many instances of people marrying within their own extended families, as did *Avraham Avinu*, and Amram in marrying Yocheved, his aunt. Marrying a person from one's own surroundings and background will help ensure mutual understanding, compatible goals, and a harmonious relationship.

❖ *A Person Alone is Incomplete*

Rabbeinu Bachya goes out of his way to emphasize that one should marry for the sake of heaven. Why this special emphasis in the case of marriage? After all, the *Mishna* in *Avos* declares, "*All of your deeds should be for the sake of Heaven.*"

To explain this point, we will return to Avraham's insistence that Eliezer swear by the "G-d of Heaven and Earth." *Ibn Ezra*, in a cryptic comment, which he calls a "secret of the Torah (*sod*)," states that the reason for this oath is found in the Talmud's dictum: "Forty days before a fetus is conceived, a *Bas Kol* (Heavenly voice) calls out and says 'the daughter of *Ploni* (so-and-so) to *Ploni*.'" The *Avi Ezer* explains that in order to understand the cryptic words of *Ibn*

Ezra, one must study *Rashi's* explanation on the *pasuk* in *Bereishis* (2,18), in which *Hashem* says, "It is not good for Man to be alone. I will make him a helpmate opposite him." *Rashi* explains, "So that they should not say that there are two authorities. *Hashem* is unique in higher realms and has no mate, and Man is unique in the lower realms, and he too has no mate." *Rashi* implies that if Man were left without a partner on earth, he would become so filled with self-importance, that he would view himself as a god. That is why *Hashem* created a partner for Man. Creation of the human female, however, differed from the female of all other species, in that she was made from Man himself and was therefore a part of him. In all other species, the male and female are completely independent of each other; the only purpose of the female is to propagate the species.

There is yet another important dimension to their creation. Man was created so weak that he could not manage alone in this world. He and his partner are completely dependent on each other to navigate the vicissitudes of life. Why didn't *Hashem* make the human a super-being, with the ability to do everything – learn, earn a living, cook, bring up children, and so on? *Rashi* is telling us that if a person would possess such capacities, able to perform all tasks himself, he would think of himself as a *yachid b'olamo* – a singular power in this world. Man must realize that he cannot do everything on his own.

Marriage is the means for bringing a person to completion, so that he can achieve his ultimate goal: Each spouse is intended to complete the other, to enable the two together to overcome their inherent inadequacies. Were the aim of marriage to be no more than simply providing a vehicle to propagate the human race, *Hashem* could have created humans similar to animals, who have little to do with one another. Rather, *Hashem* intended that each person help his or her mate achieve their assigned goals through understanding each other's needs, and overcoming obstacles so as to realize these goals. This is what the *pasuk* indicated with the comment: "It is not good for Man to be alone."

❧ *"Bashert"* – Its Meaning and Implications

This concept can be developed further by examining the term *"bashert* – predestined" and its implications. It is commonly assumed that when it comes to *shidduchim*, everybody has a *"ba shert*," a predestined partner whom he (and she) must find. But, is not everything in the world also predestined? Why is this only singled out in regard to *shidduchim*?

In fact, the Talmudic source for this concept is, "Forty days before conception, a Heavenly Voice proclaims, 'the daughter of *Ploni* for *Ploni.*'" But that Talmudic statement continues, saying the same regarding "the house of *Ploni* to *Ploni*... [and] the field of *Ploni* to *Ploni*...." The same Heavenly Voice that declares whom one will marry also proclaims which house one will live in, and which field one will acquire. These too are *"bashert."* This concept can also be seen from the *Gemora* that states: "Before one is born, it is declared whether he will be wise or foolish, strong or weak, poor or rich..." (*Nidda* 30a). If everything about the person is predestined, it would seem that even before a person is born, his circumstances are so molded that there is little room to improve or regress. Why did *Hashem* create Man this way?

We recognize, of course, that at the moment of a child's birth, a soul is sent into its body to fulfill a specific mission. The soul has a complement of tools necessary to achieve that purpose. *Chazal* are telling us that a person is provided with all that he needs to succeed in his mission in this world. If the person is to become a *talmid chacham*, he is provided with the requisite intelligence. If he is to become a *baal tzeddaka*, he is provided with the necessary wealth, and so on. Similarly, it is difficult to achieve one's purpose without a place to live; thus the *Bas Kol* declares the assignment of "the house of *Ploni*." And the same applies to *Bas Ploni* – one's spouse, for a spouse is an integral part of one's life, without whom he would not be able to act out in his assigned role in life. All of the above factors mentioned in the *Gemora*, including *Bas Ploni* – the person who will be one's life partner – are integral components in enabling an individual to achieve the specific purpose for which he was created.

This is where "marriage for the sake of Heaven" comes into play. When a person lives his life with the objective that he must achieve the purpose for which he was sent into the world, he will approach marriage with that role in mind. When seeking a helpmate, his criteria will be based on "which person will enable me to achieve my purpose?" If one becomes sidetracked from what his focus should be, and concentrates on extraneous matters – such as beauty, wealth or honor – he is in effect losing sight of the purpose for which marriage was created. The Heavenly Voice that declares *Bas Ploni to Ploni*" is saying that each partner has the potential to enable the other to achieve the ultimate purpose for which he and she were created. Herein lies the deeper meaning of the *pasuk,* "It is not good for Man to be alone." While alone, a person cannot achieve this ultimate purpose; it is only the proper helpmate who can bring him to this goal.

It was for this reason that *Avraham Avinu,* despite having entrusted Eliezer with his entire spiritual and material fortune, insisted that he swear "by the G-d of Heaven and Earth," when seeking Yitzchak's intended wife.

❧ Fulfilling One's Mission on Earth

The realm of *shidduchim* is the point where Heaven and earth meet. The ultimate purpose for which each and every person was created has been decreed in Heaven, but it is on earth that it must fulfilled, with the help of the proper helpmate. Heaven has decreed how he will be able to achieve his purpose on earth.

If Eliezer did not swear, and Yitzchak did not get the wife who was right for him, Yitzchak might not have fulfilled his own purpose, and as a result, *Klal Yisroel* as a whole would ultimately not achieve the purpose that *Hashem* had designed for them.

That is why *Hashem* created Chava, the first woman, from Adam himself. Each spouse must be able to completely understand the other, as if they were part of a larger unit. Without this deep, inner connection and innate understanding of each other, they would not be capable of achieving completion, reaching their ultimate purposes.

When seeking proper life partners for ourselves and our children, let us bear in mind the Torah's lessons on *shidduchim*: to seek a partner for the sake of Heaven. Let us focus on finding the person with whom one will be able to accomplish here on earth the purpose that was predestined for each in Heaven.

Rabbi Matisyahu Salomon שליט"א
on Shidduchim and Marriage

❧ *Introduction*

The *Shechina* dwells in the Jewish home, we are told. In fact, the two letters that distinguish the Hebrew words for man and woman – the letter "*Yud*" in the איש (man) and the "*Hey*" of אשה (woman) – combine to form the Divine Name of *Yud* and *Hey*: *Kah*. Without them, each word spells אש – fire: fires of passion, perhaps, at the onset, but ultimately fires of destruction. In a Torah-inspired home, however, the husband and the wife, together, form a basis for the *Shechina*.

The goals of setting up a *Bayis Ne'eman BeYisroel* – a home that resonates with *kedusha* (sanctity) and would be comfortable hosting the Divine Presence – may, at first blush, seem too daunting a task to entrust to a young man and woman who may (or may not yet) be barely out of their teens. Yet, *Chazal* have told us that "At eighteen one is destined for the *chupa*." Moreover, young people usually also possess fires of idealism, which can truly equip them to embark on such an ambitious undertaking.

This extremely challenging task can be brought more within the reach of a young couple if they have access to a mentor who possesses the requisite Torah-based knowledge and experience to guide them in this most crucial of life's undertakings.

The Jewish Observer thus submitted several questions to Rabbi Matisyahu Salomon שליט"א, *Mashgiach* of Bais Medrash Govoha in Lakewood NJ, formerly *Mashgiach* of the Yeshiva in Gateshead, for his comment.

The questions, with the *Mashgiach's* responses, follow:

I. **JO:** What are the important points one should research before entering a *shidduch*?
(a) Which should take priority? Are there any areas that can – or should – wait until later?
(b) Should finances be discussed before the couple meet, or can this wait until after initial meetings, when they are progressing toward making a commitment?

Rabbi Salomon: (a) Of course, there are universal concerns that everyone cares about: the prospective partner's health, family, *chinuch*.... Beyond that, a person should inquire about those aspects of the prospective *shidduch* that are important to him or her. An objective checklist is not about to follow; personal leanings and preferences count.

If a young man or woman is reading these lines in hope of finding definitive guidance in terms of which character traits are more or less important, may I suggest that at the threshold of seeking a *shidduch*, this type of search is several years overdue. For this very reason, when presenting a *shmuess* to young men of *shidduch* age, I do not offer advice as to which *middos* one should look for. There is no point in imposing my standards on someone else. It will not be helpful to them and, in the long run, it can prove counterproductive: Shmuel or Velvel will not find happiness with a wife who meets my criteria, if he does not share those same standards in his personal life.

This specific type of "preparation" for marriage should begin several years in advance of involvement in *shidduchim*. Ideally, the young *bachur* and girl should have mentors who help them formulate his and her personal goals in *middos* and character development. After that, on the basis of one's personal roster of desirable traits (and those that should be avoided), one can project a profile of the type of person one is looking for as an ideal mate. But one should not go shopping with a list that does not reflect one's personal goals. The list must reflect one's own *chinuch*.

(b) While a prospective couple will generally decide to go through with a *shidduch* after meeting with each other, and feeling secure in their choice of *zivug*, there are certain conditions in terms of background, level of observance, family, and future intentions that are to be met. These objective issues – including financial obligations – should be clarified before the couple invests time and emotional involvement in a face-to-face meeting.

This prerequisite was conveyed orally by the Chofetz Chaim זצ"ל to Rabbi Elchonon Wasserman הי"ד, as reported by Reb Elchonon in private correspondence:

> "*I heard from the holy mouth of the Chofetz Chaim* זצ"ל *that the common practice in shidduchim, to meet with each other before any prior discussion, is improper. It would be appropriate to postpone the personal meeting until all investigations and expectations are concluded and all negotiations between the two sides are resolved. Then, after that, when everything is agreed upon in all its details, then they can meet – but not before.*"

II. **JO:** How does a *bachur* who would like to devote a number of years to learning after the *chasuna* reconcile conflicting concerns of (a) meeting basic financial needs, (b) *bitachon*, (c) *mentschlichkeit*, (d) finding his true *zivug*?

Rabbi Salomon: One must think realistically in terms of minimum needs, and stop there. To escalate one's financial frame of reference to a "wish list," which become "expectations," and then are presented as "demands" is demeaning for all concerned. It also carries the risk of crossing the line into being "A person who marries a woman for monetary reasons."[1] Ideally, money should not even enter the equation when choosing a spouse, but we live in *bedi'eved*, less-than-perfect circumstances. As a result, entering a marriage with the intention of devoting oneself to full-time Torah study requires a degree of financial security, beyond typical *kollel* stipends, in keeping with "If there is no *kemach* (bread), there is no Torah." This, of course, may also involve the young man's engaging in some tutoring, the wife's teaching, and so on, to supplement the committed amounts of support. With these and other sources of support in place, the search should then focus exclusively on the quality of the individual, *not* on the size of the dowry.

In sum, financial considerations should encompass two elements: they should be formulated on a basis of *mistapek bemu'at* – a minimum standard of living – and be received with *hakoras hatov* – a deep sense of gratitude to whoever provides the support.

III. JO: Should parents of a prospective *shidduch* meet before the young couple does?

Rabbi Salomon: When such a meeting is feasible, it has many advantages – especially to help the principals resolve their doubts. When one or the other member of the prospective *shidduch* gets last-minute cold feet, a note of encouragement from his or her parents based on the pre-*shidduch* meeting can be crucially reassuring.

IV. JO: Is there a minimum number of times a couple should meet before they make a commitment? A maximum, after which they should be ready to make a decision without further meetings?

Rabbi Salomon: The couple should continue to meet each other until they feel reasonably confident in their choice, based on shared goals and appreciation of each other's company. It is ridiculous to hope to work out every detail of their projected relationship in advance, and to expect to do so is an exercise in futility.

V. JO: To what do you attribute the rising rate of divorces in *Chareidi* circles?

Rabbi Salomon: A key element in a successful marriage is *savlonus* – forbearance. After all, a marriage brings together two unique individuals, from different backgrounds, and of different genders

– which, of course, expresses itself in emotional and spiritual make-up and needs, as well as in disparate educations and different roles in the life of each. A successful marriage is thus a learning process. This is viable when the members view themselves as partners in an undertaking, with each yielding to the other partner more often than not. Should a person enter marriage with the single goal of self-gratification, with an agenda of "I'm in this for me," it is doomed to failure.

This focus on self-gratification – physical pleasure and emotional fulfillment – is often the product of oversimplified lectures or literature available on how to create a successful marriage, which promise a life of marital bliss, if you just adhere to the guidelines that follow…. This leads to chasing an elusive rainbow. Then, when the promises do not materialize, the disappointed marriage partner assumes that there's something better out there, something (or someone) to which he or she is entitled. So why continue to make do with less than that to which one is entitled?

Again: Marriage is a partnership in which both must continue to invest in a common venture, with dividends yet to come.

A young man cannot be imbued with this outlook in a single *chassan shmuess* or even in a five-session *vaad* (series of talks). It calls for long-term preparation in fashioning oneself – in Rabbi Dessler's reference – into a "giver" rather than a "taker." Then one emerges as a person prepared to found a *Bayis Ne'eman BeYisroel*. To do otherwise is to risk being either a *chassid shoteh* or a *naval bireshus haTorah*.

SHADCHANIM — MATCHMAKERS:
THE WAY IT WAS IN THE OLD COUNTRY

CHAIM SHAPIRO ז״ל

❦ *Sources for the Profession*

"Since Creation, G-d has engaged in making matches, a task as difficult as splitting the Yam Suf (Red Sea)" *(Bereishis Rabba, 68,4).*

The word *shadchan,* for matchmaker, is related to *shidduch,* match, which literally means (believe it or not) peace (of mind?) or rest (assured?). According to the *Ran (Rabbeinu Nissim):* "It stems from the word *sheket* and *menucha,* which a woman finds in her husband's house, as the *Targum* translates the passage (in *Shoftim* 5,31), "And the land was tranquil for forty years (*'Vatishkot ha'aretz arba'im shana*): *veshiduchas ara'* (*Shabbos* 12a)."

When the late Gerrer *Rebbe,* Rabbi Avraham Mordechai Alter, זצ״ל was approached by his brother regarding a *shidduch* between their respective children, the *Rebbe* said, "Go get a *shadchan!*"

The brother was shocked. "I can't talk to my own brother about a *shidduch* for our own children? I, of all people, need a *shadchan?*"

Replied the *Rebbe:* "*Hashem* offered His Torah to all the nations of the world, yet they refused to accept his offer. No deal! When He turned to the Jews, however, they did accept. Why? — because He offered the Torah through a *shadchan, Moshe Rabbeinu.* And a *shidduch* was made!"

Indeed, the Midrash is the source for this relationship: "Why did Moshe merit that his face glowed? Because he was the *shadchan* between *Yisroel* and *Hakadosh Baruch Hu*" *(Yalkut Shimoni, Yisro 1, 279)*.

Every town in Eastern Europe had a *shadchan*, while bigger cities had two or more who plied the trade. They were held in great esteem for the important position they occupied in the community. They were not just brokers who brought together two parties, as in a business deal. They were agents of Heaven, fulfilling a Divine mission, as Talmudic literature declares: "A person's mate is designated by the Holy One" *(Bereishis Rabba 68,3)*; "Heaven mates a man and his wife in accordance with his merits"; and "Mating a couple is as difficult as splitting the Yam Suf" *(Sota 2)*.

So they were respected and honored — after all, the fate of the town's children rested in their hands. And ultimately, they were loved — or hated — depending on the outcome of the individual *shidduch*.

❧ The Prerequisites of an Effective Shadchan

A *shadchan* could never lie, or he would lose his credibility. "Trust" was the foundation of his mission. But that didn't prevent him from being a thorough expert on *guzma'os* (exaggerations) — stretching the positive or minimizing a negative factor — and above all, an expert in the art of persuasion.

People know how to distinguish between hard facts and *guzma*. They could tell where the core of truth ended and the embroidery began. If they did accept everything said at face value, it was only because they wanted to hear and accept the exaggerations. The *shadchan*, then, was clearly blameless for later disappointments and complaints.

To ply their profession, the *shadchanim* stored "mental computer files" of information regarding some hundred families in various cities. Sifting through his memory, a *shadchan* had to come up with a suggestion that would work!

Matching the boy and girl, their looks and personalities, their levels of intelligence and commitment to *Yiddishkeit,* was only half the mission; matching the families was just as important. This meant dealing with the families' stature in the community, their Torah level, their charity activities, economic status, and, above all, their *yichus.*

A *shadchan* thus had to be something of a *ben Torah* to be able to evaluate Torah levels or *yichus.* As a matter of fact, some highly regarded rabbinical figures engaged in making *shidduchim* on a strictly non-professional basis. For example, Rabbi Nosson Tzvi Finkel, the revered "*Alter* of Slobodka," arranged matches between his top students and the daughters of prominent *Roshei Yeshiva* — frequently the very men who opposed his system of teaching *Mussar,* winning over their yeshivos to his ideology through infiltration by marriage! (See "Torah Pioneers," JO June '74, for some of the *Alter's* more eminent *shidduchim.*)

❧ *This Thing Called "Yichus"*

The term *yichus* — its meaning and connotations — can never be translated into another language. Pedigree? Genealogy? Breeding? These terms are suitable when buying a dog or a horse! No wonder the rabbis stated "*Ein yichus lo'akum*"; the concept does not even have a counterpart in alien tongues!

Indeed, the Jews pride themselves on tracing their *yichus* to Avraham, Yitzchak and Yaakov, all the way to *Adam Harishon,* directly to the Creator (in contrast to the atheists who trace their ancestry to the apes). And converts to Judaism become attached directly to Avraham, joining the same chain of aristocracy. Actually, there are two kinds of *yichus:* the halachic one (the legal term), and the popular expression of deep respect for a family's lineage. In *halacha, yichus* among Jews follows the father "... by their families, by their fathers' houses" (*Bamidbar* 1,2). Hence if the father is a *Kohein* or *Levi,* so are his children.

Yichus in our discussion is in terms of the popular usage referring to an aristocracy of Torah. With the birth of the Chassidic movement, the term was widened to include *Chassidus* and *tzidkus* as well. And these types of *yichus* apply to the mother's lineage as well as the father's. When a young lady is the daughter or niece of so-and-so, it is just as impressive as when the young man is the offspring of so-and-so.

Traditionally, *yichus* has figured in marriage, as is recorded in the *Mishna:* "Twice yearly the daughters of Israel would go out in borrowed white garments and dance in the vineyards. Unmarried men would also go there. The beautiful maidens would say, 'Lift up your eyes to beauty, for a wife is primarily for beauty.' The *meyuchasos* (daughters of distinguished families) would say, 'Fix your eyes on family, for a woman is primarily for child-bearing' (*Taanis* 31a)."

And so every *shadchan* knew, or made it his business to know, the *yichus* — in terms of the Torah-*Chassidus*-or *Tzidkus*-stature — of the families involved.

❧ The *Shadchan* of Tiktin

In Poland, almost every city had a nickname, which described the inhabitants of the town. Certainly it was not foolproof in its description, but it did reflect the type of the people who lived there to quite a degree. For instance, one large city in Poland was famous as the home of *ganovim*. Of course, all of its people were not thieves, but the city gained notoriety for the pickpockets, flim-flam operators, and common thieves that preyed on its visitors.

Tiktin (Tykacin) was known for its *"Tiktiner Yachsonim,"* a title that speaks for itself. Each *baal habayis* considered himself a *yachsan*, measuring his family against the others', to his own advantage. One can imagine the difficult job of the local *shadchan*, Reb Choneh (brother of my Bubbie Faigel).

Reb Choneh worked very diligently at his trade. He carried the names of hundreds of clients in his memory bank. He knew people in neighboring towns, all the way to Bialystok. Sometimes he would even wander off as far away as Warsaw for a *shidduch!*

As a rule, he would never *shadchan* together two families from the same street or village: they knew too much about each other. He preferred out-of-towners for Tiktiners. To justify this, Reb Choneh would quote a *Tiktiner Vort:*[1] "Why did the Jews make the Golden Calf? True, they thought that *Moshe Rabbeinu* had died and they needed another leader. But why didn't they pick Aaron, Elazar or Chur for a leader? Why a calf?" And *Anshei Tiktin* would reply: "Let it be a calf, as long as it's a stranger from out of town."

He would occasionally drop into the house of my *Zeide* — Reb Shmuel Leib Shapiro — to consult on a *shidduch* he was contemplating. Tall, thin, gray — Reb Choneh would stand and *shokel zich* as if standing *Shmoneh Esrei,* listening to the opinions. Seeing him leave once, I heard him whisper a prayer: *"Ribbono Shel Olam,* I know I can't split the Sea, but I'm doing Your work. *Zei mir matzliach* (Allow me to succeed)!"

Unlike other professionals, who were finished with a *shidduch* once they received payment for their efforts, he would become emotionally involved in his clients' lives, and would worry about his couples for years to come. When he would silently pace the kitchen, with a pensive expression on his face, the family knew that he was either worrying about a *shidduch* that wasn't working out, or about one that was going well, but perhaps shouldn't .... Once at a wedding, when he was congratulated by everyone about "the perfect match" he had arranged, he repeated the old *shadchanim's vort:* "Kinderlach (children), whatever you are wishing me today, let it happen to me. Whatever you will be wishing me five years from today, may it happen to you!"

---

1. A *vort* usually refers to an idea or statement of wisdom originated by a *Gaon, Rosh Yeshiva* or Chassidic *Rebbe.* Did you ever hear of a *vort* attributed to a town? In Poland and Lithuania one could hear a *"Tiktiner Vort"* making the rounds!

Another *Tiktiner Vort* took people to task for only considering the father of the bride's financial status when contemplating a *shidduch.* As "proof" they cite the placing of the account of the birth of Er and Onan just after their mother's *yichus:* "the daughter of Shua the merchant." When there is no other distinction in a person's family, an Er and Onan result.

As a rule, *shadchanim* prefer to work with young prospects, rather than with widowed or divorced people. Yet they kept lists of once-marrrieds, too, and never let a good idea pass. The personal gratification of helping an older person find a match far surpassed the joys of helping a younger couple.

When a match was successful, the *shadchan* would receive the couple's thanks and appreciation for the rest of their lives! But if it turned out tragic, then both sides would spell out his title SH-D-CH-N, as the initials of a derogatory message: *SHeker Dover Kessef Notel* (speaks false, takes money — i.e., his matchmaking fee).

❧ A Do-It-Yourself Guide to *Yichus*

And what of those not born into distinguished Torah-*Chassidus-Tzidkus* families? They can start a *yichus* of their own! As the old saying goes: "*Yichus* is admirable where it begins, not where it ends." In many families the *yichus* ended when the children went astray; the next generation did not appreciate the treasure that it had inherited. These children might boast about their *yichus*, but its value dropped to nil with them. As someone once retorted to a person who had belittled a great *talmid chacham* who happened not to stem from a well-known "*yichus* family": "He is the pride of his parents, while you are the shame of yours!"

The *Rambam* actually prescribes a course for fashioning one's own *yichus*, based on a passage in *Avos:* "The Jews were crowned with three crowns. The crown of *Kehuna* went to Aaron and his offspring. The crown of royalty went to David. And the crown of Torah is ready and waiting for everyone to come and claim it. ... Perhaps you think those two crowns are greater than the crown of Torah ... [but] the Torah crown is greater than those two" (*Hilchos Talmud Torah* 3:1).

The *chachamim* advise us: "A person should sell all of his possessions in order to marry the daughter of a *talmid chacham*. And he should marry his daughter to a *talmid chacham*; it can be compared to clusters from a grapevine with clusters from a grapevine, a thing both pleasant and well received" (*Pesachim* 49a). The *Maharsha* explains, "He too will be well received, for she will bear him fine children — just as the grapevine does not accept a graft from any other tree, so too will your children be without flaw."

If one finds it impossible to become a master of Torah, one can still build a house of *Yiddishkeit* and *tzeddaka*, for "the Crown of a good name is above them all."If one raises children, imbuing them with values that they will remember and cherish, it provides them with a *yichus* for generations to come.

And what about the *ger*, the convert? In his letter to Obadiah the Proselyte, the *Rambam* writes: "Proselytes, do not underestimate your lineage! If we trace ours to Abraham, Isaac, and Jacob, you trace yours to the Creator."

They, too, can begin to build a *yichus* family of great nobility, as we find in regard to Pinchas: one of his grandfathers was Aaron the *Kohein Gadol*, while his other grandfather [Yisro] had once fattened calves to be sacrificed to idols *(Bamidbar 25, see Rashi)*.

❧ A Shadchan in Lomza

Since I was blessed with two hometowns, Lomza and Tiktin, I am able to share with the readers information about the King of the *Shadchanim* of the entire vicinity of Lomza, Reb Ever Frankel. He even wrote a book, *Nistorei Nechbados (Secrets of Shadchanim)*, a veritable handbook for the trade: He argued that *shadchanus* is a profession, and one must study its myriad rules to become a master *shadchan*.

In that pre-telephone era, the most impressive tool at the disposal *of shadchanim* was the telegram. Its impact was much greater than that of a letter or an oral communication. Since telegrams were charged by the word, the trick was to say the most with the least number of words. Descriptions, propositions and plans had to be condensed into just a few words, so the *shadchanim* were experts in sending telegrams. The two parties would study every word for what it said and what it did not say, and every possible meaning of the word was discussed and interpreted. In absence of commas, periods and exclamation marks (there was no punctuation in a telegram), the word *stop* was strategically inserted. It was also designated to give the recipient a chance to digest the meaning of each word, and let him catch his breath. The telegram's impact was such, however, that people would read it quickly to its conclusion, without catching their breath.

Now we can understand the writing of Ever Frankel, who knew all Jewish families — their *yichus* and their secrets — "from Dan to Be'er Sheva." He writes: "Do not tell me of the first *shadchan* in history, Eliezer, who concluded the *shidduch* of Yitzchak and Rivka without a hitch — no difficulties, no arguments, no telegrams from Charan to Chevron. There the *shidduch* went smoothly because the *mechutan Avraham Avinu* did not ask for any *nadan* (dowry) from the *kallah's* side. In our day, however, they sing a different tune. Every *mechutan* is from the *Asara Yuchsin,*[*] and the wealth of Korach is not enough for these *Bnei Heichala Dichsifin!"*[*]

Then he gives a sample of one of his greatest achievements, a *shidduch* that he brought to a happy conclusion, where all other *shadchanim* had tried and failed: It meant dealing with "... the famous, highly educated lady Sarah Mintzevitz from Bialystok, granddaughter of Horav Yehoshua Leib Diskin, *Rav* of Lomza (later, Brisk and Yerushalayim). She spoke 70 languages; she was a *Bas Kohein* and carried her *yichus* with pride, and she writes a literate Hebrew which flows like a swift river. She offered her only son with 10,000 rubles *nadan,* but demanded 25,000 from the *kalla's* side in return. All *shadchanim* in the country were out looking for a suitable *kalla,* but could find none."

Frankel found a *kalla* in Riga, Latvia (in those days the three Baltic States were part of the Czarist Russian empire). He sent a telegram: MATZASI (I FOUND) STOP MISHOMAYIM HITZLICHA (HEAVEN HELPED ME) STOP KALLA NA'AH VACHSUDO (A GRACIOUS PIOUS BRIDE) STOP A PERFECT MATCH STOP TWENTY THOUSAND STOP MAZEL TOV STOP

---

[*] Talmudic and Midrashic references that defy translation.

And Sarah Mintzevitz's reply? HAVE SPOKEN STOP I GIVE MY SON STOP AS MUCH AS BEN HAMDOSO STOP GAVE FOR ALL THE JEWS STOP IN THE KINGDOM OF ACHASHVEROSH STOP WE THE CHILDREN OF AARON HAKOHEIN STOP WILL BLESS THE SHIDDUCH STOP ONLY WITH TWENTY FIVE STOP

It took the wisdom, experience, and the powers of persuasion of the King of the *Shadchanim*, Reb Ever Frankel — plus another exchange of telegrams — to conclude the negotiations. One must bear in mind that the telegrams and the haggling about money were done without the knowledge of the children. If the chemistry was positive when they met, the parents could do nothing to derail the match. And if the principals were not interested, the parents were helpless to bring them together. The pre-meeting haggling was merely a matter of planning to secure a financial future for the young couple.

❧ P'gam: A Blemish in the Family

A *shadchan* not only had to be familiar with each family's *yichus*, but also with any *p'gam* in the family, a significant factor in the matching process. The following were considered blemishes (in descending order of severity):

1) A *meshumad*, someone who converted to another faith (a rarity). 2) A *mosseir*, an informer against fellow Jews. 3) A Communist. 4) A Bundist-Socialist. It was the *shadchan's* duty to uncover the entire story, and in such cases, to report whatever was relevant to the interested parties.

Remarkable are the words of the *Maharsha*, who was *Rav* in Tiktin (1620). (I can visualize him in the old *Beis-Din Shtub* — still extant before the war — writing these words in his famous commentary on *Shas*.) "In our generation, most questions regarding *yichus* are not based on documented fact. Thus, if one casts aspersions on someone else's *yichus* to his friends, he is nothing less than a slanderer, seeking glory by shaming others. Whoever points out a *p'gam* in someone else is merely covering up his own shortcomings.

They should be chastised and warned to correct their ways. The *shadchanim*, especially, are guilty in this matter, and they should be punished" (*Maharsha, Kiddushin* 71a).

✦ A Shadchan's Shadchanus

A *shadchan's* commission was protected by the *halacha*, which in turn brings to the fore a number of questions: Who is required to pay the *shadchanus*, the bride and groom or their parents? (The young couple, as the main beneficiaries, but it's customary for the parents to pay.) When is payment due — at the engagement or after the wedding? If one does not pay on time, does one violate the Torah's prohibition against holding back a worker's wages? What if one *shadchan* introduced the couple and another one steered the *shidduch* to its conclusion? What if the couple broke off, and another person renewed the effort and brought it to its completion? Responsa are full of such problems, mainly geared to protect the *shadchan*. Community discipline was strict on the subject. In fact, some people are meticulous in giving a gift of some sort to everyone involved in bringing a couple together, to free the match from any misgivings on anyone's part. Some people take advantage of this tendency, as they tell about a *shadchan* who approached one of the fathers after the wedding and demanded payment. Said the father, "I'm astonished at your nerve to ask for payment. It was Reb Dovid the *shadchan* who made the *shidduch*, not you! You never even spoke one word about us!"

"Indeed," replied the *shadchan*, "had I said but one word about you, there never would have been a wedding."

He got the message, and paid the *shadchan*.

In conclusion, *shadchanim* are a *mazel beracha* in a community. For the thirty years that I'm involved in the *gittin* process in Baltimore, I can testify that, in the hundreds or perhaps thousands of divorces that I've witnessed, there were hardly two dozen divorces from the yeshiva community. Why such an excellent record? Of course, a Torah life offers the best antidote against the plague, with its built-in patterns of renewal. But, in my opinion, *shadchanim* are also a contributing factor, by bringing an objective third party into the selection process, and serving as a buffer between the parties, who may be too eager, too reluctant, or too inexperienced for a smooth courtship. By contrast, when a boy meets a girl casually, Jewish patterns of modesty are violated from the start, the young man and woman are unduly impatient and can't wait to get married. Too often, within six months, they can't wait to get divorced. Not so when dealing with a *shadchan*, who sees the entire picture from the start.

As the Gerrer *Rebbe* put it: "Go get a *shadchan! Mazel Tov!*"

THE PATH TO HAPPILY EVER AFTER

Rabbi Ephraim Wachsman

❦ *I. A Process That is in Galus*

The first step toward founding a *Bayis Ne'eman BeYisroel* is to pass through the *shidduch* process. The *Ran* in *Mesechta Shabbos* says that the word *shidduch* stems from the *Targum* for "*Vatishkot ha'aretz* – and the earth rested," which the *Targum* translates *v'shadichas ar'o* – denoting serenity, calm, tranquility. This raises a difficult question: Why has something that is meant to be a source of tranquility become a source of stress, of profound disappointment, of paralyzing fear and, in many cases, pure agony? The logical conclusion has to be that we lost our way. The Torah approach in this process would certainly be much more pleasant. The pain we are experiencing must be coming from the way the secular world has wormed its way into our lives – like a terrorist, who sabotaged one of our most beautiful institutions and turned it into something monstrous.

There is no subject that so preoccupies and dominates the secular world as does the man-woman relationship. And we would be presumptuous to deny that the host culture has influenced us. In *Ikvesa d'Meshicha*, the Era preceding the Advent of *Mashiach*, the *sefarim hakedoshim* (sacred literature) tell us, there will be a reincarnation of the souls of the *dor hamabul*, the generation of the Flood, in Noach's time. As a matter of course, this brings in its wake the bane of that era: *"vateshacheis ha'aretz"* – an erosion in all strata of society, even among the holiest. This may well be what we are witnessing.

We, however, are meant to be an *am le'vadad yishkon* – a nation that dwells alone. Our vulnerability to the forces of erosion can be dangerous and destructive to our essence. If we just consider the sources of what influences our conduct in *shidduchim*, that alone should give us pause.

> *Two weeks before his chasuna (wedding), a close friend of mine developed a terrible facial blemish. His mother was very distraught: "We cannot permit such a mark on your face so close to your chasuna!" So she arranged an appointment for him with one of the foremost cosmetic dermatologists in New York, a doctor who caters to the wealthy and influential. He reported to the doctor's office and sat in the waiting room with his attention focused on his open Gemora. Suddenly a female media celebrity walked in, and everybody was swept up with excitement. The fellow next to my friend gave him a nudge. "So-and-so is here!"*
>
> *My friend responded, "Who's that?"*
>
> *"What? You never heard of this person?" And he shared this with the next person. Soon the whole waiting room was buzzing about this bachur with beard and payos who's so uninformed that he never heard of this model of depravity. The word reached the inner office, and the secretaries were talking about it.*
>
> *When the young man's turn came, the doctor started baiting him: "Aha, so you're getting married in a week or two. I suppose it's been an arranged marriage. Did you have a matchmaker?" Then he started getting nasty. "So you're marrying somebody you barely know? You met her a few times …. You know, you Orthodox don't understand anything about marriage. You're listening to your rabbis and it's going to be disastrous."*
>
> *Understandably, the doctor is a Jew. Finally, he offered, "Let me give you some advice about marriage."*

My friend looked him in the eye and said, "Fine. First, however, tell me how many times you've been married."

His reply: "I'm on my fourth marriage."

Our host society has a dismal success rate, and yet firmly believes that it has unmatched expertise. It would be wise for us to do everything in exactly the opposite manner from what they do.

❧ *The Dating System: An American Phenomenon*

It is an established fact. The American approach to *shidduchim* in the non-*Chassidic* circles – the dating system, as it's known – is a uniquely American phenomenon. There is no precedent for it in our *Mesorah* (tradition), and there is no parallel to it in Europe or *Eretz Yisroel*. It is purely an American invention. A story attributed to Rabbi Meir Shapiro זצ״ל puts it into perspective.

> *A sofer (scribe) who lived in Warsaw was trying to earn a living by selling mezuzos and tefillin. Somebody advised him, "People here have no money. Take your merchandise to Berlin, where wealthy people will pay you top Mark, and you'll be able to make ends meet."*
>
> *So he packed up 150 mezuzos, traveled to Berlin, and set up shop right in the Reform community, selling his mezuzos at 50 Mark apiece. People viewed it as a good luck thing and were snapping up the merchandise. In two or three hours, he made a fortune... and had nothing left. What a lost opportunity! Then he remembered that he had brought along a Megilla (Scroll of Esther, also written on parchment). So he took his scissors, cut the Megilla into strips, rolled them up, and began selling them as mezuzos with great success. One of the purchasers decided to examine the insides of the "mezuza." He opened it up and saw "Vayezoso," the tenth of Haman's sons. It struck him as strange, so he decided to ask his Rabbiner.*
>
> *"Rabbi, I bought a mezuza, and here it says 'Vayezoso.' Is this what's meant to be written in the mezuza?"*

The rabbi responded, "That's a very deep question. I will have to ponder over it." He went into his study, removed the mezuza that he had just bought and unwrapped it. His mezuza said "Parshandoso" – the first of Haman's sons. He returned and told his congregant: "Yes. If Parshandoso is a mezuza, so is Vayezoso a mezuza."

We are suffering from a *Parshandoso* Syndrome. Our *shidduchim* system is structured according to an accepted pattern. We have been told that this is the way we operate because this is how it has always been done. Created by whom? What is the *Mesorah* on it? Nobody has any idea.

In truth, it's a relic of the 1940's, when a young and innocent Jewish America did not yet have direction, and everything was learned from the way the non-Jews do things. We are still stuck in that time warp.

It took quite a few years for the summer camps to catch up with contemporary standards. Until recently, many of the camps for boys had the same learning schedules as they had in 1950. The administrators were laboring under the misconception that *Yiddishe kinderlach* could not handle more learning in July and August. Today boys have the capacity to do much more; and they do.

In the crucial area of *shidduchim*, however, we have scarcely advanced.

✦ II. Guidelines From Gedolim Versus Common Practice in Dating: Frequency, Duration… and Kedusha

Let us contrast the views of other *gedolim* on this issue with what has come to be common practice.

Rabbi Elchonon Wasserman הי״ד quotes his *Rebbe*, the Chofetz Chaim: "It is improper for two people to meet each other for the purpose of marriage before all the researching, information-gathering and decision-making are mutually concluded, and all details are completely worked out. First they must know exactly what they can expect from each other and what their commitment would entail. Then they could meet, but not before."

This is how it has been done, and is still being done, in many circles of *Klal Yisroel* – throughout the generations, wherever Jews have lived.

Several years ago, Rabbi Elazar Shach זצ״ל wrote a letter to *bnei Torah* on the topic: "With a heartfelt cry. I see it incumbent upon myself to express a protest, *l'ma'an Hashem v'Toraso*. I am turning to all *bnei yeshiva*, wherever they may be, to express my views on what I have seen and heard. There is a spreading practice of unlimited meetings for the sake of *shidduchim*. Of course, they should meet until each one recognizes to a degree what the other person is like and what their *hashkafas hachaim* (outlook on life) is. But one should not go beyond a moderate norm, to convene meetings for hours upon hours, to go and spend time in places where no *ben Torah* should be found. Such practice is forbidden by Torah law, and no worthwhile outcome can result from such meetings.

"One should plan on a limited number of meetings, of two or three hours' duration each. Whoever adheres to these guidelines will be graced by *Hashem*'s choicest blessings, and will merit establishing a *Bayis Ne'eman BeYisroel*."

Why not lead our lives in accordance with the charge of the *gedolei hador*? Why not listen to *daas Torah* in this fundamental pillar of *kedushas Yisroel*? We have fallen victim to the *Parshandoso* Syndrome. We have unthinkingly embraced a dehumanizing system that breeds frustration and prolongs the process. It has become an accepted part of life: He or she is now "going out." Add to this the popular wisdom that directs our conduct, such as: I can't marry the first one I meet, because then I haven't gone out enough. I haven't shopped properly.

The Steipler *Gaon* once told an older *bachur*, who had not yet found his *zivug*: "Do you know what your problem is? You think that the biggest loss that you could suffer is to become a *chassan*, because right now the whole world is still open to you. The minute you choose one, you've locked out everyone else, leaving you only with that one. Your mistake is that you never had more than one in the first place. That one is meant to be yours. Your job is to find her."

❧ A Place for Parental Involvement

I n a less complicated era, parents were not only more active in their children's *shidduchim*, they were more or less in control. Nowadays, parents are often only minimally involved, especially as young men and women spend time – months or years – away from home, under the guidance of others, subject to peer pressure and norms, and in general getting older and more independent. To whatever degree possible, parents should view the decision as to whom their child meets as though they were deciding whom he or she will marry; they should be more assertive, where feasible. They should drop the attitude of, "Why not? Let them meet. They might like each other. You never know."

Their children still need guidance. Parents – and mentors, *in loco parenti* – should share their opinions with their charges, instead of permitting things to just happen. This should include dating patterns and venues. The *bachurim* do not want this extreme *laissez faire* attitude, nor do the girls. Similarly, hundreds of sterling *bachurim* do not want to haunt Manhattan's hotel lobbies. And neither do the girls. They feel it beneath them. But they have come to accept it as the unwritten law.

A European *Rebbetzin* (of Lithuanian extraction) spoke out on this quite clearly: "In truth, my daughter is not going to be taken to such places. That is not the way of aristocracy." In dealing with bona fide princes and princesses, we would understand that there are limitations. Yet we have permitted our children to adopt the ways of peasantry. As part of that unstructured approach, *shidduchim* may stretch out over months and months, and then fall apart. All because we have forgotten the *Yiddishe* way. The Jewish approach has always been to make inquiries … and then arrange that they meet each other several times to see if the match is suitable. It can – and should – still be operative.

❧ III. The Marketplace Perspective: Verbal Indicators

The popular approach to *shidduchim* can be recognized by its terminology: "Dating." Even the term itself should be considered offensive. "Dumping." Is a *bas Yisroel* "dumped"? "He's on the market." "She's off the market." Is seeking to find a partner in life a matter of entering a market?

Moreover, the competitiveness of the "market"– shopping, buying and selling – brings out the worst in us. So in one sense, we have become paralyzed; in another, we have become unduly aggressive. The endeavor has become inflated – and reduced – to a public relations issue, with so much unhealthy stress and unnecessary pain, involving a new, status-centered array of questions.

> *A very fine gentleman approached his Rav with a she'eila. Someone suggested a worthy shidduch for his daughter, but the shadchan requested a list of everybody she had already met…. The shadchan told him that everybody does this today.*
>
> *The Rav replied, "I do not have the least doubt that this is assur mi'd'Oraysa – forbidden by Torah law. By what right may one reveal classified information – private matters – without the other party's permission? And on the simple, human level, where is our concern for the privacy, the dignity in the reputation of another Yid?"*[1]

❧ Dealing With the Image Factor: Historical Precedent, Rabbinical Comments

A *talmid* of the Chofetz Chaim was suggested for the daughter of a highly respected businessman, who was searching for a specific type of boy – both accomplished in learning and pre-

---

1. The *Orchchas Tzaddikim*, 900 years ago, writes about this. He decries people who say nonchalantly, "I was '*red*' this-and-this *shidduch*, but we weren't interested."

sentable. After this *bachur* met this girl, the father came to the *Rosh Yeshiva* with complaints: "How could you suggest such a boy to me? He limps; he stutters; he's not poised. "The *Rosh Yeshiva* was stunned. The *bachur* was highly accomplished in every way. So he later confronted the young man: "What happened? I heard you were limping and stuttering."

He replied, "*Rebbe*, as soon as I met her, I realized that she's not for me – nor for any *ben Torah*, for that matter. I thought, why should I say no to her? I'd rather make myself seem unattractive than hurt her feelings."

How would that have affected his "market value" in today's *shidduch* scene?

An ugly by-product of this environment is that *shidduchim* have become a way of determining our status. It has become a scorecard. The Satmar *Rav* זצ״ל once said: "Since I came to America, I barely know anyone who did a *shidduch* for the sake of his children." What an indictment!

Factors in making choices in the marketplace include: "What will we gain from this son/daughter-in-law?" "How will it propel us upward on the status ladder?" These considerations should not even enter in the process. This may be evident in the following incident in *Chumash*:

When *Avraham Avinu* dispatched Eliezer to select a wife for Yitzchak, he made it clear that he wanted someone from a specific *mishpacha* – his family. Yet when Eliezer arrived in Charan, he focused on who would perform the *chessed* of drawing and pouring buckets of water for him and for his camels. Why didn't he follow *Avraham Avinu*'s instructions, and first have sought out the *mishpacha*, and then search for who in the family is most qualified?

Perhaps Eliezer was afraid that once he would know her *mishpacha*, he would be predisposed to see all her good features – her unmatched *middos*, the type of character we value – to back up his choice. First, he decided, I want to establish that she is of sterling character, before I know anything of her background. After that's confirmed, then – if she's from the correct *mishpacha* – it will be *invei hagefen b'invei hagefen*, a match made in Heaven.

We are so often sidetracked, blinded by external factors that are meaningless, and ignore essentials.

A horror story to illustrate this:

> *A friend told me how his sister has been seeing a boy for months. My friend is upset. The boy brings her home in the wee hours of the morning, and she has to go to work that day. Then he suddenly decided that he's not really interested. Or, perhaps he would be, if.... This is all deliberated with a cold detachment.*
>
> *"So what do you want?" I asked my friend.*
>
> *"Maybe you could speak to him."*
>
> *"Maybe I could speak to him? Are you still interested in such a bachur?"*
>
> *He replied "Yes. He's a top name. Everybody knows he's a top name!"*
>
> *My response: "You should bentsch gomel[2] that he revealed himself before anything tragic happened."*

If Eliezer were conducting the search, that much-sought-after young man would never have made it past the camel trough.

❧ *Seeking a Talmid Chacham*

There is, of course, good reason to want a budding *talmid chacham* as a son-in-law. Rabbi Elchonon Wasserman הי״ד explains this goal, as a directive to be inferred from the *Rambam* in *Sefer Hamitzvos*. The *Rambam* discusses the *mitzva* of u'bo sidbok – the command that a person should cleave to *Hashem*, by associating with *talmidei chachamim*. The *Rambam* spells out the ways of doing so in detail: A person should do business with *talmidei chachamim*; he should support *talmidei chachamim*; he should maintain a closeness with *talmidei chachamim*; and he should endeavor to have his daughter marry a *talmid chacham*. Reb Elchonon expands on this: Just as I'm advised to do business with a *talmid chacham* for the *talmid chacham*'s sake, so too am I meant to give my daughter in marriage

---

2. Thanking G-d for emerging in one piece from a life-threatening situation.

to a *talmid chacham* for his sake. Not as an ornament for myself, to parade him around, crowing, "This is my son-in-law!" On the contrary, I'm meant to raise my daughter in a manner that would make her worthy, with *siyata D'Shmaya* (we need great *zechusim* for this), of serving as a life-partner of a *talmid chacham*.

❦ *A Page From the Social Section*

The non-Jewish world has seeped into our society in yet other ways. It has become expected that the engagement period of a *chassan* and *kalla* should somehow parallel the mores of the non-Jewish world.

Rabbi Falk of Gateshead recently wrote a book delineating the proper conduct of *chassan* and *kalla*. He points out how some of the practices that have become commonly accepted, that are part and parcel of our *Parshandoso* system, can involve actual transgressions. Others can bring serious problems in their wake. As the *Chazon Ish* had commented, when a *chassan* and *kalla* spend endless hours together, they can develop an antipathy for each other. The *Radak* comments on the *passuk*: "And Rivka raised her eyes and saw Yitzchak …. She took the veil and covered herself" (*Bereishis* 24, 64-65). Says the *Radak*, "The Torah teaches *derech eretz ve'tzenius*. It is proper that a woman be shy in the presence of her betrothed."

Common wisdom today has it that if one feels that type of restraint, something must be wrong; their relationship is not solid yet. The expectation is that at that early stage, the couple should feel a type of closeness that should actually be reserved for after the *chasuna*.

❦ *IV. Guidelines for a Happy Marriage*

Unfortunately, the guidelines for achieving success in marriage are being determined by a society (as we heard before) that has a divorce rate of 50 percent. It's an astonishing figure … astonishing that 50 percent actually stay married. It is difficult to believe that – considering the superficiality of contemporary society – any marriage could possibly survive.

Rabbi Eliyahu Eliezer Dessler זצ״ל, in his classic discussion of *shalom bayis*, explains that the root of *ahava* – love – is *hav*, to give. Love for another grows out of giving to that person. One loves a child because we are endlessly involved in giving to him. A farmer loves a tree that he has planted because he put work into it. A *bayis ne'eman b'Yisroel* is founded on the principle of giving. What can be expected from a society that understands success in marriage as the result of getting the most out of one's spouse, without altering one's selfish goals one iota?

A typical example: The current era of *chassan-kalla* relationships is witness to a new *Parshandoso*-system-induced indulgence: the practice of hyper-gifting. It appears to be an exercise in giving, but sadly, it is meaningless. Its underlying message is about looking right, not looking cheap, even if extending that prescribed gift to one's prospective daughter-in-law or son-in-law means putting oneself into bankruptcy.

Chazal spoke about *sivlonos* – exchange of gifts between the *chassan* and *kalla*, a longstanding *minhag Yisroel*. But there were ceilings on the gifts.

A *yungerman* (married fellow) of my acquaintances became a *chassan* with a very special young lady who knew that he was of very limited means, and had to pay for everything himself. He could not rely on his parents. She told him, "Please don't buy me a diamond. You can't afford it and I don't need it."

He said, "You're engaged. You can't walk around without a diamond ring."

Finally she suggested, "Get me a synthetic diamond. I promise you, I'll be just as happy."

This *chassan* realized that he had a very special *kalla*. He thought: She truly deserves to wear a genuine diamond. He scraped together every cent he could, borrowed money with extended payment schedules, and bought her a genuine diamond. He could not tell her it was genuine, because she had refused to wear a real diamond.

So he gave her a real diamond, claiming it was fake. She was happy that her *chassan* did not spend more than he could afford, and he was happy that his *kalla* was wearing a real diamond, as was befitting her.

After a year and a half of tutoring and collecting *sefarim* to pay off his debt, he told her, "I want you to know, the ring that you're wearing is a real diamond, because that's what you deserve."

How much more meaningful is such a gift than the ridiculous showcasing that goes on today. Because that *matana* was an experience in giving. And these *matanos* are all about taking.

The other side of the coin of this showcasing is the lack of any sense of *hakoras hatov* (gratitude). Nobody feels grateful. "My father-in-law bought me this gift. Why not? It's coming to me." Everything has been crowned with the definite article – "*the* pearls," "*the* bracelet," "*the* watch," "*the* menora," "*the* esrog box." These trinkets have taken on entire personalities of their own. And we created these goblins.

❧ *The Spin-off: Second Thoughts*

This phenomenon of "shopping, marketing, and investing" has an impact on *shalom bayis*, creating problems that are very different from those that plagued the world of our *Zeides* and *Bubbas*.

> *My Zeide was Rav in a city in Holland. In his community, a particular couple included a husband who had a terrible temper. Once a year, he and his wife would come to him for a get. My grandfather anticipated their annual visit, and he always managed to make peace between them. One time he told them the following story of an arguing couple:*
>
> *The wife woke up in the middle of the night and she heard a noise in the house. She said, "I think there's a mouse in the house."*
>
> *The husband said, "No, it's a cat."*
>
> *She objected, "No, it's a mouse." "No, it's a cat!" "It's a mouse!" Soon they were screaming, "It's a cat!" "It's a mouse!"*
>
> *"We're going to the Rav." Finished.*

They appeared before the Rav, who heard both sides. "Listen,"
he said. "You have such a marvelous family, you have wonderful
children, a beautiful marriage. It's not worthwhile to destroy such a
magnificent palace just because of a silly difference."

They accepted his plea, and they walked home very happy. On the
way home, the husband remarked to his wife, "You know, we should
thank Hashem. We have such a wise Rav. We nearly destroyed our
marriage just because of a cat." To which she said, "No, it was a
mouse." "A cat!" "A mouse!"

Such were the *shalom bayis* problems of earlier times, reflecting
inability to get along on issues, both major and minor... part of
the human condition. In some circumstances, a person may have
thought: "My spouse is all wrong!" Never did he or she think: "I
selected the wrong spouse!"

By contrast, the system that we've created fosters a marketplace
attitude wherein people walk into marriage constantly evaluating:
Am I happy? Am I unhappy? Is this what I'm looking for? Am I get-
ting what I had wanted? Did I let something better go by? This causes
terrible, deep *shalom bayis* problems where people are not simply
annoyed with their spouses, but are intrinsically dissatisfied and
unhappy with their spouses ר״ל.

We must remember the words of the *Rambam*: Marriage is not
about rights, it's about obligations. The obligation of a husband is
to be *"ohava kegufo u'mechabda yoser migufo* – To love her as much as
himself and to honor her more than himself." The wife's obligation
is expressed in *"Eizu isha kesheira, kol ha'osa retzon ba'ala.* Who is a
worthy wife? Whoever fulfills her husband's wishes." With these
two foundations in place, a *bayis ne'eman beYisroel* can flourish.

Once we enter into the realm of demands, the scene changes.
Talk about a good husband, and the first picture that comes to mind
is a fellow wrapped in an apron, washing dishes. For the record,
he's a wonderful *Yid*, a *tzaddik,* and he should help his wife because
she is probably overburdened. But that alone does not identify him
as a model spouse. He could do the same for his mother, too. He
could hire a maid to do that chore. He must give his wife something
that only a husband can give. *Ohavo kegufo u'mechabdo yoser migufo*

– constantly conveying to her that she is precious to him, as the *Chazon Ish* writes in a letter: "*Mi'teva shel ha'isha lehisaneg al china b'ein ba'ala* – It is consistent with a woman's nature to take pleasure in the fact that her husband appreciates her." Once she knows that, and he verbalizes it day after day – he thanks her and lets her know that he understands how hard she's working for him – he will not have to do the dishes.

She will be delighted to be *oseh retzon ba'ala*, "to do her husband's will," and treat him like a king, as the *Rambam* writes. The words of the *Rambam* do not resonate well in today's society. That is because the shallow, inane ideology of feminism has worked its way into our society, too.

In the competitive arena, normal expectations become demands. A husband helping at home is not performing a *chessed*; it is demanded of him. In a well-structured, secular-type marriage, each partner does his or her share. Our marriages are meant to serve the *Ribbono Shel Olam*, not ourselves. Indeed, the *Chovos HaLevavos* describes the structure of a person's relationship with his wife, advising against extending favors to her "in hope of earning a Divine reward, or so she will reciprocate …. [His acting on her behalf should] not be because of the recognition he is going to get, nor to dominate her, but solely to fulfill his Creator's wishes, and perform the Torah's commands. Whoever performs these acts of kindness for ulterior, self-serving motives will not achieve what he strives for – not in this world or the next. His efforts will be for naught. But if he or she extends favors to the other, thinking 'that's my assignment as an *oveid Hashem*,' then *Hashem* will help them achieve the best of this world and the next."

This should serve as the guidelines for a successful marriage that we should remember.

READERS' FORUM ON "THE PATH TO HAPPILY EVER AFTER"

The previous article engendered an unusual number of responses. We therefore present several pertinent letters, with Rabbi Wachsman's response.

❧ A Path Charted by Non-Americans

To the Editor:

I found the article, "The Path to Happily Ever After," disappointing. Though I have several difficulties with this article, there is one which compels me to write. The article is addressing an American audience, yet only quotes *gedolim* from *Eretz Yisroel* or Europe.

America has been blessed with outstanding *gedolim*. It may be possible that their approach to *shidduchim* for the American *bachur* or *bas Yisroel* differed from that of their contemporaries in other countries/societies. It would behoove Rabbi Wachsman to appreciate this reality, and research their opinions before writing on this issue.

Ben Zion Ungar
Far Rockaway, NY

❧ A "Parshandosa Mezuza"
or Building a Bayis Ne'eman?

To the Editor:

In his article, "The Path to the Happily Ever After," Rabbi Ephraim Wachsman described the yeshiva world's approach to *shidduchim* – the "Dating System" – as "a uniquely American phenomenon … a relic of the 1940's when … Jewish America did not yet have direction, and everything was learned from the way the non-Jews do things." If that sweeping statement was meant to include the manner in which three generations of *bnei Torah* have sought to find their *zivug*, I would find this indictment somewhat unfair, inaccurate and even offensive. Are all the wonderful *shidduchim* of these last 50-60 years, which have succeeded in creating homes and families *bi'kedusha ve'tahara*, resonating with sanctity and purity, comparable to the fictitious *mezuza* of Rabbi Meir Shapiro's parable (the *Parshandosa* Syndrome)?

There is no doubt that the dating system requires monitoring and fine tuning, to avoid unacceptable attitudes and practices. One should bear in mind, however, that the system *per se* was accepted and then developed by the greatest *Roshei Yeshiva* and *Gedolei Rabbanim* in America, who actively guided their *talmidim* in finding their *zivug* by – yes – dating. Many American *minhagim* – indeed, our most vital *chinuch* institutions (including summer camps) – were established with the deep insight of those *Gedolei Torah* after their arrival to America. They understood that integration of Torah life within American society required ingenuity, patience, and even some accommodation. As our society grows stronger, both in numbers and Torah commitment, we may well be able to improve upon some of these systems. But that hardly justifies saying that it is a system "without *Mesora*," or dismissing it as something unworthy, "created by whom?"

Indeed, hundreds of genuine *bnei Torah* are currently consulting directly with their *Rosh Yeshiva* or *Rav* in all aspects of *shidduchim*.

It is also important to take into account that many of the young men, especially those whose homes or backgrounds do not reflect the level of dedication to Torah that these young scholars have attained, would not be able to find their proper *shidduch* relying solely on parental guidance. (This holds true for young women, as well.)

In addition, our Torah society today is very diversified and has many variables. It is not pre-War Europe, where the girls as a rule stayed home and received no formal education (and certainly had no careers), and a married "yeshiva man" would move in to his in-laws' home as he continued to learn. Our American environment promotes a greater degree of autonomy. Thus, even in many families where children and parents are "on the same page" regarding *shidduchim*, the children do not want decisions made for them. They hope to ultimately arrive at crucial decisions for themselves, especially with regard to their *shidduch*. Therefore, more time is required "until each one recognizes to a degree what the other person is like and what their *hashkafas hachayim* is." (Quoted from Rav Elazar Shach זצ״ל.)

We should encourage and admire *bnei Torah* and *bnos Yisroel* who are exercising much caution while dealing with the most important decision of their lives *bekedusha u'vetahara*. Certainly, Rabbi Wachsman is correct in admonishing those who abuse the system by dating too often, for too long, or deliberately seeing many girls. Similarly, we must also decry those parents who are not seeking what is best and appropriate for their child, but rather a *shidduch* that will bring stature or prominence to the parents.

The main challenge in *shidduchim* is to strengthen our *emuna* and *bitachon* – our faith in *Hashem*. We must truly believe that all our *shidduchim* are subject to *Hashem's* divine will and that He brings them to fruition. Then we will certainly conduct ourselves in His ways, and merit the right *zivug*. We will also achieve the calm and serenity, which is how the *Ran* (cited by Rabbi Wachsman) defines the source of the word *"shidduchim."*

Rabbi Moshe Halberstadt
Passaic NJ

❧ Challenges Lack of Source or Legitimacy of the American Dating System

To the Editor:

I read with much interest Rabbi Ephraim Wachsman's "The Path to Happily Ever After." Rabbi Wachsman, an erudite and articulate *talmid chacham*, has an entertaining style and provides edifying insights and perspectives. Nevertheless, I disagree with both his premise and his proposal.

Rabbi Wachsman asserts: "It is an established fact. The American approach to *shidduchim* in the non-Chassidic circles — the dating system, as it's known — is a uniquely American phenomenon."

It is not clear, at least to this reader, how this "fact" became so established. I do not see any historical evidence brought to bear. To the best of my knowledge, the system of courtship practiced in Eastern and Central Europe bore strong resemblance to that which is in effect today.

In any event, I think we must take into account the vast differences between the expectations that a contemporary couple has from marriage and those once harbored by a strictly Chassidic or otherwise isolated couple. Even the most exhaustive background checks cannot substitute for direct exploration and work on the nascent relationship. Horror stories of short-term divorces, despite extensive "homework," abound. In the intense and complex (and, we hope, rewarding and fulfilling) relationship that our contemporary couple will likely develop, many problems may arise if proper premarital groundwork for the life they will live together is lacking.

Even if one believes the entire milieu must change, this realignment cannot begin from the "dating" process. It is first necessary to argue why the current state of love and marriage in our world that led to the current state of the courtship process should change. After such arguments have been made, other core issues, such as love before or after marriage, must be considered as well. If our society is then convinced that the new perspective is correct, then, and only then, may we advocate curtailing the courtship process.

Continuing to Rabbi Wachsman's proposal, it seems to consist of two elements: more parental involvement and less face-to-face meetings. I question the former element: What is to be done with children of non-Orthodox, modern-Orthodox, or, for that matter, dysfunctional parents, who are either unused, unwilling, or unable to engage in the extensive background checks and negotiations that underlie the model espoused by Rabbi Wachsman?

But my real problem is with the second element of Rabbi Wachsman's proposal. Rabbi Wachsman cites several *Gedolei Torah* as advocating fewer meetings of shorter durations. Precise numbers are not forthcoming, but one senses that we are talking of no more than two to three "dates" of two to three hours each. I do not wish to quibble on numbers. I have heard that the Brisker Rav זצ״ל prescribed no fewer than six meetings, and that Rabbi Bick זצ״ל recommended a minimum of eight. It is, however, the quality of the courtship process that should be our concern. The goals of that process should dictate its relevant length in each case. Rabbi Wachsman seems to hold that since "suitability" has been determined already by the parents, what remains is to confirm that compatibility: to ensure that both sides find their respective mates reasonably presentable. This may work for some Chassidic circles, but I do not believe it will work for the majority of the American Torah community.

❦ *Applying the Rambam's Three Levels of Friendship*

The ideal marriage is captured by the *Rambam* in his commentary on Rabbi Yehoshua ben Perachia's advice, "Acquire a friend for yourself" (*Avos* 1:6). The *Rambam's* explanation of the *Mishna* is based on three levels of friendship: The lowest level is a friendship built on mutual benefit, such as the relationship of two business partners. The *Rambam* divides the next level into two: friendship based on pleasure, and friendship based on security — both comprise friendship based on a sense of equilibrium, but the latter sublevel is higher. Friendship based on security is such that each person finds in the other a person whom he can trust; someone with whom he can let down his defenses, and share profound matters and innermost thoughts — good and bad — without fear. The highest level of friendship is of a lofty character — both friends yearn and aspire for true good, and each helps the other in that quest. That last level is the type of friend that Yehoshua ben Perachia urges us to acquire.

It seems that the courtship process should parallel the *Rambam*'s ladder of friendship. The initial stages of courtship are much like "sounding out" a potential business partner: You go out to lunch and make small talk. Thus, the initial stage consists of such small talk between the prospective mates: comings and goings, education, experiences, even *"vertlach"* and matters of general *hashkafa*. Little nuances — politeness, consideration, refined expression, sense of humor, etc. — are clues as to the potential partner's suitability.

The next stage consists of the higher sub-level of the *Rambam*'s Level Two. The two individuals courting each other need to make a conscious effort to bring out and discuss intimate — even painful — emotional and experiential developments in themselves and in their counterparts. They each must take risks, yet simultaneously attempt to make the other feel safe and secure. Together they should share their exhilarating sensations of success and their demoralizing feelings of failures, their strengths and their weaknesses.

The final stage should flow naturally from the first and second stages. If a couple shares a general *hashkafa*, then proceeds to feel open – yet secure – bonds, they should begin to sense that elusive "chemistry" that is the basis of Level Three. The merger of souls that grows throughout marriage has been well grounded. Rather than facing each other (figuratively), a couple should have a sense of common, united, directed advancement toward their complementary goals in *Avodas Hashem* and *Kiddush Shem Shamayim*. Whether realization of that high-level relationship can precede or only follow marriage is an important question that does not lend itself to a ready or uniform answer (but may be a good topic for the prospective couple to discuss!). The general direction, however, is clearly along the *Rambam*'s road.

There is a considerable amount of *Torah she'b'al peh* that can and should be added to this brief outline. For example: Generally, sustained "eye contact" leads to greater bonding. On the other hand, there are obvious *tzeni'us* issues that surround such intensity. There are doubts, real or imaginary issues of compatibility, expectations and dreams. While the prospective couple must deal with these "stumbling blocks," a *moreh/ moras derech* (*rebbi, rebbitzen* or other experienced mentor) is imperative.

This much seems clear: Parents cannot forge such bonds in lieu of their children. Expecting such work to occur in either side's living room may also be unfair; perhaps a neutral, public yet private, location is better suited for this *avoda kasha she'ba'Mikdash*.

In short: The courtship process may be flawed, but not because of a lack of parental involvement nor because of some excessive time frame. We have not educated potential *chassanim* and *kallos* to apply the process of "Acquire a friend for yourself" to the goal of creating *rei'im ahuvim* – beloved partners in marriage. We need to counsel our young men and women about how their courtship – however short or long it takes – may comprise a solid foundation for the *Bayis Ne'eman b'Yisroel*.

Yosef G. Schochet
Ramapo, NY

❧ *Rabbi Wachsman responds:*

Before addressing the specific issues brought up by the letter-writers, I would like to clarify a few points. The article "The Path to Happily Ever After" has generated a torrent of response, much of it positive. People have expressed their frustration and disenchantment with the *shidduchim* process as we know it. Many were grateful that the issue was being opened up for discussion.

The purpose of the article was not to express my own opinions on the subject. They are irrelevant. My intent was only to determine, to the best of my ability, the position of *Gedolei Torah* on the matter. Continued discussion ought to be more of the same. What did our *gedolim* hold, and are we following their *daas Torah,* or not? The letters that I am attempting to respond to all take issue with the part of the article that dealt with the dating process as it is commonly practiced today.

To quickly review, the position advocated in the article was built around two quotes. One was a letter written by Rabbi Elchonon Wasserman זצ״ל, quoting his *Rebbe,* the Chofetz Chaim זצ״ל: "… Meetings should not commence before all the research and investigation has been completed by both sides and all the details and negotiations have been agreed upon by both sides. After they have come to full agreement on all the issues, only then should they meet, and not before …." The other quote was taken from a sharply worded, deeply emotional letter written by HaRav Shach זצ״ל addressed to *bnei yeshiva,* decrying the current custom in *shidduchim* as *"pesula ve'asura"* (invalid and forbidden). I asked why we were clearly straying from their directives, and I questioned the wisdom of not heeding *daas Torah* on such a fundamental issue.

The letters printed in this issue of JO raised some objections. I will attempt to respond point by point.

❧ *Not a Matter of Geography*

Ben Zion Ungar objects to quoting only *"gedolim* of *Eretz Yisroel* and Europe" regarding a matter pertaining to an American audience. Firstly, *gedolei olam* (world-renowned Torah giants) like the *Chofetz Chaim* or Rabbi Shach must be listened to regardless of where they live. More importantly, the *gedolim* themselves chose to address the American audience. Rabbi Shach begins his letter saying, "I feel compelled to raise an outcry for the sake of *Hashem* and His Torah, and I turn to all *bnei yeshiva* in any place they may be found." The letter from the *Chofetz Chaim* זצ״ל was circulated in this country by no less a personage than the revered Manchester *Rosh Yeshiva,* Rabbi Yehuda Segal זצ״ל. The *Rosh Yeshiva* would often publicly and tearfully protest against what he called the American system of *shidduchim.* Surely these *gedolim* were aware that "America is different," yet they still conveyed their opinions to us with great force and clarity. Obviously, they felt that their *daas Torah* was not limited by a geographic or cultural divide. What could possibly be objectionable about publicizing what our Torah giants had to say to us? Shouldn't we want to know?

This brings us to a deeper, far more transcendent issue. That of *emunas chachamim* – trust in Torah sages. What do we do when the words of *gedolei olam* appear to go against our deep-seated convictions and perceptions of sense? Do we scurry about to find more agreeable *gedolim*, while dismissing others as being out of touch (*challila*)? Or do we say, "I may think one way, but those who understand the *ratzon Hashem* – G-d's will – think otherwise"?

As for the opinions of the *gedolim* who lived in this country, there is little written on the subject. While many *Roshei Yeshiva* guided their *talmidim* through the *shidduch* process as we know it, they were obviously dealing with facts already on the ground, as Rabbi Halberstadt correctly pointed out. There is nothing to indicate that they were happy about the situation. I was told by a *talmid* of Rabbi Moshe Feinstein זצ״ל that Reb Moshe had told him that if he had the power, he would change the system, but it's so ingrained in society that it would be too difficult to accomplish. Rabbi Matisyahu Salomon שליט״א, the *Mashgiach* of Bais Medrash Govoha, Lakewood, told me that Rabbi Avrohom Pam זצ״ל told him the same thing. Certainly one could argue that if these *gedolim* despaired of changing the process, we might as well leave it alone, too. But to argue that the system is correct, sensible, and encouraged by *gedolei Torah* on its own merit, is an entirely different matter, is contrary to the evidence, and would certainly require documentation. Mere speculation is not a basis for one to just ignore clearly written, signed, and *uncontested* directives of our greatest Torah leaders.

Moreover, the American scene is blessed with a group of *Roshei Yeshiva* who maintain close contact with their *talmidim* after they have left their institutions – during their subsequent time in *Eretz Yisroel*, and then when they return to America and embark on *shidduchim*. Whenever it is realistic, these *Roshei Yeshiva* guide these *talmidim* along the very lines that the article proposes: extensive research in advance, a limited number of dates of reasonable duration, and avoidance of compromising places for dating.

Of interest, incidentally, should be the *psak* of Rabbi Moshe Feintein in *Igros Moshe, Even Ha'ezer* 4:65, where he prohibits, *lechat'chila* (preferred choice), *yichud* (a couple sitting in isolation) in a car "even during the day, and certainly at night." Reb Moshe concludes, "Only in a case of *shaas hadchak* (extenuating circumstances) can one rely on the lenient opinions." Rabbi Yaakov Kamenetzky is also known to have held that driving in a car at night is only permitted with the dome light on. In view of these *p'sakim*, it is difficult to imagine Reb Moshe or Reb Yaakov condoning a system that often involves violation of their halachic rulings. Apparently, the system is following the opinions of other authorities – *the gedolim of Eretz Yisroel* – (see *Shevet HaLevy* 5:202 and Rabbi Shlomo Zalman Auerbach, quoted in *sefer D'var Halacha* on *Hilchos Yichud*) who ruled that there is no prohibition of *yichud* in a car on an open road.

Rabbi Halberstadt criticizes what he calls my misuse of Rabbi Meir Shapiro's parable, and claims that I compared wonderful, true *zivuggim* to fictitious *mezuzos*.[1] This is clearly not what I said or meant. There is no mention in the article about the truth or fiction of anyone's *zivug*. The only point I was making was that the *system* that we so tenaciously adhere to has no inherent holiness or traditional meaning to it. It is purely cultural, and nobody should feel obligated to follow it. Questioning its sense or efficiency does not amount to an attack on a religious institution.

⤌ *Dating ... Leading Toward What?*

Rabbi Halberstadt and Rabbi Schochet both contend that the diverse nature of our society and culture demand a more lengthy and extensive type of courtship that cannot be done the

---

1. The parable involved a "*mezuza*" made from fragments of a Megillas Esther scroll, with "Vayezasa" written on the parchment, which is presumed to be kosher by virtue of another mezuza with "Parshandaso" on it. Similarly, the current dating system is presumed valid based on an old, worthless precedent.

way our *zeides* did it. Rabbi Halberstadt concludes, "Therefore, more time is required 'until each one recognizes to a degree what the other person is like and what their *hashkafas hachaim* is' (quoted from Rabbi Shach צ״ל)." Rabbi Halberstadt fails, though, to quote *the very next line* in that same letter of Rabbi Shach, which continues: "Know, my brothers, this custom [of excessive dating] is invalid and forbidden. More than three or four meetings is not necessary. Also, the duration of the meetings should not be longer than two or three hours each."

The point is that while all the talk of relationship development, sharing, bonding, merger of souls, *et al* may sound very sensible, *daas Torah* does not subscribe to it. The author of *Avi Ezri* (Rabbi Shach) states unequivocally: By the third or fourth meeting, you'll know all you need to know. (See also *Kuntrus Ve'alehu Lo Yibol* which quotes Rabbi Shlomo Zalman Auerbach to the same effect.) I understand that other *gedolim* may have held that more meetings are necessary. That is why I made no mention of numbers in the original article. As Rabbi Schochet points out, however, numbers are not the issue *per se*. The point is the attitude and *hashkafa*. If Rabbi Shach and Reb Shlomo Zalman held that three or four times is enough, that means that dating is not about bonding or merging of souls. That's what marriage is about.

It is precisely on this point that the difference in *hashkafa* is so compelling. I will illustrate this with a question. Suppose someone feels that he needs fifteen meetings to make a decision. Fine. Why do these meetings have to be spread out over a period of fifteen weeks? Why not in two or three weeks? The answer is, obviously, because one cannot develop a relationship within so short a time span. And herein lies the core of this discussion. Why do we meet before getting married? Our *gedolim* tell us that we meet in order to ensure that we know whom we are marrying. The meetings are essentially an exercise in *information gathering*, necessary to verify the extensive research done beforehand, and to determine *nesi'us chein* (compatibility for marriage).

The "fifteen-week system," though, has a different objective. In that system, they meet in order to develop a relationship to the point where the couple feel so close that they are ready to graduate to marriage. That, I believe, is an alien idea that has surreptitiously worked its way into our psyche, along with the foreign terminology of "dating." The results can be tragic. If it takes weeks to decide on a "no," it can take months upon months to meet just three or four people. That can add up to an awful lot of precious life slipping by. People who have endured this process concur: Proper research and selectivity could have condensed these years into mere *weeks*. Considering that many people are marrying their twentieth or even fiftieth *"shidduch,"* they could be gearing themselves for a catastrophic delay until they finally reach the *chupa*.

In light of this, we need to address Rabbi Schochet's next point. Rabbi Schochet mentions "other core issues such as love before or after marriage." It appears that he is suggesting that there are different opinions on this issue. Are there any Torah sources that advocate love before marriage, or any that even indicate that such a phenomenon indeed exists on any meaningful level? I am not aware of any. In fact, the words of the *Malbim* in *Parshas Ki Seitzei* are most illuminating on this subject.

> The Malbim writes "... concerning those who laugh at the ways of our fathers whose custom of shidduchim was for the parents to investigate the family and the character of the girl and decide on the match, and have the chassan meet the kalla only just before the wedding.... For the fact is that the main love comes only after marriage. In those days, love was planted like a tiny seed that would grow and blossom like a flowering tree. Because couples knew so little about each other beforehand, they entered the marriage with an attitude of acceptance toward one another. Later they would start to notice each other's noble qualities and good attributes – thereby increasing their love ... In those days only a disaster would cause a divorce .... But with today's new customs, the young are taught to capture each other's hearts and show each other love that is without foundation on earth, only sweet talk and fantasy – like on an actors' stage. And later, when they realize how they've fooled each other, their love cools off bit by bit – until it becomes nothing and meaningless ...."

The penetrating wisdom of the *Malbim* should give us pause.

❧ Are There Any Exceptions?

Rabbi Halberstadt and Rabbi Schochet both ask: What about all the people for whom such a system is not always feasible? Of course, I understand that there are many segments of our society that could never adopt such an approach. The culture shock would be impossible to overcome. I also recognize that for some individuals (for example, older boys or girls) it would not be very practical. There is often a geographic factor in America that can make prior meetings between parents and prospective in-law children not feasible. Also, as the letter-writers pointed out, some yeshiva and Bais Yaakov products come from irreligious families, or – even when their parents are observant – do not fully share values and life goals with their parents. They are often left to their own resources, which can limit prior research.

So, yes, there are countless good reasons for exceptions. That is still not a reason for the rest of us to doggedly stick to a system disdained by *Gedolei Yisroel*. Many of us could seriously contemplate a change in practice and attitude.

❧ Postscript

Recently I spoke to an exceptional yeshiva *bachur* about his *shidduch* prospects. A *shadchan* had given him a list of thirty "names." The same list was given to his friends. One friend was up to number six. Another had already "covered" (met with) eight. "Research" was a five-to-ten-minute phone call to a teacher or friend who informs him that "she is a very nice girl." I told him that at this rate, it would take him at least five years to get married. "Covering" one name could take weeks. Why not invest five hours in finding out if someone is for you, rather than wasting fifty hours to discover that she is not for you? (Consider if a *bachur* knew he had to meet three or four times in one week. The decision to meet would automatically be a much more serious and well-researched one. It is a far greater commitment to give up a full week than it is to take the weekly Sunday "give-it-a-try" excursion ....)

Contrast this with the European scene (which I have had the opportunity to observe up close). In Europe, no self-respecting *baal habayis* would ever allow a young man to meet his daughter without his and his wife's meeting him first. Most impressive, however, is the *seriousness* of the whole process there. After extensive research, the parents go to meet the prospective mate. The children stay home until the parents feel certain that the *shidduch* makes sense. It's 90 percent done before they even meet. Exactly the way the *Chofetz Chaim* wrote it should be done.

Why would anyone find that objectionable? What would we be giving up? Perhaps we are reluctant because secular society has taught us that we are entitled to be swept off our feet, etc. We feel that we will be missing a thrilling part of life's drama of which we must not be deprived. The price, however, is too heavy to pay. The tragic suffering of countless older singles who have paid with the best years of their lives to facilitate a dysfunctional and humiliating process is too agonizing to contemplate. Only *Hashem* knows how many oceans of *Yiddishe* tears have been shed by heartbroken parents and children. The current epidemic proportions of this problem are a direct result of the dating system. In circles where the classic approach is employed, the problem of older singles is marginal, almost non-existent.

The upshot of it all is that our children are being victimized and horribly misled. Eagerly and innocently, they do everything they think they're supposed to be doing, trusting us that the system is controlled and sanctioned by *Gedolei Torah*. Obediently, they sit in trendy lounges and garish hotel lobbies (compromising their own deep-felt *tzenius* sensibilities); naively believing that this is the way of Torah and *talmidei chachamim*. They *nebach* do not yet know that the system is grossly inefficient and will fail countless numbers of them, as it has already failed thousands before them, who are still anxiously waiting for the *yeshua* to come.

It's time to follow the advice of *gedolei Torah*. "*Derocheha darkei noam v'chol nesivoseha shalom*: Its ways are ways of pleasantness and all its paths are peace" (*Mishlei* 3, 17).

(Rabbi) Ephraim Wachsman

UNDERSTANDING LIMITATIONS

A CLOSER LOOK AT TWO DIFFERENT PATHS TO "THE BROKEN PLATE"

PROFESSOR AARON D. TWERSKI

❧ When Parents Carry the Responsibility

All social institutions have their limitations. A school is not a home. A summer camp is not a school. A playgroup is not a classroom. Each institution has things that it can do very well and others not so well and often not at all. Dating in the Torah world is an institution for bringing young men and women together so that they can make the all-important decision about whether they are compatible with one another. Thousands of youngsters enter the doors of this institution every year but rarely with any insight as to the limitations that inhere in it.

At the outset I should indicate that within the Torah world, the method for bringing *shidduchim* to fruition is not monolithic. Within the Chassidic community the responsibility for making the choice of mates lay primarily on the parents' shoulders. They do all the screening, and in the vast majority of instances, when the young man and woman are brought together, the couple ends up as *chassan* and *kalla*. They may see each other two, or at most, three times. Only if the couple find something objectionable do they part company. On occasion that happens. However, the task facing the young man or woman is clearly defined. No one expects the couple to develop any relationship in that short period of time. And since, for the most part, there is little contact between the couple prior to the wedding, there is not much second guessing that goes on during the engagement period.

It is not my purpose in this article to advocate the *Chassidishe* dating model over the classic yeshiva dating model. I understand that "one size fits all" is unrealistic. Coming from a *Chassidishe* family, my children all followed the age-old Chassidic tradition. I do believe that when parents properly fulfill their responsibilities, this method works very well indeed. Admittedly, divorces occur from *Chassidishe shidduchim*, but they don't appear to exceed the divorce rate from the yeshiva dating model and may well be less. However, my point here is that the responsibilities of the parents and the young man and woman are very clearly defined in the Chassidic *shidduchim* model and the expectations about what they can get from such limited interaction with each other is circumscribed.

❦ *The Non-Chassidic Approach*

When one examines the classic yeshiva dating model, the picture is somewhat murky.

Almost all *shidduchim* have screening of some sort. For some the screening is quite substantial for others it is less intense. However, I believe it fair to observe that the screening is not as intense as within Chassidic circles where the young man and woman do not expect to develop a relationship. For example, within the Chassidic model the parents will almost always have met the young man or woman and their parents before the prospective mates meet for the first time. Within the yeshiva dating model, it is extremely rare for the respective parents to have met, and aside from the glimpse that the parents of the young woman get of the young man when he comes to pick up their daughter for the date, the parents have almost no opportunity to make any assessment of their own until the *shidduch* appears to reach the serious stage.

The prospective couple carries an enormous burden. They have to decide whether they are for each other. Since the dating process cannot go on for any great length of time, their task is even more daunting. In a period of five or six (seven or eight or whatever number) dates, they must establish not only whether their personalities mesh but also whether they share common goals in life. There is nothing easy going about this process. They are dating not *chas veshalom* to have a good time, but rather to make a decision of monumental importance. In a jocular mood I once observed that the probing that goes on is not unlike the cross-examination that a party to a lawsuit undergoes from the opposing lawyer. If you have undergone cross-examination (I have), you would understand that one develops a quick antipathy for the lawyer who is putting you through the mill. Often, when counseling a couple who have dated several times and are unsure about their feeling toward each other, I observe that if they feel even slightly positive toward each other after the intense grilling that they have undergone, they must care for each other quite a bit. Normally, they ought to dislike each other intensely for having put each other through such an ordeal.

❧ No Bells or Whistles

Not all-prospective mates feel this way about the yeshiva dating process. Many are able to develop a very positive relationship in a short time. However, many do not. They are not to blame. They are not being picky. They simply cannot, within the constraints of a system that demands that dating is for *tachlis* and *tachlis* only, develop a sufficiently positive relationship to make their decision an easy one. They lament that they would like to be in the comfort zone before deciding to become engaged. Many youngsters will freely admit that they have parted on numerous occasions with a prospective mate because they have not felt sufficiently positive to make the decision. My psychologist friends tell me that the inability to commit may evidence problems that are more profound. And certainly in some cases they are correct. However, my own experience is that the problem is often not personal but rather institutional. The institution of dating – the process that is supposed to bring a couple together – has the capacity to keep them apart and distant.

When I share this observation with singles they often come back at me with the following rejoinder. Assume that you are right – what is the alternative? What do you offer us as a resolution to our dilemma? More dating will not help because the atmosphere is too heavy. Indeed, as time goes on, it becomes unbearably so. Well, I suggest why not go to the top of the Empire State Building and wave the American flag? They look at me as if I had just descended from Mars. No, I say, you won't do that because it won't help. Well, neither will anything else. You must honestly confront the question as to whether you belong to the class of persons for whom the only dating process you can engage in will not provide you all the positive bells and whistles that you desire. The reality is that many couples do make the decision to go ahead when they find that the *shidduch* is appropriate and makes good common sense. If they share common Torah goals as to how they wish to build their lives, even if the relationship is lukewarm, they make the plunge. Few will announce this to the world. But what I am relating is fact. At some point, the youngsters have learned the limitations of the system and have decided that despite its limitations, they have to decide or else face an endless cycle of dating leading to nowhere.

A person must be a *maven* on himself. If you are having difficulty operating within the *shidduch* system, perhaps you are a person who will never develop the ability to make easy decisions within the existing system. And if that is true, there is nothing wrong with you. And there may be little we can do with the system. The institution has its limitations. It works easily for some and with great difficulty for others. The only choice is to recognize that the decision to marry will have to be made with a lesser degree of comfort. Institutions have their limitations. But we, as thinking sensitive *bnei Torah*, can rise above institutions. We have the freedom to choose, and choose we must.

NOW YOU SAY IT,
NOW YOU DON'T

RABBI YITZCHOK BERKOWITZ

So here you have it – the paramedic's guide to neurosurgery. Yes, that is precisely what a concise summary of Hilchos Lashon Hara regarding shidduchim is like. In deciding when to speak up, what information to disclose, precise choice of words, and even tone of voice, one may very well be affecting the lives of individuals and families for years to come. The most subtle nuance – even unintended – could seal one's fate for a lifetime. No article – nor even an entire sefer, for that matter – could possibly take the place of consultation with a competent, sensitive, experienced Rav. The purpose of this article is merely to call attention to several basic guidelines that must not be overlooked by anyone involved in a shidduch in any capacity. And to alert the reader when to consult a Rav, and on which issues.

❧ Suggestions and Advice: Eitza Hogennes

The first principle to keep in mind with regard to *shidduchim* is the commandment *"Lifnei iver lo sitten michshol* – not to cause the blind to stumble"; or as *Chazal* interpret it – don't give bad advice (*eitza she'eina hogennes*). For the *shadchan* or adviser, that means neither suggesting nor promoting a *shidduch* that one does not believe the party he is speaking to would be interested in, were they made aware of all pertinent information. In the case of a parent or the prospective *chassan* or *kalla,* it would be wrong to request that a *shidduch* be arranged with a party who – if properly informed – would not choose to be involved.

According to the *Chofetz Chaim,* this is true even when the information in question does not necessarily reflect on the appropriateness of the *shidduch*. One does not suggest a *shidduch* to a family that is known to be especially particular about *yichus,* withholding the fact that the perspective's grandfather was a well-known *apikores.* Instead, after explaining the situation, one could proceed to point out that some of *Klal Yisroel's* most prominent families have favored character over genealogy…. Rather than truncate a decade or two off the prospective partner's age, one could attempt to show that the person in question is exceptional and worth meeting despite the age difference. (Needless to say, one should not suggest a *shidduch* that he does not believe is a good idea for either of the involved parties.)

So what does one do when he feels that a *bachur* has "unrealistic expectations," is "living in a fantasy world," and "isn't getting any younger"? The proper approach is one of reason – not manipulation. Occasionally, a *poseik* (authority in *halacha*) may allow for information to be withheld temporarily when there are grounds for assuming that the person is subconsciously waiting to be tricked into meeting someone, rather than admit to having made an issue of something trivial.

Additionally, the common practice of the inaccurate reporting of age is not considered dishonest in a society or situation where one is expected to do so. Not unlike "Jewish Standard Time" on wedding invitations (which for better or for worse has become a fact of life), using the number 29 for a 32-year-old will probably be understood quite accurately in many circles – much as, in those very circles, 32 could easily be taken to mean 36. (This would obviously not apply when it can be assumed that the information will be taken at face value.) Because of the temptation to be extremely liberal in applying this rule, one cannot help but insist on having a *rav* decide the matter. On the other hand, where information is taken at face value, one should be precise in these details.

A serious issue in *halacha* is that of defining whom the relevant parties really are. Is it right to suggest a *shidduch* where the prospective *chassan* and *kalla* are within the parameters of one another's standards of acceptability, but outside those of their families? On the one hand, it is the couple and not the families that is contemplating marriage, and indeed *halacha* does not leave the final word with the parents. Nevertheless, one must consider why he has chosen to assist the couple at the expense of the parents' wishes. Furthermore, there are those who maintain that although children are not bound by the preferences of their parents with regard to *shidduchim*, they do not have the right to do anything that could embarrass their parents. In such cases, you must consult your local *poseik*.

⁕ Information: What to Reveal

Unlike the *shadchan* or adviser, who would be violating *lifnei iver* by promoting a *shidduch* while concealing information about one party that the other would have found objectionable, the person to whom a *shidduch* was suggested is not considered offering advice, and would therefore not have to volunteer facts that may be of concern to the other side. Similarly, a visit to a *shadchan* does not call for revealing information that could interfere with one's prospects. The *halachos* that apply here are those of not causing harm to another – which would require the revealing of only issues that could pose a serious threat to the future of the couple should they marry; and *midvar shekker tirchak* – even when information can be withheld, one may not lie outright about anything that could in any way be relevant. Included in the category of facts to be revealed are physical, psychological, and psychiatric conditions that could interfere with the person's ability to function properly as a spouse or parent, as well as any serious condition in the family that is hereditary. Such information, however, need not be revealed at an initial meeting; one does have the right to wait and see if the prospect is worth considering seriously before making oneself vulnerable. What is absolutely prohibited is to conceal a serious condition until the point where the other person is emotionally involved and will find it difficult to make an objective decision. (It may be a strategic mistake to withhold even less-critical information as the couple considers engagement, considering the fact that the other party could one day feel deceived.) An individual or family that is aware of a condition that may have to be revealed should be encouraged to discuss the subject with a *rav* before entering the era of *shidduchim*.

An acquaintance who is aware of a condition that must be revealed has the responsibility to see to it that the information will be communicated at the proper time, and if it seems that no one will communicate it, he (or she) must do so himself. This responsibility is included in the prohibition *"Lo saamod al dam rei'echa* – Do not stand by as your brother's blood is being spilled." Conditions of this type – whether those that cast doubt on one's abilities as a spouse, or hereditary illnesses – are to be reported even if the other side has made no effort to find out. Other issues need not be brought up, even when approached as a reference, as there are no objective grounds for assuming they should be reasons for concern. When asked directly concerning some other issue, one must not be dishonest – but one could choose to be evasive.

- *A girl on medication for manic depression must inform the bachur she is meeting before things get too serious. If she confides in a close friend that on the advice of a parent she has decided not to tell, the friend should try to convince her that such an approach is wrong – or more correctly, should direct her to a rav. If it becomes apparent that the girl is adamant on not telling, the friend would be required to do so. A sensitive, competent rav must be sought out for guidance on just how to go about that.*
- *A bachur has a history of losing his temper with chavrusos and roommates, and does on occasion get violent: His friends should*

have been in touch with the mashgiach who – in turn – would have had to see to it that this bachur get the appropriate help in dealing with his temper. If the bachur *has entered shidduchim showing no signs of major change, the friends must seek the advice of a rav to determine who should tell, and precisely how to describe his personality.*

- *A young woman has mentioned to friends on countless occasions that she is just petrified of the thought of getting married, as she never learned to cook. Not only would neither she nor her friends have to mention anything about the situation to someone she is meeting, when questioned explicitly about her culinary abilities a friend can simply say, "I don't know."*

In all situations where potentially damaging information is to be revealed, one must be careful not to cause any undo harm. If the father of a girl who is meeting a severely problematic *bachur* is known to be indiscreet and could be expected to make the information public, he may not be told about the *bachur's* problems. This rule holds true even if there seem to be no alternative means for preventing a potentially unhealthy marriage.

❧ Finding Out: Who Asks Whom and How

This brings us to the most complicated aspect of *shidduchim* in *halacha*: How do you find out about someone? If all but drastic conditions can be concealed by everyone involved, how does one obtain the necessary information in determining whether or not the *shidduch* is worth one's while in the first place – and how does one protect himself, his children, and his students from marrying the wrong person?

Indeed, *zivuggim* (pairing people in marriage) are from Heaven. Often, the oddest combinations have made for beautiful marriages. Our own assessments of who is for whom are far from definitive. Nevertheless, a competent *mechanech* or parent should have a relatively good idea of what his child or *talmid* is like, what he needs in a spouse, and certainly what kind of spouse could be problematic if not outright destructive. When such a person asks pointed questions, it is understood that these are not mere matters of preference – rather, substantive issues of concern deserving of an accurate response.

As said, questions must be pointed; general questions are an invitation for miscommunication. One man's *talmid chacham* is another's *am ha'aretz*. The forty-year-old mother of seven has totally different standards for what it means to be organized than does the newlywed. And what precisely do you mean when you ask if someone is "good," "neat," or "friendly"? These are all unquantifiable terms for which we are without common vocabulary. *"Is he on time for seder?" "Does he bother making his bed in the morning?"* These questions leave little room for error. Even *"Does she have close friends?"* – when asked of someone mature – is a valid way of inquiring about one's openness to relationships.

Whom to ask is an issue of its own. Ideally, what could be better than asking a *mechanech* or *mechaneches*? In reality, many a *rebbi* or *rosh yeshiva* defines his role as that of giving a *derech* in learning *Gemora* and may not find the time to gain an understanding of all his *talmidim* (especially if he has many). Even a *mashgiach* may be familiar with only the more positive side of a *talmid*; after all, the *talmid* probably does not conduct himself in the presence of the *mashgiach* the way he behaves in his dorm room. And then there is the tendency among *rebbe'im* and teachers to be protective of their students to the point where they would not consider saying anything that could possibly "ruin a *shidduch*." If a *mechanech* is to be consulted, it should preferably be by a peer, colleague, or other acquaintance to whom he feels some level of responsibility.

The obvious next choice would be friends of the person in question. In light of issues raised with regard to relying exclusively on *mechanchim* alone, it would stand to reason that a roommate or close friend would be an invaluable resource in obtaining pertinent information. Many *gedolei Yisroel*, however, have voiced serious concerns over the practice of asking *bachurim* about one another. Not every twenty-one-year old *bachur* possesses the necessary judgment to interpret the behavior of his contemporaries accurately and objectively. Such a reference must himself be checked out for maturity, accuracy of perception and integrity, and could only then be approached. As previously discussed, it would have to be made clear to the reference that the questions are coming from one who understands the issues crucial to the *shidduch*, and as such are worthy of an honest response.

One could logically conclude that every eligible young man and woman should have a responsible, well-connected person to research suggested names by way of pointed questions asked of the appropriate references. If parents don't feel they can play that role, they should enlist the help of those who can. Singles on their own must find a *rebbe* figure to do the research for them, and concerned, capable people would be doing a great *chessed* by offering their services to those who do not have family looking out for them.

In gathering information about a family, one resorts to networking – seeking out among one's own acquaintances someone familiar with an acquaintance of the family. A neighbor is not required by *halacha* to be open with a total stranger about any issue involving the family – with the exceptions of serious hereditary diseases and actual questions of *p'sul* (halachic ineligibility for marriage). That would not be the case when questioned by a responsible acquaintance attempting to clarify specific concerns relevant to the particular *shidduch*, where one should be forthright. One should, if possible, try to establish the person's credentials. On the other hand, one should be forthright when questioned by a responsible acquaintance attempting to clarify specific concerns relevant to the particular *shidduch*. It is also necessary to first establish that a neighbor to be consulted as a reference is not on bad terms with the people one is inquiring about. (Similarly, when inquiring about a divorcee, one would not contact the former spouse or his friends and relatives, unless a *poseik* has ruled that the specific situation allows for it.) If you are the "total stranger" contacting the neighbor, you would be well advised to have a respected intermediary introduce you or make the inquiries on your behalf.

❧ Reporting Back:
Avoiding Lashon Hara and Rechilus

A most sensitive area in *shidduchim* regarding *lashon hara* is the debriefing by the *shadchan* of the young man or woman following a meeting. When unsure of how to proceed when in need of advice, the prospective partner should discuss the issue with the person he feels is in the best position to help clarify matters for him – whether that is the *shadchan* or someone else. Having made a decision not to continue with the *shidduch*, one owes an explanation to no one but *Hashem* and himself. The *shadchan* can attempt to convince the party that he may be mistaken and that it may be in his best interest to share his concerns with the *shadchan*, but unless he feels that is the case, one does not owe it to the *shadchan* to explain his decision.

Furthermore, if it is clear to the person that his decision is final, he should not tell the *shadchan* anything negative about the other party without clarifying with a *rav* that it is important to do so. The *shadchan* himself must be extremely cautious in what he communicates to the other party. Any negative comment said over in the name of the first party constitutes *rechilus* – gossip – and is prohibited. If the *shadchan* feels the need to communicate constructive criticism, it must be done tactfully, to ensure that it will indeed be constructive, and not angrily brushed off as the subjective – and perhaps warped – perception of the other party.

And finally, following an unsuccessful *shidduch* attempt, all involved must be careful not to allow their frustrations to be expressed in the form of accusations and labeling. Not every *shidduch* is meant to work, and there does not always have to be a culprit.

After all the investigating, consulting, and intuiting, entering marriage is still very much a mystery; can anyone really know what kind of spouse and parent he will turn out to be – let alone this stranger with whom he is about to build a home? The feeling of vulnerability and helplessness is countered only by *bitachon* – trust that ultimately *Hashem* is looking out for us. Going about things in accordance with His will is a first step in enlisting that *siyata diShmaya*.

WHEN SOMEONE'S LIFE
IS IN YOUR HANDS[1]

JUDITH MISHELL, PH.D.

The Stern family was searching for a shidduch for their daughter Malkie, and Moshe seemed a very suitable prospect. The young couple met twice, and it seemed to be a promising shidduch.

After their third meeting, Malkie was much more subdued. She learned that Moshe had gone through a period when he got very anxious – so anxious that he had trouble sitting still and concentrating on his learning.

He had gone to his family doctor and was prescribed some medicine for anxiety that really helped him. He didn't want to keep taking the medicine, so the doctor had referred him to a psychologist. He had learned a lot from the psychologist about how to deal with anxiety, and now, even without the medicine, he was much calmer and able to concentrate.

Malkie was quite sure that there was no problem, but her parents were quite worried. They didn't want Malkie to get into a difficult marriage. They wanted to know what the chances were that Moshe's anxiety would return. They told Malkie that before the shidduch would continue, they were going to do some checking.

---

1. This title is used with the kind permission of the Chofetz Chaim Heritage Foundation.

Malkie was very disappointed. Her parents sympathized but they pointed out that life gets a lot more stressful after marriage, and they wanted to be sure that her husband would be able to take care of her and, b'ezras Hashem, a family.

✦ A "Hit or Miss" Process

The Sterns are one hundred percent correct in being concerned about Malkie's future and wanting more information before they let the *shidduch* proceed. Most of us would want to find out more about the implications of the fact that the young man had trouble functioning and had been treated for anxiety. The questions are: 1) What information do we need? 2) How do we go about getting the information? 3) How do we assess the information once we have it?

I am addressing this issue as an Orthodox clinical psychologist who serves the Orthodox Jewish community. I have been professionally involved in many cases like the one described above. Over the years I have become increasingly concerned about the stigma surrounding mental health problems and the "hit or miss" process for getting the necessary information about a prospective *shidduch* who has been in therapy and/or on psychotropic medication. Unfortunately, I have seen fine, vibrant young people, *baalei middos*, who have been deeply hurt by being *passuled* (disqualified) because of irrational fears and inadequate information. Let me tell you about the "hit or miss" process that is common today.

We'll use the fictional situation above as an example. The Sterns talked to the *shadchan* about their concerns about Moshe's problem with anxiety. The *shadchan* talked to Moshe and his parents and they agreed to allow the Sterns to get information on his condition from the therapist. The Sterns were not too confident in their ability to process the information, so they asked their family physician to serve as their *shaliach* (designated agent), and both called the therapist for information about Moshe. In response, the therapist gave the callers relevant information[2] about Moshe. Up to this point everything proceeded smoothly.

Within a few days, however, another *shaliach* – this time a mental health professional – called. It seems that the Sterns, or whoever was advising them, either didn't trust the therapist, didn't feel the *shaliach* asked the right questions, or didn't think the *shaliach* was qualified to evaluate the information. In some cases, I myself have been called by as many as five people, including family members, rabbis, mental health professionals and physicians. The family may want to say, "Enough is enough. Evaluate the information you have and make a decision." They are afraid, however, that it will seem as though they are trying to hide something, so they permit the process to go on and on.

If the psychotherapist is not the one who prescribes the medication, the *shlichim* will often want to speak to the consulting physician or psychiatrist. In one of my cases, after speaking both to me and the prescribing psychiatrist, the *shlichim* still did not feel satisfied with the information they had collected. Therefore they advised the prospective *shidduch* to copy the client's psychiatric records so they could see them. Even though the family was concerned that they might be perceived as trying to hide something, they felt they had to draw a line. After seeking counsel with their rabbi, they allowed the prospective *shidduch* to go to the psychiatrist's office and *read* the record – but they did not allow it to be *copied*.

At this point, the psychiatrist and I felt that the situation had gotten out of hand. First, the records kept by professionals are subject to misinterpretation when read by laymen. Second, there may be issues addressed in the record that involve other family or community members that are not at all relevant to the question of whether the client is a good marriage prospect. This becomes a matter of *lashon hara*. Third, even though the client has written a release allowing the record to be read, they may also reveal private matters that are irrelevant to the *shidduch*. Fourth, who can guarantee that

---

2. The information given should conform to the halachic guidelines in *Sefer Chofetz Chaim*. See also the Companion Study Guide to the video, *When Someone's Life is in Your Hands*, published by The Chofetz Chaim Heritage Foundation.

information in the record will be treated with complete confidentiality outside of the therapist's office?

The young person involved in this particular incident felt dehumanized and violated by the information-gathering and evaluating process, which ended up including as many as four rabbis, medical and mental health professionals, and friends of the prospective spouse. The person was understandably much more guarded in subsequent sessions with me and faced future *shidduchim with dread.*

❧ The Stigma Problem

Obviously, everyone involved in this process was trying to do a *mitzva* and help the person find a good *shidduch*. Nevertheless, there are problems raised by the stigma attached to mental health treatment and this intrusive process of information collecting, such as:

1. Family members and other interested parties who are not qualified to make recommendations often strongly advise young people not to take medication and/or be in therapy because it will interfere with getting a "good *shidduch*."
2. People in therapy and/or on medication often feel deeply ashamed of their need for help.
3. People may terminate therapy prematurely to avoid having to say that they are in therapy.
4. Many people who would benefit from therapy and/or medication do not seek help for fear of not getting married.
5. People sometimes hide the fact that they are, or have been, in therapy, and that they are using, or have used, psychotropic medication.
6. As a result of the above, problems that could have been resolved show up later and cause much suffering and unhappiness.
7. The unresolved problems affect the next generation.
8. People sometimes do not seek help for family problems for

fear that a record of parental problems will interfere with *shidduchim* for their children.

It seems obvious from the list of problems above that the potential harm of this slipshod information-gathering process can far outweigh the good. I have spoken to *rabbanim* who are very involved with *shidduchim* and with other mental health professionals who work with *frum* clients, and all told me of similar situations. Therefore, I think that this is an issue which needs to be addressed by the Orthodox Jewish community. We need a process for helping people get the information required to make informed, rational decisions about prospective *shidduchim* who either are, or have been, in psychotherapy, and/or are using, or have used, psychopharmacological treatment.

It is important to understand that one of the effects of the recent advances in psychopharmacology and psychotherapy is that medication and therapy are now prescribed for far less serious disorders than in the past. Therefore, some people who in the past might have turned exclusively to *tefilla, Tehillim, mussar,* or a *shmuess* with their *rav,* now turn to professionals for additional help. I'm a firm believer in the ultimate power of the Torah-based methods mentioned above and I think that any therapy that leaves out the spiritual component is deficient.[3] Nevertheless, there are many *frum* people[4] today who, for one reason or another, feel that they need therapy and/or medication in addition to (*chas v'shalom* in place of) these time-honored methods.

It is beyond the scope of this article to discuss whether or not medication and therapy are over-prescribed-and-utilized. The fact that is germane to our subject is that more and more *frum Yidden* go to physicians and mental health professionals to seek relief, not only from serious problems but from everyday problems-in-living such as anxiety, tension, minor depression, relationship difficulties,

---

3. See Mishell, J. & Srebrenik, S. (1991) Beyond Your Ego: A Torah Approach to Self-Knowledge, Emotional Health, and Inner Peace. CIS Publishers: New York, London, Jerusalem.

4. There are cultural differences in the pattern of utilization of mental health services by *frum* Jews, with Americans most likely to seek professional help.

and *parnassa* problems. And, more and more of these people are successfully treated with psychotropic drugs and therapy.

The point I wish to emphasize here is that there is no reason to *pasul* someone for a *shidduch* just because they have received mental health treatment, either in the form of psychotherapy or medication. Being in therapy or taking medication is not necessarily an indication that a person is dysfunctional in any way. In fact, many people who have undergone psychotherapy have learned skills that make them better prepared than average to cope with stress, communicate effectively, and take responsibility for their lives. They are to be admired, not condemned, for trying to improve their lives and the lives of their families.

⤝ What is a Major Problem and What is a Minor Problem?

There are, of course, conditions that are more debilitating and more chronic than the everyday "problems-in-living" we all encounter. Psychoses, bipolar disorder, and major depression, to name a few, may require ongoing psychiatric and psychological intervention and have far more profound effects on daily functioning. *But let us not confuse minor and major problems!* Is there anyone who doesn't have his or her ups and downs? Who hasn't had trouble making a transition? Who hasn't felt discouraged? Who doesn't sometimes feel jumpy? Who isn't occasionally irritable? Who hasn't felt the need to air difficulties with a sympathetic listener and get objective feedback? Are we really going to *pasul* people just because they get help from professionals?

So, how can concerned parents get the information they need in order to decide whether a problem is minor or major? What questions should they ask? How should they go about asking? And how should they evaluate the information once they have it?

First, however, let us ask ourselves the following question, in hope that the other party will pose the very same question to himself or herself:

Does a person have an obligation to disclose their own mental health problems?

If one is currently being treated for mental health problems with psychotherapy and/or psychopharmacology, one might be obligated to disclose this information, either personally or via a second party. When and how to disclose this information depends on many factors, such as the severity of the disorder, how it affects functioning, and how likely it is to cause difficulties in the marital relationship. Because of the number and complexity of the factors, it is impossible to give specific rules as to when and how to disclose. Each case needs to be assessed on an individual basis by competent *rabbanim* and mental health professionals. (For further information on this matter see the article by Rabbi Yitzchok Berkowitz preceding this article.)

The following general guidelines were suggested by Rabbi Aryeh Beer (of Lakewood, NJ).

1) For relatively minor disorders, e.g., mild anxiety and/or depression, the information should be personally disclosed at the point that the relationship is getting serious. The disclosure should occur before either party is completely emotionally involved.

2) For more serious disorders, e.g., clinical depression, severe anxiety disorders, cyclical mood disorder, and borderline personality disorder, the information may need to be disclosed earlier. If the condition is so severe that it will almost certainly interfere with normal functioning and/or will cause relationship difficulties, the disclosure should be made in advance of the initial meeting. However, if the condition is being effectively managed by medication, the disclosure need not be made in advance but it should be made before the parties are emotionally involved.

3) Withholding information about current mental health problems may undermine the marital relationship by:

a) creating trust problems,

b) fostering regret, resentment, and disappointment,

c) putting a person in a situation with which he or she is unable to cope.

4) Personal self-disclosure is preferable whenever possible, because it eliminates issues of *lashon hara* and confidentiality, should the source reveal more than is called for. If a person is unable or uncomfortable to personally reveal the information, however, a *shaliach* can be used.

What questions should parents ask?

Parents, or those advising them, should ask for the diagnosis and the severity of the disorder, duration of the problem, type and dosage of medications used, response to psychotherapy, prognosis, genetic factors, implications for fetal development, advisability of nursing, effect on functioning and relationships, and motivation of client. All of these factors have to be weighed carefully in order to assess the suitability of the person as a prospective *shidduch*.

How can they get the information they need?

At the present time, the best strategy is to ask a *gadol* for guidance and have a qualified *shaliach* gather information from involved mental health professionals and other people who know the person well, e.g., a boy's *mechanech* or Rosh Yeshiva, a girl's *mechaneches* or Seminary Director.

How shall parents assess the information they gather?

The information should be assessed by the *shaliach* with the help of experts, if necessary, and discussed with the *gadol*. Recommendations should then be made to the parents as to the suitability of the prospective *shidduch*, whether more information is needed, and whether a waiting period is needed in order to evaluate the efficacy of treatment before making a final decision. Once a decision is made, it should be communicated clearly and sensitively to the prospective *shidduch* and his or her family. Discussions of the information should be limited to those who are qualified to evaluate the data.

❧ Recommendations for a New Approach

Because of the hazards mentioned above, and the seriousness of the matter of helping people to find *shidduchim*, I strongly recommend a task force to: 1) establish an advisory board[5] composed of experts on psychopharmacology, genetics, psychiatry and psychotherapy. These experts would provide the background knowledge needed to evaluate the data requested above; 2) form a panel of well-trained *shlichim* qualified to collect the data in a sensitive and halachically correct manner; and 3) develop a procedure to counsel parents or surrogate parents, answer their questions, and make recommendations.

This is an extremely delicate matter. The lives of precious young people (and others not so young) can be deeply affected by being involved in such a procedure. All of the steps above require the utmost sensitivity, *kavod habrios,* and *yiras Shamayim.* May *Hakadosh Baruch Hu* give us *Siyata DiShmaya* to be able to help every *Yid* find his or her *zivug* and establish a *bayis ne'eman b'Yisroel.*

---

5. In preparation of this article, I spoke to Rabbi Aaron Weitz of the Echo Institute for Health. He had heard of many such cases and was keenly aware of the problem. He spoke to a *Gadol B'Yisroel* and was told that it would be a big *mitzvah* and a great benefit to the Orthodox Jewish community to establish such an Advisory Board. The *Gadol* recommended that mental questions be included as well.

ON THE ROAD TO THE CHUPA: NAVIGATING THE POTHOLES

❧ A PRISONER IN CINDERELLA'S CASTLE

❧ FROM A SHADCHAN'S PERSPECTIVE

❧ LE'TORAH LE'CHUPA ULE'MA'ASIM TOVIM

❧ TIME TO MOVE ON

❧ "HELP ME GET MARRIED"

❧ THE RUCHNIUS APPROACH (EVEN WHEN ALL ELSE FAILS)

❧ FACING REJECTION IN SHIDDUCHIM … WITHOUT FEELING REJECTED

Life's road can be full of stumbling blocks and unanticipated obstacles. How do we wend our way around the pitfalls, and — if we slip — how do we get back on our feet, and proceed to our goal of a happy and fulfilling marriage?

A Prisoner in Cinderella's Castle

Thoughts on Being Single

Miss Anonymous

When I was young, my father took my brother and me to a theme park based on fairy tales. My brother and I decided to take a ride in Cinderella's pumpkin coach. After a fun-filled ride, the coach stopped at Cinderella's castle to allow all the riders off. My brother and I, along with a dozen other laughing children, tumbled out of the pumpkin coaches, and ran across the moat via the open drawbridge. The drawbridge closed and we were left to our own devices inside the castle. We joined the other children as they ran around looking at this, climbing on that... then one child discovered a staircase. A minute later, we were all enthusiastically climbing up the steps to find ourselves on a beautiful terrace with climbing towers and a splendid enclosure overlooking the castle's moat. Again, we all ran around laughing and talking as would any group of rambunctious youngsters. My brother and I were especially enthralled as we ran wildly from tower to tower pointing out the exquisite architecture. Suddenly, I stopped and looked around. All around us was quiet. We were alone.

A little flustered, we decided that perhaps the others had gone back downstairs and so we ran quickly down. Nobody was in sight. Rushing upstairs again, we looked around. Where could everyone have gone? We walked around the railing looking at the moat below us. And then we saw it. There was a second drawbridge leading out of the castle. We were just in time to glimpse the tail end of our group tramp across the bridge and happily rejoin their parents. But how did they get there?

"There must be another doorway downstairs that we missed," I told my brother. While my brother waited upstairs, I ran down to check. It looked a little darker than before and somehow the mannequins of the fairy-tale characters didn't look as cheerful as they had a few minutes earlier. Nor was there a door. I rushed back upstairs, eager to rejoin my brother and to escape the dingy indoors of the castle and the ominous stares of the evil stepmother. My heart was pounding and fear was mounting.

As we once again looked over the railing, we could see my father down on the ground signaling to us. But what was he trying to tell us? He was motioning to us and mouthing well-meant advice, but up on the terrace we couldn't make sense of his animated gesticulations. Frustrated and disappointed, I looked away. I desperately tried to blink back my tears. After all, I was the brave, older sister.

Of course, we found our way out of that castle eventually. We turned a corner and there, in one of the towers we had circled dozens of times, was a doorway we hadn't seen before. We stepped through the doorway, walked down the spiral staircase we found and joyfully dashed across the drawbridge.

The incident was safely in the past. Yet, I never forgot it. The overwhelming feelings, the stinging unfairness, and the overall fear and the disappointment are as entangled in my memory as the intricate charm of Cinderella's castle.

❧ Putting the Situation in Perspective

In recent years, I have come to relive this episode albeit with a slight variation. A number of years ago, I came home from seminary ready to embark on the next stage of my life. I was excited and a little bit nervous as I anticipated my next year or so ... finding a job, *shidduchim*, and of course ... marriage. I was sure the last step wouldn't be long in coming. After all, my siblings all married quickly, and I was confident that I would be no different. I anxiously awaited the day.

But it was not to be. Bewildered and disillusioned, I watched as friend after friend happily tramped across the drawbridge, and for the second time in my life, I was left alone on the terrace all but forgotten. With an aching bewilderment firmly lodged in my throat, I was left to wonder. *What happened? How were they able to do it and I just don't seem to be able? And why me?*

However, I'm not the 6-year-old anymore that I was in the castle, and after a few years of frustration and bitterness, I concluded that there was supposed to be another part to the story. I understood that I was meant to take the pain and the heartache and to go one step further.

So I did. It wasn't a quick step; nor was it painless. I've found that it is much easier to indulge in self-misery than to take a predicament and grow from it. It is also more convenient to blame circumstances for your unhappiness than to learn to be happy within a situation. But I assume that if I can learn, now, how to be happy regardless of my situation, then I have got it made for life!

One of the things I have tried to do over the past few years is to put my predicament in perspective. What will five or ten years mean to me when I am 100 years old? Furthermore, what significance does this *nisayon* have in light of the enormity of some others' *nisyonos*? In fact, once this period of my life is over, that's it – it'll be over. That cannot be said for every *nisayon*.

❧ *Learning From My Predicament*

I once heard Rabbi Frand say, "Suppose everyone were to come to a long collective table, and each individual were to place his *pekele* on the table. If I were allowed to pick up any *pekele* and leave the room, I would end up leaving with my own." Why is that? It is because my *nisyonos* were custom made for me. I was given what I can handle.

My friend and I were the last two from among our friends still single, and I remember her telling me, "I hope you get married first, because I can handle it and you can't." I agreed. She could definitely handle being alone better than I could. Apparently, *Hashem* felt differently....

It's a terrific feeling to know that *Hashem* believes in you. Still, I couldn't help but wonder – do I really need all this anxiety?

The answer is *yes*. I need this *nisayon* in order for me to properly fulfill my *tafkid* (mission) here on earth. R' Bachya describes the *neshama* before it is placed in its body. The *neshama* understands what it needs to accomplish in this lifetime. Then the *neshama* is taken and shown its body. It's shown the body's family, financial status, talents, looks, strengths and weaknesses. It's shown everything. And then the *neshama* agrees. It agrees to everything because it knows that it will need every one of those elements in order to properly accomplish its goal. If I knew the whole picture, I'm sure I'd also agree. I have found it helpful to acknowledge that there is a bigger picture that I simply can't comprehend.

Not comprehending the big picture, though, certainly hasn't stopped me from seeing how I have grown from this experience. Many people spend their lives running a marathon. They have to get married first. They have to have children first. Their homes must be the nicest. Their children have to be the brightest, the cutest, the most talented ... and the list goes on and on.

I was forced out of this marathon at the starting line. And for that I am thankful. For the rest of my life now, I am free to concentrate my energies inward and to utilize *my* talents and *my* gifts to fulfill *my* potential.

And oh, how many lessons I have learned over the past few years!

For one thing, I have learned to wait. In an age where messages are sent across the world within seconds and people can travel in a few hours what used to take months, I have learned to wait for something I want. Just for that reason, this all would have been worth it.

There's more, though. I have come closer to *Hashem* through *tefilla* and by learning to rely more on Him. Although I must turn to *shadchanim*, friends and *rabbanim* for help, I know that, ultimately, it is He Who has put me into this predicament and it is He Who will take me out.

I have learned to try and use this time wisely. I know I won't always have it. This is the time to work on myself and to help others.

I have learned to stop comparing myself to others. I have what I need. If I don't have it, I don't need it. I do not have the same life's plan as my friends, even my best friend ... even my siblings! I am unique.

Finally, I have learned that in order to receive *Hashem's berachos*, I must be ready to accept them. One who is prepared to accept *Hashem's berachos* is not one who is filled with doubt or cynicism.

And so here I stand. I am still alone on the terrace, but I am no longer bewildered or disappointed. I know that one day in the near future, I will round a corner and there it will be – the door I somehow hadn't seen before. And I, too, will dash joyously across the drawbridge to the world beyond.

FROM A *SHADCHAN'S* PERSPECTIVE

RABBI ZVI SCHACHTEL

❧ The Crisis

Thousands of Jewish Orthodox singles between the ages of 20 and 60 are searching for their soul mates. Many attend social events, lectures, *shuls*, and other venues where singles congregate with the hope of meeting "the right one." Unfortunately, however, these attempts often prove to be unsuccessful. These along with many others fail to make the connections necessary to create the long-standing relationships they seek. As a result, there is tremendous frustration and despair, not only for the singles, but also for their families, friends, and communal leaders who are dedicated to ensuring the growth and survival of the Jewish community.

Further aggravating the issue, a large number of singles are rightfully apprehensive about enlisting the aid of professional matchmakers who could potentially be helpful in making appropriate introductions. As a result, some Orthodox Jewish singles eventually turn to alternative communities or resources to find their *zivug*. They may begin to seek their soul mates in non-Orthodox settings *chas v'shalom*.

This has resulted in a crisis, one that signifies the complex issues of the modern age and threatens to become increasingly problematic in the future. It is a crisis that demands an organized, effective and timely response on the part of the Orthodox community.

❋ Suggestions for Singles

To be sure, there are areas where singles could benefit from reassessing their approach and attitude, and some are discussed at length in other articles in this issue. I will summarize my own suggestions in brief:

A) **Make time** – Keep *shidduchim* as the top item on your agenda, even when it is a source of disappointment and frustration. Lighten up your heavy schedule so you can be available when the call comes. Plan your week with time for *shidduchim*.

B) **Build a support system** – whether it is a mentor, good friend, Rabbi, Rebbetzin, or therapist. This mentor should preferably be married. This chosen guide or mentor should help you carefully resolve past relationships and fears, and for many, this includes the fear of failure and the fear of commitment.

C) **The "LIST"** – Try constructing a list of ten items or qualities you are seeking in a spouse. This construction project should be carefully considered. If you find someone with seven of the ten items on the list, then wisely *compromise*.

A compromise is not *settling*. To settle is to give up. Compromise simply means forgoing the more trivial attributes while retaining the priority requirements.

A mentor can help the single person formulate this list. Try not to be too dogmatic about the list since many people end up marrying someone who negates many qualities that they had considered necessities. By deciding to change their lists, they found their *bashert* and are happily married.

D) I always emphasize it is most important to **let *Hashem* into the process**. Never, never underestimate the incredible power of *Avinu Shebashamayim*. *Daven* – the *Kol Yaakov* is imperative in the process.

✦ Analysis: *Shadchanim* — What Are the Major Problems?

Many singles are dissatisfied with their experiences with *shadchanim*. From my conversations with them, the following problems are among the most disconcerting:

A) Focus – Honesty and "focused introductions" are often missing. Instead, many espouse the theory that since he is a man and she is a woman, that's reason enough to match them; the chance of infatuation and marriage are there.

B) Separate – Many work completely alone and are wary of speaking to any other *shadchan* for fear of losing a client.

C) Favoritism – Some exercise favoritism and promote one individual repeatedly instead of recognizing the different qualities of each *neshama* being special in its own right.

D) Organization – They may lack organization and training.

E) Pressure tactics – They can be guilty of pressuring singles into unwanted matches.

I had a couple recently who met on a Wednesday night and, to my utter surprise, were engaged by Monday night. I had another couple who dated for over six months until she felt comfortable entering a lifelong commitment.

> *I recently had a lady who was pressured by the shadchan after a few dates to commit herself. She was understandably very nervous. So I invited the chassan to be my Shabbos guest. He was unstable and, as it turns out, beset with serious medical problems. Within a few hours after Havdalla, I advised her to break the engagement. Bechasdei Hashem, she is since married to someone else and the original chassan recognized his problem and is receiving counseling.*

⁂ Suggestions for *Shadchanim*

To succeed as a *shadchan*, you have to really care about people. In addition, you must realize that every *neshama* who comes your way is equal. Favoritism or promoting an individual to every possible candidate is not professional, ethical, or honest.

I have found that it is best to conduct a ten-minute pre-interview on the telephone. I then do a scan of my database to see if I have anyone to offer. Then, if we mutually agree to meet, it is a personal interview of substance. I firmly believe that a "focused" introduction is the only way to go, since rejection is very painful. It is simply *g'neivas daas* (misleading) to set up an unfocused meeting.

I then pray for *siyata diShmaya*, and, *Baruch Hashem,* there has been much *siyata diShmaya.*

⁂ *A New Initiative: The Need for Project Marriage*

Project Marriage intends to address this crisis in an innovative, effective manner. There is a need for a new, national organization exclusively focused on helping singles to meet suitable mates through a nationwide network of carefully selected, highly motivated and well-qualified matchmakers. These will help their clients to develop realistic expectations and to provide positive reinforcement and guidance until they succeed in finding their soul mates. The project will utilize a variety of avenues through which singles can meet, including:

1) A direct, nationwide registry of matchmakers who attend events and personally acquaint themselves with each couple they attempt to match.

2) Provide mentors and/or therapists who could counsel singles, matchmakers, and couples as they go through the dating process. Maintaining hope and having an objective third party as a sounding board can make all the difference in keeping a positive attitude, leading to success.

3) Classes and seminars conducted by rabbis and relationship experts that address relevant issues for creating healthy, long-term relationships and which create the opportunity for singles to meet. These will include sessions on how to act and respond on a date, and how to communicate feelings.
4) Informational materials in the form of pamphlets and tapes, which inspire singles and address relevant relationship issues.

The process of creating a network of trained matchmakers and connecting them appropriately with singles will make an important impact on today's Orthodox singles' community.

There are few *mitzvos* where a person is called a partner with *Hashem*. One of them is the *shadchan*, of whom it is stated, *"Na'aseh shutaf im Hakadosh Baruch Hu."* I have tremendous admiration for the *mesiras nefesh* of all *shadchanim*.

The ultimate success of a *shadchan* is to realize you are a pawn on *HaKadosh Baruch Hu's* chessboard. The credo must be to give *chizuk* and compassion to all who come to you for assistance, and to *daven* to *Hashem* for *siyata diShmaya*.

LE'TORAH, LE'CHUPA U'LE'MA'ASIM TOVIM
CHALLENGES TO OUR CHILDREN'S SHIDDUCHIM

SHAYA OSTROV

I. ENCOUNTERING THE PROBLEMS

Over the past decades we have all become painfully aware of a phenomenon unfolding in every frum population center throughout the world. Many parents have been experiencing increasing difficulties in finding appropriate shidduchim for their children. They have found that something so vital to the hemshech (continuity) of Klal Yisroel, and to the well being and happiness of these young people, can become a frustrating and even painful nightmare. This article attempts to analyze this phenomenon and define its sources, tracing how living in contemporary society has an impact on us as bnei Torah.

May I begin by sharing some vivid images that left indelible impressions on my mind and heart.

Scene I. On a Quiet Brooklyn Street

Walking past a Flatbush home on a sunny summer day, I noticed a father and son sitting on the steps of their home, preparing the young boy's Bar Mitzva Haftora. It was a "private lesson." But the moment was available for the discreet pedestrian to see and hear. It seemed that this father had been preparing his son for kabollas ha-mitzvos from the moment he was born, in keeping with the beracha expressed on the birth of a child: LeTorah, le'chupa, u'le'ma'asim tovim. The first stages of this beracha were being realized, and this young man's next stage in fulfilling this beracha will bring him to the chupa.

But we live in a world that invades our lives as at no other time. And nowhere do we see it more poignantly than in the world of *shidduchim*. Passing by this scene, I asked myself: Will what is happening to *Am Yisroel* affect this young man's ability to find his *basherte*, his predestined mate?

Scene II. Motza'ei Shabbos

It was late Motza'ei Shabbos when I received a call from a father – a *mechanech* in a well-known yeshiva. His 27-year-old daughter, who has been in *shidduchim* for more than eight years, and dated more young men than he would dare to count, has been seeing a young man for three months. He fits all her criteria for a *zivug* (perfect mate). After all these years of frustration, hurt and disappointment, it appeared to have finally been worth it, all for this opportunity. Yet, at this very last moment, she was considering calling it off and walking away. True, he was all she ever thought she wanted. He was a *masmid*, thoughtful, and from a very fine family. But there was something missing. It seemed slight to everyone else, but for her it was disturbing and disappointing. As a *ben Torah*, he was not used to articulating his feelings about himself to a woman. He was unable to communicate in a way she had become accustomed to in her professional relationships.

She was an actuary, and a very successful one, at that. Her success was not flaunted. But she was aware that she had become valuable to the financial success of others. It never compromised her *tzenius*. But success impacts on many levels. Perhaps earlier in her life she would have felt more comfortable with and even admiring of this young man. Now, this *bachur* was not at all the way she thought her *chassan* would look and act. She's been out there too long as a single professional woman. She's seen too many polished young men – both *frum* and not *frum* – and communicated with countless intelligent and articulate colleagues with impeccable credentials. In the process, she has come to define herself more clearly and has developed a sense of sophistication. This young man may have been all she ever wanted, perhaps five or six years ago. Now, the idea of marrying him leaves her feeling sad, disappointed and unable to escape her unhappiness.

So, this father who has dedicated his life to teaching Torah to others is desperately calling out for help, understanding so fully that his beloved, talented and wonderful daughter – a *tzenua* and true *baalas middos* – is also a very mature and responsible professional. There is no question that her career has helped her survive these years of disappointment and rejection. But it has also molded her perception and appreciation of the personal qualities she is looking for in a young man. She may very well spend the rest of her life as a single woman, never knowing childbirth or the love of her husband and children.

This father reached out to ask for my guidance, suggestions and even intervention. I knew that this young woman would be struggling with a challenge that went far beyond her own perceptions and even her freedom to make a choice in her own best interests. I knew this, because the lives and perceptions of the many young men and women I have encountered have been altered in their determined efforts to find success and self-esteem while waiting to find their *basherte*.

Scene III. Eretz Yisroel

We spent Sukkos in *Eretz Yisroel* for a family *simcha*. Sukkos is a time of great joy, especially in Israel. But this year, it was also a time of fear, with the escalation of Arab violence. As we visited old friends in their *sukkos*, however, we heard of another kind of torment. It was the hurt of parents, old and dear friends, who shared their long-suffering frustrations and deep concerns over their children. Many of these children were now in their late 20's, early 30's and still unmarried. These were *frum*, Torah families, with children from homes filled with *yiras Shamayim* and the best our *chinuch* has to offer. Yet these parents were expressing the same pain and dismay that I have come to hear time and again in America: "What have we done wrong? Why are we and our children suffering so?"

During the waning moments of *Yom Tov*, an Israeli-born Bais Yaakov graduate, now approaching age 30 and still not married, came to visit. Not only was she pained and helpless over her inability to meet her *basherte*, she was equally troubled over the hurt experienced by her parents. She felt at fault. With every date that failed, beyond her own palpable disappointment, she experienced the burden of telling her parents of another "failure." Worst of all, she knew that once again their response would oscillate between accusing her of being too "picky" and blaming themselves for some unknown crime committed as parents that could have contributed to this tragedy. When I returned to the States, this young woman called me. She had become a *kalla*. The *vort* had been set to take place that very evening. But she was unable to go through with it. She was calling it off. The reason? The young man left her feeling disappointed and depressed. She felt she was marrying beneath herself and giving up too much. I calmed her down and encouraged her to proceed. She was clearly a very frightened young woman.

Scene IV. The Empty Hall

On a cold and blustery winter night, I traveled to a Long Island wedding hall. I very much wanted to participate at the wedding of a young man, a distant relative who was now in his late 20's. Marriage had not come easy. He had been trying to discover his *basherte* for a number of years. I had not been involved in the process, and I was never asked to help out. I was deeply interested in his well-being, however, as he was raised without a father. Having been raised without my father, I have always been sensitive to his difficulties. I therefore wanted to get to the *chupa* on time.

When I arrived, I noticed the absence of cars in the parking field. As I approached the building I realized that the lights were out and the hall was empty… the wedding had been called off just two days ago! For some reason, I was not notified. My heart sank. I couldn't leave the hall. I was lost in my sense of pain for the young man, his mother, the *kalla*, and all those who have been hurt by this tragedy. I finally pulled myself together and left.

I am hesitant about sharing quick-fix commentary, but even without the facts, I instinctively knew what had happened. At life's critical junctures, such as preparing for a wedding, we need all the help we can get. Whatever happened to call off that wedding, it was not because he had all the help and guidance he needed. Very much the contrary, he could not have had enough.

✳ *Obstacles Along the Way*

Through the process of helping my own children marry, I have come to understand that, while every phase of the *shidduch* process is delicate, the final phases, right before engagement and the period before marriage, are the most delicate of all. The potential for cold feet, panic attacks, struggles over money, seating arrangements, *frumkeit* issues, lifestyle decisions, in-law differences – all expressions of anxiety and panic – are potential sparks in a tinder box. Without the steadying voice and guiding hand of parental wisdom and maturity, the desire to build a life together is easily lost through a small misunderstanding – just a "small fight" that sets off a fusion reaction worthy of Los Alamos.

It's not only the end of the dating process that is so difficult for single parents. It's also at the beginning. Arranging the right dates can be daunting. Financial demands can be impossible. I know of a young woman whose mother died when she was 19; she did not marry until she was 31. And a young man whose father died when he was 12; he's now close to 40 and still unmarried. How many singles never had the benefit of an even playing field! One parent was just not enough to guide them through. A child growing up without two healthy and caring parents is at a clear disadvantage. *Chazal* realized this a long time ago. That's where surrogate parents, a *rebbe*, *rav* or mentor come in.

And then there are yet other disadvantaged singles who need outside help. Both parents may still be alive and physically well, but personal crises, including divorce, financial pressures, illness and long-standing feuds between couples, have left them ill-equipped to help their children during this crucial period of their lives. These are children from homes experiencing instability and ongoing marital tensions. Many don't have the financial means to undertake a large wedding or commitments for financial support. How many of our children's futures are lost on the shoals of the financial and emotional stress, particularly around the period before the wedding!

In addition, there are others who require assistance to help them negotiate dating and marriage. First there are a growing number of *baalei teshuva*, many of whom come from marginally Jewish or totally assimilated backgrounds. *Yeshivos* such as Ohr Somayach, Aish HaTorah and seminaries for women, including Neve and She'arim, help numerous young, educated people turn to Torah life. Yet, becoming *frum* is just the first step. Dating for many of these individuals is immeasurably difficult. There are also a growing number of young people who were raised in modern *frum* homes. After a year or more in *Eretz Yisroel*, their lifestyle and *hashkafos* have become decidedly *yeshivish*. They require a guiding and wise hand in dating. Their parents may be very willing to help. But they are at a loss to understand the subtleties of dating in the Torah world. The result is that the deep desire of these young people to create a Torah home is so frequently frustrated by the difficulties inherent in the dating process. (And certainly, we cannot forget the increase of *geirim* and *geyoros* who also require assistance in this area.)

The *Mishna* in *Nedarim* tells of how Reb Yishmael took in a poor girl who was unable to find a *chassan*. He realized that because of her poverty, her appearance was not flattering. So he gave her a gold tooth where one was missing, provided her with new clothing, and cared for her needs until she found her *basherte*. Reb Yishmael then bemoaned how poverty was responsible for hiding the beauty of our *bnos Yisroel*. These same *bnos Yisroel* cried bitterly over the death of Reb Yishmael. He understood their pain.

Today's poverty, which hides beauty, is not only financial poverty. It is social, familial. It deprives our children of the ability to demonstrate their beauty and to recognize the beauty in others.

✦ Challenges to Parental Responsibility

Even as *frum Yidden*, we live in a society that challenges our dreams for spiritual growth and undermines our ability to fulfill our responsibility to our children. True, there are many other concerns that we deal with, but the rise in the number of mature singles across the spectrum of the *frum* community bears witness to forces that affect families of all lifestyles and levels of *frumkeit*. It is also a phenomenon whose impact is felt continuously and deepens with every passing day, and leaves its mark through every date that fails to materialize into a lasting relationship.

To relate to this phenomenon, we must address a few questions: What are the contributing factors and events that could have left such an impact on our Torah world – across this continent, reaching Israel, Europe and every Jewish center throughout the world? How can parents appropriately and effectively respond in a manner that enables our children to find new sources of hope and strength in their search for their basherte, while reducing friction and anxiety?

II. SOME OF THE CAUSES

✦ Erosion of Marriage in Western Societies

Let us begin by taking a look at a very sobering statistic: The number of individuals living in non-nuclear families – that is, without a husband and wife – has grown in just 40 years from 25 percent in 1960 to 48 percent of the population in 1999. America today has almost 70 million singles between the ages of 25-55. And even those who marry do not have such an easy time keeping their relationship intact. According to a *NY Times* report, of the 270,000

Americans who married this past June, almost 55 percent will divorce. No wonder so many opt not to marry! In Israel, as well, current statistics place the divorce rate at 30 percent. This is an unprecedented number for a predominantly Jewish society. All statistics project an increase in singles in the next decade, some by as many as an additional 25 percent.

These are just a few statistics at play, which come to mind when a distraught father calls, or when I see an empty wedding hall on the night of a scheduled *chasuna*. No matter how insular our culture, there has always been seepage of host-culture values that have impact on us –*"Vie es krystelt zich, yiddelt zich."* It is clearly part of being citizens of the richest nation in history. Let us take a closer look at how it trickles down to our children.

❧ *Technology and Transformation*

The rapid technological changes over the past four decades have transformed our culture, impacting on people's commitment to their careers and the professions our children choose to pursue. When men and women reach marriageable age, they frequently also enter the workforce. Until this generation, work was always viewed as secondary to starting a family. Today, however, when *frum* singles discover that after a couple of years marriage is not coming so easily, they decide that they cannot forever wait for that "right person" to come along. They crave stability, security, self-esteem and an opportunity to advance. Many feel compelled to make a choice to become more involved and committed to their careers. It's perhaps the only choice they have.

Even if the choice is not consciously made, it occurs because of the present reality. Today's workforce is an all-consuming environment. Professional offices, businesses and corporations have become intense environments where all concerned are competing for their market share and profits. Young people are expected to contribute to this growth in a serious and disciplined manner. As years go by without marriage, they become increasingly affected by the professional roles, tasks and relationships that now become more central to their lives. Their identities, appearance and even personalities are shaped by these roles – roles that are crucial to their success as responsible adults.

But so frequently, these very same commitments color their expectations and create new pressures which contribute to their entrapment as singles. CPAs are not very available between January 1 and April 15. Lawyers are always under the gun. Teachers feel the constant pressure of lesson plans. When the frustrations of dating accumulate, commitment to career pressures can serve as a convenient reason to back away.

I recently visited an old friend who heads a software development unit for a well-known bank. I was exploring the possibility of employment for a young man I knew. The young executive said to me: "Look around here. Who do you see? [I saw many young people, quite a few of whom were Asian-Americans.] They are all single," he said. "We are demanding of our employees here. If you have anyone *frum*, you certainly don't want them to work in a place like this, where there is no night or day."

It's the modern-day version of the sweatshop. Only this time the laborers are all happy because they are making enough money to lead their lives as single adults, with plenty of disposable income and perhaps some stock options.

I got the message. But I also learned how the technological revolution is hostile to family life. It is not just in software units. It is anywhere that the role of corporate competition and earnings plays a more important role than that of the family.

❧ New Economy, New Affluence, New Values

Along with the new culture of commitment to career, profession and corporations, American society has also given us the opportunity to reach undreamed-of levels of affluence. The pursuit of the "New Economy," as we come to characterize the staggering acquisition of today's wealth, has left its unmistakable imprint on the yeshiva and *Chassidishe* world. It colors our decisions, perceptions and the way we value ourselves. It has an impact on the lavishness of our *simchos*, the frequently outrageous prices paid for homes, new luxury cars, and a relentless pursuit to amass staggering financial holdings. The deepest impact is that since wealth is within the grasp of the masses, it has become an acceptable measure of one's personal value as a human being. Indeed, money and luxury have become our currency for judging quality and success. Precious few have the maturity and *eidelkeit* to understand the deeper meaning of wealth and know how to handle it.

Many within our community can no longer imagine that a life of personal sacrifice and material discomfort can be worth living. American culture's correlation of wealth to happiness and personal fulfillment has crept into our own definition of personal *shleimus*. Emphasis on the material leaves us more vulnerable to making mistakes about *middos* and the deeper issues of personal character. Perhaps more young people remain alone because dating partners lacked the "required" attributes. And far too many who do focus on these "essentials" come to realize their error, leading to an increase in broken engagements and – even more tragic – divorces.

An outstanding young man may be told that his years of *hasmada* (diligence) have earned him the right to expect a high price in the *shidduch* market. But we are amazed at the number of these young men still dating after years of seeking such an arrangement. And then we take note of countless outstanding young women who were passed up, and it pains us to the core. Sadly, the value placed on externals – height, weight, money, etc. – blurs our vision to perceive and appreciate those *middos* that we have valued and searched for since Avraham sent Eliezer in search of Rivka. Perhaps the emphasis on the material has led to a cataract on our *neshamos*. The result is that countless young men and women are spending years of fruitless dating, focused on everything *but* the essentials that have made us an *am segula*.

There is no escaping the fact that the "New Economy" and consumerism have created a gold standard where the wealthiest, slimmest, and most beautiful are universally prized. Moreover, for far too many, the absence of these requisites creates a feeling of depression and disappointment. As consumers, we are unprepared for anything short of perfection. Anything less than the new luxury auto lease is unacceptable as a means of transportation. One scratch on this shining new beauty and the heart sinks. So it goes with *shidduchim*. The values of our society interfere with our inherent appreciation of *penimius* and prevent so many of our children from seeing beyond the superficial, leaving our most prized children with a sense of spiritual deprivation.

Yet, as parents and adults, we know better. Our life experience has taught each of us what *Chazal* have been saying since Sinai: Personal happiness, stability and fulfillment are the result of our *middos* and *ruchnius* – character and spirituality. Personal wealth, professional accomplishments and physical beauty are only of value when they serve the Torah's more sublime goals. Every Friday-night *seuda*, we sing *"shekker hachein v'hevel hayofi,"* that externals are secondary. We need to truly believe it once again.

The age in which we feel "we can touch opulence and not be touched by it" is over. For the great majority, the trappings of wealth resonate too deeply, and few if any escape its influence. And the true *korbanos* are the children. It has thrown them off their natural ability to select a *zivug* with relative ease and comfort. It has filled far too many with attempting to achieve adulation for making "great deals" through *shidduchim* related to money, status and other arrangements. And these arrangements have nothing to do with what is really required to build a *bayis ne'eman beYisroel*.

❖ The Younger-Versus-Older Dilemma

One of the results of this process of seeking the "great deal" or the right physical attributes is that more and more of our children are sifting through more and more dates, and getting older in the process.

Many frustrated parents ask: "Why do younger couples have an easier time making up their mind?" Their perception is correct. *Chazal* clearly understood this when they suggested: *shemona esrei lechupa* – "18 (plus) is the ideal time to marry." It's the transition period between dependency and understanding your own needs and preferences. It's ideal because our children's lives are not yet complex, careers have not yet begun, identities have not yet been fully defined, disappointments have been kept to a minimum, and most important, they still listen to us. After this window, which lasts for a few years, it becomes decidedly more difficult to help them make the leap.

Beyond these reasons, there is another compelling reason why younger couples can decide more easily than older couples. The most frequent statement I hear, particularly from young women is: "He's really a very nice person. But I just don't feel certain. I'm not enthused or moved by the idea of marriage to him." This is heard far less frequently from younger singles, who are involved in a world of boundless excitement, with fireworks going off continuously all around them. A multitude of cameras is clicking with snapshots of friends getting married, engagements, *vorts*, *Shabbos kallos*, the excitement of friends and relatives waiting to see "who will go next." It's a time of contagious anticipation, filled with a million dreams of young lives starting out new – in *kollel*, in *Eretz Yisroel*, in new homes and communities waiting to greet the young couples. Whatever the doubts, these are frequently papered over by a *zeitgeist* to be part of this wonderful atmosphere of *simcha*, the desire to say, "Guess what, we're engaged!" This atmosphere can only add to a feeling of hope and enthusiasm, as it very well should.

But just two or three years later, the scene has changed. Did you ever listen to popcorn in the microwave? In the second and third minutes the action is furious. After the fourth and fifth minute there is hardly a pop. All is quiet. Older couples no longer hear the kernels, which had been exploding so frequently just a short time ago. And as they mature and grow into their lifestyle as singles, they become more aware of the multitude of changes that will have to occur should marriage happen. They are also more aware of the hurt and disappointments, which are now a part of their personal history. And they find themselves saying: "If I waited this long, I'm going to make sure it's for the right person."

III. SOME GUIDELINES FOR PARENTS

The observations and impressions I have shared were intended to provide the reader with insights, which can make a difference in how you assist your child's progress toward marriage. As in all other areas of parenting, the more you understand, the greater the opportunities for helping your children marry.

Here are some guidelines which parents may find helpful in dealing with children who are single.

1. In real estate we say: location, location, location. In *shidduchim*, we must say: *middos, middos, middos*. All else is a very distant second. So when your child talks about dress size, personal or family wealth, or even being "more outgoing," we can't really argue. But, we as parents can realize that it's *middos* that will ultimately create the relationship that builds a happy and loving home.

2. Whatever your financial means, your goal is to help a young couple slowly build a home. We can't buy a *bayis ne'eman*. They have to build it. Lavish spending on weddings, *vorts*, homes, and jewelry never help a couple. They also disturb those with less to spend, and distort our values as a community. We all know what is required to achieve our most cherished results. Beyond this, we are actually hampering a natural process from unfolding.

3. If you are a parent feeling frustrated and deeply concerned, try not to express your negative emotions to your child. Parental pressure, guilt or feelings of parental depression are all of highly questionable value. After a certain age, your child is experiencing his/her own hurt. Singles also have fears of turning their own lives upside down to make room for another person. They need to feel clarity and courage. This is when your support is most important.

4. Respect your child as a mature adult, capable of making mature decisions in his/her own best interest. Self-esteem is critical in maintaining a sense of emotional balance through this difficult period.

5. Accept that the older and more accomplished they are becoming in other areas of life, the more they are defining themselves and their own individuality. Your mature son or daughter is not being "picky," just making sure that the relationship fits personal needs and interests. The older they become, the more we must give them the ability to feel that sense of certainty about their prospective marriage partner.

6. Never aggressively question the decision to end a relationship. You can and should understand that anxiety and fear play a key role in this decision. Challenging them will only increase tension and mutual feelings of hurt. You can and should suggest discussing the decision with a trusted friend, or someone in the field with expertise and life experience.

7. Frequently parents will try to show that they are even handed and objective by voicing fears and doubts about a specific relationship. They hope this will win the trust of their children. I suggest you not voice your doubts. It will kill the relationship immediately. Mature singles have enough inner doubts without parental hesitations.

8. Never trivialize a doubt about a prospective marriage partner that your child believes to be a serious issue. Be attentive to hesitations and understand your child as part of the natural feelings of anxiety.

9. If your child is feeling hopeless, encourage a sense of optimism. Your understanding will provide the courage to defeat loneliness and frustration. You are frequently an important source of strength, which enables your child to take a chance at a serious relationship.

10. Encourage membership in a community of other singles with whom they can share friendships. Otherwise the isolation can be staggering.

11. Make sure holiday weekends and *Yamim Tovim* are well planned, with the option of being with either friends or family.

12. Understand that the older parents get, the more pressure they place on their children to care for them, both emotionally and physically. Many parents do not feel that their age and dis-

abilities restrain their single children from marriage. Yet it's an inescapable reality, particularly where there is only one surviving parent. The sense of loyalty and protectiveness are enough to occupy the hearts and mind of any responsible and loving child. It's therefore important to seek guidance as to how to help your single child feel a greater sense of freedom to pursue a relationship that can lead to marriage.

✦ *Beyond the Scope of Parents*

These suggestions have been offered to help parents maintain more productive relationships with their single children while being aware of the impact that our culture has on us. Hopefully, we can enable our single children to feel a sense of self-respect for who they are, rather than shame for who they are not. The solutions to this growing problem reach beyond the ability of parents to heal the emotional wounds suffered as a result of endless dating. The answer, like any other problem we face in life, lies with a comprehensive effort to bring singles together in a responsible manner, enhancing their self-esteem and communication skills, and guiding them every step of the way, without leaving any stone unturned.

TIME TO MOVE ON
A FORMULA FOR CHANGE AS AN AID
TO GETTING MARRIED

DR. YAAKOV SALOMON

❧ *Nobody Said It's Easy*

True. Nobody said it was going to be easy. But then again, nobody warned you about how long and painful the trip would actually be, either.

But how could they have known? After all, each journey is so unpredictable; there really is no way to properly prepare for it.

The voyage, of course, is *shidduchim*, and the seas have never been more turbulent than they are now. The plight of ever-increasing numbers of older singles in our midst assumed major proportions.

"*Ki ayn bayis asher ayn shom....*" Practically no home exists that is not, in some way, affected by this growing epidemic; if not directly within the nuclear family, then certainly indirectly – through extended family, friends, or neighbors. Not surprising then, that well-meaning people everywhere ask, "Why? How did the situation become so serious? Can't we figure out what happened? Why are *many thousands* of serious, capable, and mature young men and women in the Torah community finding it so difficult to find their life partner?"

And yet, the etiology of this crisis seems, to this writer, to be rather moot. The causes are probably so diverse, so complex, and so beyond consensus that it appears fruitless to expend endless energy to "solve" the mystery of the unmarried. Instead, let's focus on solutions. *Why* they find themselves in this dreadful predicament is far less important than relieving their pain and helping them build their own *binyan adei ad*. If my son has a fever, I don't ask, "Why?" I give him some Motrin, pump him with fluids, and send him to bed. *Later*, I might conduct the investigation. Remember. We're looking for solutions. We're not trying to assign blame to anyone.

❧ *The Most Frightening Word*

With that in mind, let's talk about one of the most frightening six-letter words in the English language. It is *"change."* Do you feel the pain? Are you frightened? C-H-A-N-G-E. It's terrifying. It's alarming. Most of us physically cringe when we hear the word. Panic sets in.

"Change? I should change? Why should I change? What did I do wrong? Maybe the change will be worse? *What am I supposed to do? Can't I just try again? Give me one more chance. I'll try harder this time. I'll do anything, as long as I can keep doing it the same way."*

You and I, we humans, are creatures of habit. We like uniformity. We like consistency. We like familiarity. We even like repetition. We like knowing what to expect from the world. We like knowing what to expect from one another; and what to expect from ourselves. It makes us feel safe and secure … in a world of diminishing safety and security.

Truthfully, all of us practice this habitual behavior in ways that are both subtle and apparent.

"This is where I buy my fish. This is my fish store."

"Why not try going to …?"

"Oh, no. Why would I want to do that? I always go here."

And in case you're not much of a fish lover, try on one or more of these ever-so-common habitual and ritualistic declarations.

This is when I wake up ... every single day.

This is how I drive. That's just the way I do it.

This is where I buy my coleslaw. Why would you go anywhere else? I like this coleslaw. That's just how I like it.

This is when I go to sleep.

This is the vort that I say at the table about this parsha every single year. Over and over and over again.

This is how much tzeddaka I give. That's how much I give. It doesn't matter what the appeal is for. That's how much tzeddaka I give. (Which is fine if you're giving $50,000 to every appeal, by the way.)

You know what? This is me. I like me. I like the way I've been doing it, so I'm going to keep on doing it. Every day, every week, every year, erev, v'voker, v'tzohorayim.

And that's how we go through life.

And you know what? There's really nothing wrong with it. It's called consistency. It's beautiful. *I'm a consistent person.* They call it k'vius.

"*Es hakeves ho'echad ta'asaeh ba'boker, v'es hakeves hasheni ta'aseh bein ha'arbayim* – the sacrificial order in the *Mikdash.*" ... every single day. And that's how we are.

❧ *The Downside of Change*

But like most things in this world, there is a downside to this life-*gestalt*. A side effect. Our *Chazal* warned us about it. Our *Nevi'im* warned us about it. They called it *mitzvos anashim melumada*, doing things the same way. The dangers of *hergel*, doing things by rote, without thought or contemplation. Almost robotic. Regular. From the word *regel*. "Be careful," they said. "Don't do that."

"But if it's working," you're saying, "what's wrong with it?"

And you're right.

But that's exactly the problem. If it's working, why fix it? True. But let's say it's *not* working. What do you do *then*? Let's say you're *not* married. Let's say your children are not married. Is there anything more painful than that? Let's say they're not *close* to getting married. Or let's say they're *always* close to getting married … both are equally difficult.

Let's say you're not even being *redd shidduchim*. And we know people like that. Or always being *redd* the wrong ones – people who don't share the same goals, the same values, as you. What do we do then? Isn't there a time, as difficult as it is, that we have to look at ourselves, and look at our children, or look at our grandchildren, and say, "You know what? This is not working." There's something wrong.

Again, let's be clear about our intentions. We're not talking about *blame* here. No fingers are being pointed and no hypotheses of fault or responsibility are even being suggested. Nobody really knows.

But there is a time when you have to be honest with yourself. You have to say something is wrong, and something is not working. That is very hard to do. Why? Admitting that something is really not working implies that something needs to be changed. And that can be upsetting.

Now, how does this relate to *shidduchim*? For that, let's go to the source.

✦ The Source for it All

Let us take our example from the prototype of all *shidduchim*, from the Torah – Eliezer in his search for a suitable wife for Yitzchak.

Eliezer has concluded his pursuit. He witnesses enough miracles and attributes of *chessed* that he is certain he has found "THE ONE." There could be no doubt that only Heavenly intervention brought him to Rivka. But as the agreement is about to be consummated, Eliezer utters an astonishing charge to Lavan and Besuel.

"*Ve'ato im yeshchem osim chessed ve'emes es adoni, hagidu li….*" If you think this is a good idea, and you're ready to do *chessed ve'emes* with my master, tell me about it.

"*Ve'im lo, hagidu li…,*" and if not, tell me.

"*V'efneh al yemin o al s'mol*" ... and I will turn to the right or the left. Amazing. He sees all the indicators. He has *kefitzas haderech*, experiences a miraculously expeditious trip. He sees *nissim*, the waters are rising from the well! He sees Rivka performing countless acts of distinguished *chessed*.

"*VaHashem hitzliach darki*," declares Eliezer. *Hashem* has made my mission a success. There's no question in his mind. This is it. And what does he say? "Tell me if it's good. Because if it's not, we'll move on. *V'efneh al yemin o al s'mol*." Rashi says, "We'll go to *Bnos Lot* or *Bnos Yishmael*."

Rabbi Avraham Pam adapted the particulars of the story to a not-uncommon situation. Eliezer could not have been more certain that Rivka was the right *zivug* for Yitzchak. The *Hashgacha* could not have been more clear. And yet he was fully prepared to seek elsewhere, should it not work out for some reason. The flexibility was extraordinary!

How often, says Rabbi Pam, have we been witness to a situation when a *shidduch* is as close to completion as is possible ... when suddenly it breaks up, *rachmana litzlan*. Everyone involved is crushed, and understandably so. Depression often sets in, and blame is quickly assigned to an assortment of persons, sometimes only remotely involved in the process.

But while the situation feels and certainly seems tragic, we cannot lose hope or the ability to transcend the pain.

"*V'efneh al yemin o al s'mol*." Eliezer had every single sign you could imagine. And what does he say? Sometimes you have to re-assess and redirect one's efforts. We'll go to *Bnos Lot*. We'll go to *Bnos Yishmael*. If that's what we have to do, that's what we'll do. We'll move on. A lesson of immense proportion.

Admitting that we were truly stuck is enormously difficult, but the key word here is flexibility. We've got to be ready to act on "*V'efneh al yemin o al s'mol*." And not necessarily with a major meta-morphosis; just with enough reformulation to give the *Hashgacha prattis* a new opportunity in which to work.

✦ *When Reassessment is on the Agenda*

The changes relevant to these circumstances – reassessment and reformulation – fall into two basic categories: attitude and action. While no one can lay claim to a declaration that any single attitude or action is "wrong" or "inappropriate," it can be said with certainty that adhering to any attitude without knowing *why* it is that way is unhealthy and counterproductive. A person's mind-sets need to undergo periodic scrutiny and investigation to ensure their validity and relevance.

Attitudinal examples that demand examination and analysis can include any of the following:

I only want a tall boy.

I need a rich girl.

I don't like blondes. It's just not me.

I cannot marry someone with a beard. It's impossible. I just can't do it.

And we convince ourselves that it's impossible; simply because we've *always* thought that way. It is the syndrome of *"This is where I buy my coleslaw."* I know a lot of people who got married without a beard, but things do change!

I will never marry a boy with an up-hat… or a down-hat.

Never say never.

I will only go out with a "professional."

While similar intellectual pursuits can often add luster and compatibility to a marriage, this factor is far from being definitive. How many people do we know who are employed in businesses, but also happen to be great teachers, at home or with their peers? And how many social workers or nurses are there who are stymied by apprehension, yet constantly dream about entrepreneurship? Let's remember how terribly unscientific relationships really are.

I could never marry a baal teshuva.

Again, this is another ill-advised "philosophy" or "myth": that the differing backgrounds of those who have been *frum* all their lives and those who have "joined the fold" spell marital disaster. Nothing could be more untrue. Often times, it is precisely the combination of the two divergent experiences that nourishes and nurtures the relationship. A true fulfillment of *eizer kenegdo*.

Had *Boaz* been wary about *Rus*, the lineage of *David Hamelech* (and *Moshiach*) would have been inexorably altered. Something to think about.

What? You're "redding" me this girl? Wasn't she once engaged?

Yes, she was. What does that mean? Is she not allowed to make a mistake? Even a major mistake? Of course, there are times when a broken engagement may be a signal that a certain problem (probably not insurmountable) may exist, but it does not and should not imply a patent disqualification. Previously engaged men and women deserve a chance.

Those who have *never* been married often have a particular resistance to marrying those who *have* been married, especially if they have children. Divesting yourself of *all* candidates in that category is yet another illustration of the *"coleslaw* condition."

A true change in attitude means focusing on the *person*, not on the "baggage."

❧ *Redesigning Our Mode of Conduct*

Changing our *actions* in pursuing a mate can, at times, be a relatively minor challenge. Maybe it's a simple thing. Maybe it's a tie, a dress, a hairstyle or a different location for a date. Maybe your dates should be shorter. Maybe your dates should be longer. There are people who are day people and people who are night people. Perhaps you should consider dating more in the daytime, instead of at night.

Maybe *what* you do on the date should be different. Maybe you should be a little more open on your dates; or a little *less* open on your dates. Maybe you need to ask more questions; perhaps you are too busy trying to impress, instead of finding out more about the person you are considering. Or maybe you need to go to *Invei Hagefen*, the sensitive and wonderful address for serious, older singles – daunting though it may seem.

It is true. Dating is not coleslaw. And changing time-honored patterns in attitude and action to improve one's marriage potential is far more challenging than changing the *dvar Torah* we might say on a particular occasion. But questioning our habitual behavior, even in a small way, can open the door to the more significant alterations that we need to make.

Of course, sometimes your action needs to be a little more dramatic. Today, networking is the engine that moves the *shidduch* process along. And, difficult as it is, a change of venue may be indicated. New people. New *shadchanim*. New opportunities. New *mazel* …. Moving to new neighborhoods cannot be ruled out.

Some older singles have a desire for greater introspection. Are there subconscious, underlying causes that may be creating a barrier to getting married? Or are there specific thought patterns or behaviors that need to be understood or modified? When called for, therapy with a licensed, qualified, and Torah-true psychotherapist can at times be of help; often through a short-term modality. Conversely, singles who have been in therapy for a while may need to consider a change in therapists or even terminating treatment, if stagnation has set in.

← *"This Is My History"*

A final consideration involves a serious review of your dating history. All too often, a name of someone you met years ago is dismissed as "not for me." But people do change. Your needs may be different now. His priorities could have shifted. The passage of time, life experiences, and a solid dose of reality can accelerate the maturation process. Taking a careful look at each name on that list can be surprisingly prudent. Many stories exist where two people, having met 10 or 15 years previous, have later gotten married. You could be the protagonist of one of those stories.

Nobody is very comfortable with change. Those old house slippers, threadbare and holey though they may be, still feel kind of snug and cozy. But if you're serious about adding another pair of slippers to your closet, and a devoted partner to your life, those torn relics may need to be discarded. In their stead, just might be a shiny new pair of dancing shoes.

"HELP ME GET MARRIED!"
AN ORTHODOX PSYCHOTHERAPIST SHARES HIS OBSERVATION ON THE GROWING NUMBERS OF OLDER SINGLES IN OUR COMMUNITY.

DR. MEIR WIKLER

❦ *The Referral*

The most recent attempt at *shadchanus* (matchmaking) has failed. It wasn't that far off the mark — they did meet each other twice but the "chemistry" wasn't there.

Now it is time to report back to the middleman, the *shadchan*. The single person is asked for feedback on the *shidduch* (match).

'Thank you very much," comes the reply, "I really do appreciate your efforts on my behalf, But ... it's just not for me,"

The *shadchan* sighs deeply and audibly. The *shadchan* tries, unsuccessfully to elicit more details. Then the *shadchan* tries a different approach, reviewing the *maalos* (advantages) of this particular *shidduch*. At the end, the answer is the same: "Just not for me."

In exasperation, the *shadchan* launches into the all-too-familiar *mussar shmuess*, which goes something like this.

> *"You know, _____ (fill in first name of single person), you're not getting any younger. The longer you wait, the less choic-*

es you will have. What are you waiting for, anyway? Are you look-
ing for perfection? That just doesn't exist. You don't need perfection
to be happy. My _____ (fill in "husband" or "wife," as indi-
cated) has plenty of faults. But we're still happy together. Are you
expecting to see stars or hear bells? That's totally unrealistic. You
know that _____ (fill in name of mutual friend who just got
engaged) was even ready to call things off after the first date, and
look how well things worked out.

"I really hate to tell you this, and I know you'll probably be angry
with me for saying it, but… I think you're just too picky, if you ever
hope to get married, you're going to have to learn to settle. If you
don't, you may never get married, chas v 'shalom."

The single person now bites a lip or clenches a fist behind his
or her back. A weak smile is forced to appear and some pseudo-
appreciation is expressed, before the single person retreats to lick
the wounds that were just inflicted.

Deep, gut-wrenching soul-searching follows, often in the company of a close friend, equally victimized by the singles' scene.
Sometimes, the friend is married and offers a different perspective,
in addition to heavy-duty empathy.

"Is there really something wrong with me?" the single person
asks. "Am I really too picky? Am I looking for the wrong things or
in the wrong places? Am I unrealistic? Am I asking for too much?
It has gotten to the point where I just don't know anymore! Maybe
I should just 'settle' and get it all over with! At least then I'd be
able to feel that my life is moving on. Maybe I don't have enough
bitachon (trust in *Hashem*)? Maybe I should just trust in *hashgacha*
(Providence) and marry the next halfway normal *shidduch* that
comes along? I used to think I was normal and that I just hadn't
met the right one yet. But now I'm not so sure. Tell me, honestly,
what do you think I should do at this point?"

The friend is overwhelmed with the dilemma, and even more
so with the heavy responsibility placed on his or her shoulders. A
long, agonizing pause follows. Then, the friend responds in a halt-
ing voice, filled with hesitancy and apprehension:

"I don't know, _____ (fill in the name of single person); I just don't know. I hear what you're going through. I _____ (fill in "went" or "am going," as appropriate) through the exact same thing. I know just what you're talking about. But I simply don't know what to tell you. Maybe you should discuss this with someone more objective? Maybe you should see a professional?"

Weeks or even months pass. The bitter pill is avoided, and then, finally swallowed. The single person thinks. "Well I've tried everything else. I suppose I might as well try this, too." Inquiries are made. The professional is called. An appointment is scheduled.

❖ *The Initial Consultation*

The single person comes to the initial consultation loaded with intense, mixed feelings of eagerness and anxiety. Hoping for assistance and fearing disappointment, the single person takes a seat in the office.

The professional begins with a few words of small talk and then poses the obvious question. "What can I help you with?"

The single person does not answer right away. Some background information is provided, supposedly as an introduction. In reality, the single person is testing the waters by assessing the professional's empathy. Some of the events and much of the feelings that precipitated the call for an appointment are presented. Now the single person is ready to answer the question posed at the outset.

"Maybe I have the wrong idea about what you can do. But what I really want is *for* you to help me *get* married. Everything I've tried already obviously hasn't worked. I've attended singles' events, even though I've hated them. I've gone to public lectures and I've even contacted professional *shadchanim*. Nothing has worked for me.

"One friend suggested that I take courses to improve my job skills and advance my career. I've done that. Another friend suggested I circulate more for Shabbos and *Yom Tov* meals. I do that now, too. It seems that people are always suggesting some new method or approach that I haven't tried. Since I am sincerely eager to get married and I don't want to appear unmotivated, I usually try to implement whatever reasonable advice I am offered.

"Recently, a friend recommended that I meet with you. To be quite honest, I don't really see how this is supposed to help. But frankly, I'm so desperate that I'm willing to try almost anything. At first I felt a bit insulted at the very idea. But after a while, I thought to myself, 'Why not? What have I got to lose?' So I called you, and that's why I'm here."

❧ Negotiating the Contract

Whenever someone meets with a psychotherapist, there should be full and explicit agreement upon the goal of the therapy. No successful outcome can be achieved if either party has a fuzzy notion of how the treatment goal is to be defined. Ideally, a clear definition of the problem to be addressed should be agreed upon in the very first session. The negotiation around just how the problem is defined represents the first, and often the most crucial, stage of the treatment process.

After validating the single person's feelings of stress, loneliness and profound frustration with *shadchanim, shidduchim,* and humanity at large, the therapist begins the process of negotiating the definition of the problem to be solved. Therapists call this process, "negotiating the contract."

"I'm not really sure that getting you married, *per se,* is something we can work on. After all, just getting married is something you could do yourself, right now. But what you're really after is getting *happily* married. To achieve that requires the input from someone else whom neither of us has met."

The single person then asks the understandable next question. "Well, does that mean that I made a mistake in coming ... that there is really nothing you can do for me?"

The therapist then proposes a more realistic contract. "A happy marriage is a goal that is not totally within our control. It would be frustrating for both of us to try to work toward such a goal. It would be as if you and I were to agree to change your mother. (Single person laughs nervously here.) It might be possible, but it would be awfully difficult.

"So I prefer to work on things which are more within your control. For example, we might try to see if there is anything in your life now that is holding you back from getting married; any obstacle. Or, we might review together what steps you could take to improve your dating style, manner and attitude. Those are goals which could help, but would not *guarantee* your getting married. But at the very least, your chances of getting married might be improved and we would be working toward more realistic, attainable goals."

For some, the process ends here. When they hear that marriage itself is not an acceptable goal for therapy, their interest dries up like freshly cut grass. These people, of course, are told, "Since marriage has eluded you thus far, perhaps we should examine why." Nevertheless, their minds are not changed, and they do not return.

For others, the contract is successfully negotiated to address a realistic goal. The following case vignettes illustrate just what can, at times, interfere with getting married, and just what can happen when those barriers are removed.

The *shidduchim* problems illustrated by these four cases are not unique to "older" singles, but are found at all age levels. For some, these problems do not interfere with becoming engaged and getting married. For others, such as the individuals described below, these problems do impede the process of getting married.

(While the material presented here is drawn from real-life cases, it must be emphasized that considerable effort has been made to disguise the identifying characteristics, so that the true identities of these individuals are adequately concealed. If the reader suspects that he recognizes the true identity of any of these cases, it is probably an indication of the widespread nature of these issues rather than a poor job of camouflage.)

❦ *Benny*

Although Benny was mildly depressed, that was not his reason for seeking help. In fact, his symptoms were not even sufficient to warrant a diagnosis of depression. Rather, at 33, Benny was "not getting any younger" and he wanted help in getting married. Benny readily accepted the therapist's proposal during the initial consultation. The contract was negotiated amicably, and Benny agreed to work on discovering what stood in his way.

Benny was a former *yeshiva bachur* who was working at a steady, but low-paying civil-service job. "I'll look for something better," Benny assured his therapist, "just as soon as I get engaged."

Changing jobs, however, wasn't the only thing that Benny was putting on hold. His therapist soon discovered that Benny planned to update his wardrobe, improve his personal hygiene and grooming, and increase his evening *sedarim* with *chavrusas*, "just as soon as I get engaged." The therapist pointed out to Benny how self-defeating his postponement of these self-improvements really was. "Maybe if you started these projects now instead of waiting, you'll be able to upgrade your *shidduch* appeal."

That was easier said than done. But Benny applied himself diligently to the task, and with the gentle but firm support of his therapist, he did manage to increase his learning schedule, improve his appearance, and even land a better job. He met Shulamis a year and a half after entering therapy and today they are very happily married.

✦ *Rochel*

At the initial consultation, 26-year-old Rochel practically denied having any problems. Why, then, had she come? Rochel made a half-hearted gesture to explain by saying something about wanting to learn more about herself. As a graduate student in the mental health field, this seemed plausible enough.

Eventually, her true agenda emerged, which was to finally "get married, already!" As with her real motives for entering therapy, her true feelings about her troubled childhood did not surface right away. It took Rochel a good four months to really trust her therapist, whom she repeatedly tested in creative and often annoying ways.

The therapist never agreed to help Rochel get married. But they did agree to examine the nature of her relationships more closely.

Rachel's parents, especially her father, had been somewhat emotionally abusive. Rochel resented her father for the abuse but also adored him for the good times they had shared when Rochel was growing up. This attraction/distrust conflict was often played out with the *shidduchim* Rochel met. It was even replicated in her feelings toward her therapist.

After a year of intense "hot and cold" therapy Rochel learned a lot about herself. She learned, for example, how she often treated men with the same ambivalent feelings she had toward her father. She even learned to recognize and eventually stop some of her provocative behavior, such as her tendency toward sarcasm and barbed criticism. As a result, her relationships with *shidduchim* became less turbulent. In addition, her feelings toward her therapist began to include more even tones of gray, and less black and white.

Rochel felt that she had gained enough and the therapist supported her decision to end treatment. He did not hear from her again until she called for a joint appointment with Michel, an accountant to whom Rochel was seriously considering becoming engaged. During that session, the therapist needed only to strike a few familiar chords, which Rochel recognized immediately. Three months later, the therapist *shepped nachas* as a guest, at Rochel and Michel's *chasana* (wedding).

✦ *Shlomo*

Shlomo's friends considered him to be a very funny guy. In fact, most of Shlomo's friends from home and in yeshiva cited his sense of humor as one of Shlomo's most endearing qualities. The jokes, however, were a mask covering low self-esteem, feelings of inadequacy, hopelessness, and even depression.

At the initial consultation, Shlomo, 31, reported that he was having difficulty with *shidduchim;* he didn't really know why, nor did he care. All he wanted was to get married so that he could "be like all of my friends." Shlomo was quick to point out that the consultation was not his own idea. A married friend had suggested it. "Why do you suppose that your friend thinks therapy is the solution for you?" the therapist asked.

It was only later, toward the end of the hour, that Shlomo hesitatingly quoted his friend who sometimes chided Shlomo for his self-effacing one-liners, even if they were hilarious.

The therapist quickly negotiated the contract with Shlomo to directly address his hopelessness, and not his spouselessness. Shlomo reluctantly agreed as he was finding the depression unacceptable, at times.

Shlomo became highly motivated to get to the bottom of why he was so often morose, albeit in an entertaining way. "I make them laugh," he confided, " but inside, I'm crying."

Shlomo really threw himself into the therapy by doing all the "homework" suggested by the therapist. Each session was amply filled with the fruits of Shlomo's efforts in between sessions. By the time Shlomo ended therapy, not only had he conquered his bouts of depression, he had even reconciled his ties with his parents, from whom he had grown somewhat alienated in recent years.

The main reason Shlomo ended therapy was not the progress he had achieved. He was going to learn in a yeshiva in *Eretz Yisroel*. He did promise to keep in touch whenever he returned to the States for a visit. Shlomo kept his promise six months later when he called his therapist with the *besura tova* (good news) of his engagement.

❈ Chana

From the initial consultation it was clear that Chana, 29, had had a deeply troubled childhood. Not the least of her misfortune was the fact that her mother was *niftar* when Chana was only 7 years old. Because of her mother's passing, Chana's father could not keep her and her siblings at home. So she went to live with a maternal aunt, then her grandparents, then a neighbor …. You get the picture.

Now, various members of the community were trying to help Chana get married. They were arranging *shidduchim* without much success. After a few years, the lady with whom Chana boarded recommended therapy.

At the initial consultation, Chana was brought to tears as she spoke of how eagerly she wanted "to build her own *bayis ne'emon b'Yisrael*." After what she had been through as a child, Chana felt terribly impatient with the snail's pace of the *shidduchim* process for her. With Chana, the contract was negotiated to deal with her blatantly low self-esteem. She readily admitted, "never liking herself," and she was eager to try to build her self-confidence. Even before therapy. Chana had enough insight to understand that nothing attacks the self-esteem of a child more than impermanence and insecurity. How could she feel good about herself after having been shunted around as she had? Chana's treatment, therefore, did not involve a lengthy process of uncovering and analyzing feelings to promote insight. Instead. Chana and her therapist worked on more task-oriented solutions to her self-esteem problem. Under the therapist's patient tutelage, Chana's self-confidence blossomed, gradually. At first, only Chana could recognize the change. Then her landlady also noticed the improvement. Eventually, even her posture reflected her new self-esteem. Instead of always slumping over and looking at her lap when she spoke, she was now able to sit up straight and make eye contact. It was then that Chana met Mendel. They hit it off immediately and became engaged in less than two months. Although Mendel had been informed of Chana's therapy and even approved of it, Chana decided to terminate her therapy after the wedding. From the few lines she adds at the bottom of her annual New Year's cards to her therapist, it is clear that Chana and Mendel remain happily married to this day.

❧ Therapy is Not Necessary

While it may be obvious to everyone, it must still be emphasized here that older single people are not always at fault for their unmarried status. Those whose *shidduchim* options have been narrowed by major illness, or familial defects, for example, should never assume full responsibility for their difficulties in getting married. Clearly, some conditions are well beyond the control of the individuals involved.

For this reason, therapy is not necessary or even appropriate for all single people eager to find their *basherte*. Nevertheless, there are many things that all singles can learn from those who have sought therapy for help in getting married. Based on the experience of those people described here, as well as many others, the following advice could help turn at least some older singles into young marrieds.

1. Don't put your life on hold until you get engaged. If it will be worth doing then, chances are it's worth doing now. So if you move up the timetable on your self-improvement plans, you just may shorten the time you have left being single.
2. Don't expect marriage to differ greatly from other relationships you've had. If your relationships with others have been conflicted, tense, or chaotic, correcting that now will only help you handle yourself better with *shidduchim.*
3. Don't ignore depression, anxiety, hopelessness, low self-esteem, or feelings of inadequacy. They may interfere markedly with your ability to put your best foot forward on a date. If they are temporary and transitory, they should be ignored. But if they linger, they should be taken care of so that you can then move on to build your own *bayis ne'eman beYisroel.*

⋆ *"Just Too Picky"*

But aren't there some older singles who are still unmarried only because they are just too picky, and overly critical of the minor human flaws in the *shidduchim* they meet? Isn't that really the main reason so many of these older singles are still unmarried?

It is unfair to lump all singles who appear "too picky" into one pile. Furthermore, it is inaccurate to point to this careful scrutiny as a cause. It is rather a symptom of one of two conditions.

1. **Concerned Caution:** As every parent knows, children generally become more cautious as they grow older and mature. The recklessness and irresponsibility of childhood gives way to improved judgment, as children grow up. This process continues throughout life. The impulsive business or career decisions a young man makes, for example, are not nearly as carefully planned as the more thought-out moves made by his senior colleagues.

The same is true regarding decisions about marriage. A 19- or 20-year-old becomes engaged with greater ease and less reservations than a 25- or 30-year-old. The additional five or ten years of life experience naturally produce increased caution and concern for possible negative consequences which a younger person would never consider. This caution normally tends to increase with age. It is for this reason, for example, that car insurance premiums are lower for drivers over 24 years of age than for those under 24. Insurance companies have studied collision statistics and know that drivers under 24 tend to take greater risks and therefore get into more accidents than drivers over 24.

So older single people may be very cautious in *shidduchim* because of their increased maturity. That is inevitable and unavoidable. But it is not a cause for alarm. When the right person comes along, they may require additional support "to go through with it," or "to have more *bitachon*" instead of being overly anxious about financial matters, but they can and do get married. After all, many single people were considered "too picky"... until they got married. Then people said that they were "just waiting for their *basherte.*"

2. **Hidden Hindrances:** Caution can be taken too far. At times, older single people are ruling out *shidduchim* for very minor flaws, or seemingly insignificant reasons. To their friends and family, these singles appear to be "too picky." In these cases, more than discretion is at work. Here, what appears as "picky" on the surface is only a symptom of some other obstacle to marriage.

For example, someone may be living at home and finding the separation from parents too threatening, for one reason or another.

Perhaps he or she has it too easy at home. Or, maybe the parents are not ready to allow their child to achieve the ultimate independence of marriage. In either case, the child may manifest this unreadiness for marriage through "being too picky." When this happens, no *mussar shmuess* about "being more realistic" will be helpful. When being too picky is a symptom of some other underlying hindrance to marriage, addressing the symptom will not accomplish anything. In such cases, like those presented above, the underlying obstacles will have to be identified first and then removed before the single person can successfully move on into marriage.

At this point, the reader may be wondering, "How can I tell whether my friend/relative is too picky because of a concerned caution or hidden hindrances?"

The answer is that it is often extremely difficult to make that distinction accurately. For this reason it is usually best left for those *ba'alei eitza* (sages, veteran advisers) who have the experience and *da'as Torah* to differentiate between these two categories.

✦ *How You Can Help*

If you cannot accurately diagnose the reason why an older single is too picky, can you still be helpful? You most certainly can help by following these practical guidelines:

1. Accusing older single people of being "too picky" is never helpful. Even if they are, they won't stop just because you point it out. It is often heard as an attack, and wounds deeply.

2. Don't hesitate to point out barriers that you see which are hindering the single person from getting married. Just because you see them clearly does not mean they are so obvious to the single person himself/herself.

3. Don't expect the single person to open up to you simply because you make yourself available. Older single people have the same right as anyone else to choose with whom they share their private concerns and feelings.

4. Show them a copy of this article. It just may help them take more responsibility for their situation and take more control

over their lives. If they do, you may be pleasantly surprised one day with a phone call that begins, *"Es kumpt mir a Mazel Tov* (I get a Mazel Tov ...)!"

THE *RUCHNIUS* APPROACH TO FINDING ONE'S *ZIVUG*

EVEN WHEN ALL ELSE FAILS

ZELDA CUTLER

✦ *No One Believed Me*

"Oh, no! Not another article from a married person giving advice to singles on how to find a *zivug* (soul mate)!"

That's probably what the single reader is thinking. Or: "Just because she got married doesn't mean it'll help me!" To avoid these responses, I almost didn't write this story. But since I was a perennial single who was involved in *shidduchim* for nearly 20 years, my husband convinced me that other singles might gain from my experience.

And so I write about the *derech* I took, a path that I feel catapulted me into *Hashem*'s heart to find a husband – and child. By changing my attitude and behavior, I believe I changed my *mazal* (fate). Though the specifics of my journey may not be relevant to everyone, the concepts can be applied to anyone looking for a *shidduch*. There are thousands of older (over 25 years of age) Jewish Orthodox singles. Rabbi Zvi Schachtel, director of Partners in *Shidduchim*, has a mailing list of nearly 5,000 Orthodox Jewish singles, and that's just the tip of the iceberg.

No previous generation has ever claimed such numbers! If even one single person (divorced, widowed, or not-yet-married) can glean insight from my experience, this will be worth the effort.

It's no exaggeration when I said I looked for a *shidduch* for 20 years. As an older single, I met many *shadchanim* who were sympathetic and helpful. Others were less so. I heard remarks such as "You're too fussy," "You don't want to get married," "You have to compromise," "Take anybody!" and "You're still not married? You must be emotionally unstable!"

I often wondered what was harder – looking for a *shidduch* or dealing with certain *shadchanim*. A frequently asked question – which appeared to be more like an accusation – was, "Why aren't you married?" I tried to explain that being single was a matter of circumstance, not choice. I hadn't met the right one, I explained. No one believed me.

In the two-year period prior to my marriage in 1994, I traveled to 24 cities, two countries (Canada and Israel), met 160 families and spoke to 210 *shadchanim* – my little black book bears witness. I was the Queen of *Hishtadlus* (effort). Or so I thought.

While vacationing in Israel during Sukkos '93, I discovered that I had my priorities all wrong. My education came about after I spoke to Sarah Mushka Honig, a Jerusalem resident. I had been given her name by an American rabbi who said she would give me "*chizuk* (courage)." "*Chizuk?*" I had asked, "I don't need *chizuk* – I need the names of *shadchanim!*" But the *rav* didn't know any matchmakers in Israel and neither did I, so I looked up Mrs. Honig. I was glad I did.

❧ *The Ruchnius Emphasis*

"**D**o you know any *shadchanim?*" I had asked Mrs. Honig shortly after we met. "I can give you names," she said, "but don't ignore the *ruchnius* (spiritual) aspect of looking for your *basherte* (intended one). That's even more important."

Her words, said slowly while we sipped peppermint tea that afternoon, were to change the entire direction of my life:

Notwithstanding the importance of *shadchanim*, I realized I had put my faith in people instead of in *Hashem*. It's the *ruchnius* that provides the foundation for everything. In spiritual matters, there are no middlemen – there's a direct line to *Hashem*.

My *ruchnius* journey began with that vacation to Israel nine years ago. And though some of my wanderings involved *davening* at the *kevarim* (gravesites) of *tzaddikim* (righteous sages) and at the *Kosel Hamaravi* (Western Wall), one doesn't have to go to *Eretz Yisroel* – one can talk to *Hashem* from anywhere.

Looking back after eight years of marriage, it appears my *ruchnius* quest for a *shidduch* had basically three elements – *teshuva* (repentance), *tefilla* (prayer), and *tzeddaka* (charity). This makes sense, since on *Rosh Hashana* and *Yom Kippur* we say, "Repentance, prayer, and charity remove the evil decree." I feel each of these aspects is essential, though I've slightly changed the order here for purpose of chronology.

I. *TESHUVA* (REPENTANCE)

"The magnitude of one's repentance will be commensurate with the magnitude of his heart-searching."
– SHAAREI TESHUVA (GATES OF REPENTANCE),
RABBEINU YONA (THIRD GATE: I)

It's easy to blame others for not finding a *shidduch*, but in all honesty, I figured the main reason I wasn't married was that I had to *improve as a person*. If I could somehow raise my level of spirituality, this might make me a *keli* (vessel) to receive my *basherte*.

I tried to do this by various means – going to Torah classes, reading *mussar sefarim* (ethics books) for self-improvement, keeping a *cheshbon hanefesh* (daily accounting of my behavior), and doing *chessed* (good deeds).

Torah Classes

Step one of my self-improvement plan was to learn Torah. Living in Borough Park at the time, I attended evening classes at Bais Yaakov Seminary. The concepts were food for my *neshama*. If I get married, I thought, Torah classes will help me become a better person; and if I *don't* get married, Torah classes will help me become a better person. Either way, I win.

Cheshbon Hanefesh (Daily Accounting)

"... All who are engaged in repentance [should] keep a written record of those areas in which they have gone astray and of those mitzvos in the fulfillment of which they have fallen short, and to review these memoranda daily."

— SHAAREI TESHUVA (GATES OF REPENTANCE),
RABBEINU YONA (FIRST GATE, VIII)

In the month of *Elul* I began reading the classic *mussar sefer Shaarei Teshuva (Gates of Repentance)*, by Rabbeinu Yona. I realized these concepts were not just preparation for *Rosh Hashana* and *Yom Kippur,* but for every day of our lives. Rabbeinu Yona implores us to keep a written record of our deeds and review our behavior daily. I began doing both immediately. On my way to work, I would sit on the subway, abbreviating and color-coding various character traits into the minuscule squares on my pocket calendar – negative traits in red, positive ones in blue.

Not only was my *cheshbon hanefesh* a spur to self-improvement, it was a factor in my *shidduch* as well. Later, my husband told me that when he heard from our *shadchan* that I was keeping a *cheshbon hanefesh,* that was what prompted him to meet me.

Realizing the Value of Each Person I Dated

How else did I change? As the years went by, the phone calls decreased. One *shadchan* told me, "Older men want younger girls." When I did go out, I dreaded each meeting. If nothing materialized, it was almost traumatic – the build-up for the letdown. It would take weeks, if not months, to get out of the slump and emotionally prepare myself to start the process all over again. I began to think I would never get married.

It was only after I had developed a strong foundation of *emuna* and had changed my attitude that I started to project more positive vibes. It's positive vibes, after all, that make us attractive to people. At the same time, I began to look harder for positive qualities in others. I saw the *tzellem Elokim* (Hashem's image) in each person, and appreciated what each had to offer. Gradually, I no longer dreaded going out on dates.

Feeling the Joy of Another Single's *Simcha*

"Dancing at a wedding sweetens the force of the harsh judgements in the world."

— LIKUTEY MOHARAN

How do we measure spiritual growth? I measured mine by my reaction when a friend became engaged. On hearing about another single's *simcha*, I was happy for my friend, but my honest reaction was, *"Why not me?"* As I progressed in my development, I stopped asking the question. My friend's *chassan* (groom) was meant for her; my *zivug*, G-d willing, would be meant for me. I began to feel the *kalla's* joy. In fact, I remember dancing at one friend's wedding with such unabashed delight that it was almost as though it were my own *simcha*.

Chessed: Hachnasas Orchim

My *rav*, Rabbi Noach Orlowek, *mashgiach ruchani* (spiritual adviser) of Yeshiva Torah Ore in Jerusalem, had always stressed the importance of working for the *klal* (community). My life revolved too much around my own needs. Walking in the street one day, I looked upward and silently asked *Hashem* to help me get involved with the *klal*. Within days, I was asked by an organization if I'd volunteer to do *hachnasas orchim* (hospitality) for Pesach. I accepted. Realizing later that the need went far beyond Pesach, I continued placing people – mostly singles – all year round, for meals and sleeping accommodations for *Shabbos* and *Yom Tov*. This project continued for ten years, until I got married and moved out of the community. (Now, *baruch Hashem*, our family has the *zechus* to host many guests.)

There is no doubt in my mind that *chessed* contributed to my growth; instead of focusing on myself, I was busy helping others. I think I gained more than the people I accommodated. Some of the hosts, sensitive to my being single, invited me to join them for meals. I went, and some of these women are now my closest friends.

II. *TZEDDAKA* (CHARITY)

"Charity is the remedy for all wounds."

– *Likutey Moharan II*

Giving to All Who Ask

One evening I walked with a friend through *Me'a She'arim*. She *davened* to have a first child, after many years of marriage. I *davened* for a husband, after many years of waiting. As we walked, I noticed that she gave money to each and every person who approached us – and there were many. In fact, she went out of her way to give. "You're generous," I said.

"Giving *tzeddaka* is a *segula* (mystical remedy)," she explained. "Rav Chaim Pinchos Scheinberg said I should give to everyone who asks me."

I wondered if giving *tzeddaka* might also be a *segula* for finding a mate, and when we approached a telephone on the next block, I called Rabbi Scheinberg. His answer: Give to everyone who asks, without fail. Suddenly I felt a large weight drop from me. I didn't have to analyze whether anyone deserved it – I had to give without reservations. Maybe this would mean that *Hashem* would give to *me*, whether or not I deserved it! My friend and I continued our walk, nearly chasing after anyone who remotely appeared to be asking.

The *Kosel* was my next stop. I went with a bag full of change. A recent *kalla* had told me she had *davened* at the Wall and had given substantial *tzeddaka* to a woman beggar. The woman then gave her *beracha* after *beracha*. I usually felt annoyed when interrupted during *davening*. Just then a woman approached me during *Ashrei*. This time, I was more generous in my thoughts as well as my purse. She broke into a grin and showered me with *berachos.* Her smile warmed me. Charity creates a bond, I thought.

III. *TEFILLA* (PRAYER)

Berachos From *Tzaddikim*

"Each Jew must bind his prayers to the tzaddik of the age, be-cause they know how to raise every single prayer to its proper place, and out of all the prayers they build the structure of the Shechina, which brings the coming of Moshiach closer."

— *LIKUTEY MOHARAN II*

Realizing the importance of receiving *berachos* from *tzaddikim*, I visited many. Rabbi Levi Yitzchok Horowitz (the Bostoner *Rebbe),* for example, gave me a *passuk* (verse) from the Torah that started with *Zayin* and ended with *Aleph,* as did my name, Zelda. Saying a *passuk* related to one's name during *Shemoneh Esrei* is supposed to be a *segula* for good *mazal.*

In a meeting with Rabbi Avraham Pam זצ״ל, I said that I heard that a person's *mazal* lies in one's name. Did he feel I should use my Hebrew/Yiddish name instead of the secular one I had been using? I added that I had never liked my Hebrew name, Zelda.

"Zelda!" he cried. "That's a beautiful name!" He said it with such feeling that the name took on new significance. From then on, I was Zelda. Whereas Carol could not find her *zivug,* Zelda just might.

Davening in *Shul*

"Intense prayer can help a person find his marriage partner."
– *LIKUTEY MOHARAN I, 9.*

Every *Rosh Hashana* and *Yom Kippur,* I *davened* at Agudath Israel of 16th Avenue in Borough Park. When Reb Daniel Goldstein ז״ל offered his emotional *"Unesaneh Tokef"* plea to *Hashem,* during that *Mussaf* of *Rosh Hashana* in 1993, I felt inspired to *daven* with tena-cious concentration. I had a strong feeling that the prayers of the entire congregation, together with Reb Daniel's, would be heard and answered by *Shamayim*.

There were five older single women *davening* in *shul* that *Yom Tov*. Could it be mere coincidence that each one of us became a *kalla* within a year? The power of *tefilla*!

Our sages stress that *tefilla* can change the *mazal* of a person. "There's an incredible force of *tefilla* that can zoom the *shidduch* through the window even if you don't see a single *shadchan*," Mrs. Honig had said. "Even a single person who feels that decades have passed by, and the *mazal* seems for one to remain forever alone, should that person intensify his or her efforts in *tefilla*, and then boost these efforts with *berachos* from *tzaddikim*, then even that single person can burst out of the previous *mazal*."

Her sentiments, backed by Torah sources, gave me *chizuk*.

Davening for Oneself – *Hisbodedus* (Personal Prayer When Alone)

"Hashem is close to the brokenhearted; and those crushed in spirit, He saves."

– TEHILLIM 34,19

There were long periods when I hardly went out at all. I was beginning to feel the strain. I met one day with Rabbi Nachman Bulman, a respected sage in Jerusalem. "I know everything that happens is for the good," I told him, "but sometimes I feel *Hashem* has forgotten me – or is punishing me. What should I do?"

Rabbi Bulman said, "*Daven*. Ask *Hashem* for what you want. *Hashem* can do anything. If He wills it, you can walk through this wall!" I realized his answer was *emes* (truth) and that I had to put more *kavana* (concentration) into my *davening*. It gave me hope. And hope was what I needed.

I remembered hearing that the good we get isn't because of our merits, but because of *Hashem*'s will. In *davening*, I began adding a phrase recommended by our sages: "I don't ask for anything because of my righteousness, but because of Your *chessed* and Your *rachamim*." Rabbi Yitzchak Kirzner ל״צז also suggested I do this.

I began engaging in *hisbodedus*, personal prayer in solitude. I talked to *Hashem*, pouring out my heart to Him. Though I considered myself a relatively happy, upbeat person, there were often times when I would cry about being single. I remember one night just lying in bed, imploring *Hashem* to help me. As my tears flowed freely, I thought of Rabbi Avigdor Miller זצ"ל who said we should cry out to *Hashem* when we're in pain. "It's not that *Hashem* needs our cries," he had said. "We need *Hashem*."

I spoke out loud to G-d. "Am I so terrible?" I asked. "Is this why You brought me into the world – to be by myself? I'm doing Your *mitzvos*. Do you *want* me to remain single? If so, give me a sign and I'll save myself the time, effort and money I'm spending to find a *shidduch*. But if You want me to be married, why is it taking so long? What must I do? I need You to show me the way. Give me the *da'as* to know who my *zivug* is and give him the wisdom to recognize me. I don't care if he was never married or divorced or a widower – as long as he's a good man. And if he has a child, that's fine – especially a girl. I'll try to be a good mother to her. And as long as I'm asking, maybe she can be about 8 or 9 years old – that was my campers' age when I was a counselor – it's my favorite age."

Shortly afterward, I met the man who was to become my husband. He was a widower with a charming daughter. She was 9 years old.

In *Chovos Halevavos* (Duties of the Heart), we're told, "Words that come from the heart, enter the heart." I believe *Hashem* had great *chessed* and *rachamim* for me. Three months later I was married.

Chessed: Machsom Le'fi
(Shmiras Halashon – Guard Your Tongue)

Whether it was *chessed* or survival guilt, I don't know, but shortly after I was married, I began working in *shidduchim* – and still do. But somehow I felt that a *ruchnius* approach might produce more matches. For that reason, I began a *machsom le'fi* (guarding one's speech) group, in which each person would take on two hours a day of not speaking *lashon hora* (gossip), in the *zechus* that a particular single would find a *zivug*. I started this group *l'ilui nishmas* (in memory of) a friend of mine, an older single. Never bitter about being alone, my friend Barbara (Breindel) ע״ה was always delighted to hear about someone's wedding or engagement.

In the past three years, our *machsom le'fi* group has seen 35 *kallas* – all over the age of 25, and many over 30; eight of these women now have babies. I'm convinced the success of our project lies in my friend Barbara's merit. New groups, including some for single men, are springing up from coast to coast, all *l'ilui nishmas Breindel bas Preyda, aleha hashalom.*

I say this to older singles: miracles do happen. They happened to me, *bli ayin hara,* and they can happen to you. Maybe it helps to *believe* they can happen. There are no guarantees to the *ruchnius* approaches of *teshuva, tefilla* and *tzeddaka,* but aren't they worth trying? Perhaps my story will show that it's never too late; there's always hope. Just cry out to *Hashem.* He can do anything.

Facing Rejection in Shidduchim ... Without Feeling Rejected

An Orthodox Psychotherapist Analyzes a Neglected Aspect Of The Dating Process

Dr. Meir Wikler

A shidduch is suggested. Both sides give ample consideration and then agree to meet. The meeting goes well and both parties decide to meet again. After a few more dates, marriage is proposed and accepted. Mazel Tov!

That is the ideal scenario. It happens like that sometimes. But for the vast majority of shidduchim that are suggested, the ending is not as pretty. More often than not, after the first date, one or both sides does not want to continue. What should you do then? What are the guidelines? Marriage manuals seldom address these questions. This article will.

❧ Hakaras Hatov

The first consideration must always be *hakaras hatov*. Regardless of the reasons for rejecting any *shidduch*, both parties must not overlook their obligations of gratitude to whoever took the time and made the effort to suggest the *shidduch*. Although this may sound elementary to some, it is sufficiently neglected that it must be mentioned.

> *One of my rebbeim told me about a shidduch he tried to arrange over twenty years ago. After one meeting, the young man did not feel that a second time would be worthwhile. A few weeks later, the bachur met his Rav, who asked what happened. The young man replied, "Oh, Rebbe, she's not for me at all!"*
>
> *In a gentle tone the Rav taught that bachur a valuable lesson. "When I suggested that shidduch, I did not mean to guarantee that she would be the right one for you. I only meant that she might be for you. I'm sorry if there was some misunderstanding."*
>
> *The young man immediately apologized for his rudeness, as well as his failure to get back to the Rav sooner.*

Single people often fail to understand and fully appreciate the time and effort that go into *redding shidduchim* (proposing matches). That is why they often neglect their obligation of *hakaras hatov*.

❧ A Chassidic Tale

Word was out that a *Chassidic Rebbe* was looking for a *shidduch* for his daughter, and *shadchanim* from far and wide trooped to the *Rebbe's* door. One *shadchan* presented the Rebbe with all of the relevant details about a particular young man. When the *shadchan* was finished, the Rebbe indicated that he was not interested, and handed the *shadchan* some money. "What is this for?" asked the bewildered *shadchan*.

"That is *shadchanus gelt* (the matchmaking fee)," the *Rebbe* answered.

"But I am not entitled to *shadchanus gelt*, the *shadchan* protested. "The Rebbe did not even agree to meet the young man."

"That is *true*," the *Rebbe* replied. "But just as we believe that every match is decided in Heaven, we also believe that it is predetermined just how *many* proposals we must listen to until we hear the right one. Your suggestion brought us one closer. For that you are entitled to *shadchanus gelt*."

Even if you don't feel any appreciation towards the *shadchan*, it is nevertheless to your advantage to thank him or her. Not to do so just doesn't look good on your resume. Moreover, you may have to wait a long time before that same *shadchan* thinks of you again.

✦ *When You Are Rejecting*

In addition to expressing *hakaras hatov,* you have an obligation to let the other person know if you wish to continue or not as soon as possible. Be clear. If the answer is "No," don't say "Maybe." If you are not sure, then by all means say so. But do not leave the other side hanging any longer than is necessary. You need not decide whether or not you want to marry this person; only whether or not you are interested enough to meet again.

Sometimes, in the interests of "not hurting" the other side, the rejector will hedge, hesitate, or evade the *shadchan*. When this is done, the rejected person is never spared, but often gets hurt even more.

> *A young man I know dated a young lady three times. After the second meeting, they decided to bypass the shadchan and communicate directly. When he called her for a fourth date, she told him she was busy. They had a pleasant chat and then he said he'd keep in touch. Not one to take things personally, he continued this procedure for a total of five weeks.*
>
> *So when she told him she was busy for the sixth week in a row, he finally became suspicious and asked, "Tell me, are you really busy or is this your way of telling me you're not interested in going out again?"*
>
> *"Well, uh, to tell you the truth, " she practically whispered, "you're right. I'm not really interested. "*
>
> *"Did you just decide now, or did you feel that way six weeks ago?" he asked.*
>
> *"I felt that way after our last date."*
>
> *"Then why didn't you just let me know when I asked you out the following week?"*
>
> *"I didn't want to hurt your feelings. "*

Guess what? ... His feelings were just as hurt. Had the *shadchan* still been involved, this misunderstanding could have easily been avoided. But this anecdote illustrates the importance of letting the other side know as soon as possible of your decision not to continue.[1]

❧ When You Are Rejected

Suppose there has been only one date, a longer relationship, or even no dates at all. You felt the *shidduch* was right for you — for your son or daughter, or for your friend — but the other party did not feel the same way. What do you say to yourself? What do you say to your child? What do you say to your friend that can ease the pain of the rejection?

If you're like most people, you probably say something along the lines of "Well. I guess it just wasn't *bashert* for you." Of course, you would be absolutely correct in that analysis. But if sharing that evaluation with a rejected suitor ever lifted his or her spirits, then you would be eligible for entry in the *Guiness Book of World Records.* ("First person to lift spirits by saying, 'Well, I guess it wasn't *bashert'*...")

So what can you say to yourself or someone else who has just been turned down by what seemed to be the ideal match?

The first thing you need to do is acknowledge the disappointment. *It does hurt.* Ask anyone who has been rejected and they'll tell you. It can be a crushing blow to the self-esteem of the most confident person. By acknowledging the validity of the feelings, whether your own or someone else's, you are starting the process of healing the emotional wound.

---

1. Generally, the *shadchan* acts as a go-between, conveying your decision to the other party. When doing so, however, the *shadchan* must avoid sharing your reasons if that would, in any way, constitute *rechilus.* (See *Guard Your Tongue*, p. 180, #14.) Later, however, the *shadchan* might be able to use your comments (without attribution) as a basis for coaching the other person, while not inflicting the pain of embarrassment. (For example, "Do you ever try to initiate conversation instead of merely responding to questions?")

✦ *A Meaningful Metaphor*

The next thing you can do is try to put the disappointment into proper perspective. No, it wasn't *bashert*. But how can you get this message across in a helpful way? I like to use the following metaphor.

We all remember the tragedy of the Challenger, the first space ship to explode in midair, seconds after takeoff, killing everyone on board. One of the passengers was not even an astronaut. She was a public school teacher who was supposed to give the first elementary school lesson from space.

This teacher was selected from approximately 10,000 applicants — all of whom had to request, complete and submit an extensive written application. It is safe to assume that all of the 9,999 applicants who were rejected — especially those who had also been interviewed — must have felt varying degrees of disappointment.

Then, in one brief flash, all 9,999 rejected applicants must have gasped in unspeakable gratitude when they heard about the disaster. Suddenly, instead of seeing their rejection as the missed opportunity of a lifetime, they realized that it had been nothing less than lifesaving. The Challenger rejects were able to see the great blessing of their being denied inclusion on that ill-fated flight.

Even if we *never* see exactly how we benefit from a rejection (whether in *shidduchim,* yeshiva, seminary, or job applications, or any other disappointment), we must endeavor to accept it as though it were as beneficial to us as the rejection letters received by the 9,999 applicants for the Challenger mission. As Rabbi Akiva was wont to say: *"Kol de'avid Rachmana le'tav avid* —everything that *Hashem* does is for the good" *(Berachos* 60b).

✦ Who Makes *Shidduchim*

In the final analysis, we can really find strength to cope with rejection in *shidduchim* by remembering Who is responsible for making all *shidduchim.*

Chazal have declared, "*Kashye zivugam shel adam kekrias Yam Suf*" — Matchmaking of people is as difficult as splitting the Red Sea (*Sota* 2a). How can any task be referred to as "difficult" for *Hashem?*

The *sefer Simcha Bime'ono* offers the following explanation: Matchmaking is no more difficult for *Hashem* than any other daily miracle He performs. The difficulty in *shidduchim* arises when people delude themselves into thinking that *they* are in charge of the process. That is why *Chazal* emphasize that, "Matchmaking *of people* is as difficult … " When people think that the process of *shidduchim* is really up to them, then it truly becomes as difficult as *krias Yam Suf.*

✦ The Power of Prayer

I recently had a private chat with a well-known Torah personality. He is respected throughout the world as an inspiring orator, sagacious adviser, and expert in matters of *shalom bayis* (marital harmony). He made the following self-disclosure:

"When my first child was ready for *shidduchim*, I thought that it would go easily for me. With my years of experience with so many couples, I would be able to find the perfect *shidduch* for my daughter. And when she got married, I was convinced that I had, indeed, selected the best son-in-law in the world. Two agonizing, torturous years later, when she finally received her *get*, I understood how foolish I had been.

"Do you know, Meir'l, how good *shidduchim* are really made? Only through *tefilla*. If you and I were successful with our own *shidduchim*, it's not because we were smarter than anyone else. It is because of the tears shed by our *Bubbies* and *Zaidies* when they said *Tehillim* for us to find good *shidduchim*. I learned the hard way. The only way to find good *shidduchim* for our children is to pour our hearts out with *Tehillim*. "

May *Hashem* hear and answer all of our *tefillos* for good *shidduchim*, and may He ease the pain of our disappointment when we are rejected by *shidduchim* that we mistakenly thought would be good for us.

THE UNBROKEN GLASS
TWENTY-TWO YEARS OF AVERTING TRAGEDY IN KLAL YISRAEL

RABBI SHIMON FINKELMAN

❧ Success: Discovering Incompatibility

For years, the children's ward for genetic diseases at Kingsbrook Jewish Medical Center would house as many as sixteen Tay-Sachs victims, and often, there was a waiting list for beds. In 1996, the ward had not one Tay-Sachs patient. This good tiding is surely indicative of the achievements of the Dor Yeshorim organization and of the great *siyata diShmaya* with which its work has been blessed since its founding in 1983.

Over the last two decades, it has become routine for yeshiva students and Bais Yaakov girls to have their blood tested for possible carrier status, through Dor Yeshorim's anonymous testing program, and to check the compatibility of a *shidduch* when it has been suggested.[1] Since its founding, Dor Yeshorim has found some two hundred prospective matches incompatible. As anyone familiar

---

1 It cannot be stressed enough that testing and checking for compatibility should not be postponed until engagement is seriously being considered. In any event, it should be understood that exchanging Dor Yeshorim i.d. numbers to check compatibility is not a commitment toward engagement; it is simply the wise thing to do.

with the history of a baby stricken with Tay-Sachs (or other genetic disease) can testify, the suffering of such children and their families is indescribable, ר"ל. Even if only one incompatible match had been avoided, it would have been well worth the founding of Dor Yeshorim for that alone. On the other hand, those who have married after having ascertained that they are genetically compatible, have the peace of mind of knowing that the diseases for which they have been tested will not afflict their children.

✦ Key to Success

The key to Dor Yeshorim's phenomenal success has been its system of confidentiality, which is the cornerstone of its program. This has served a threefold purpose: It has made genetic testing in our community a routine matter without stigma; it has saved carriers of genetic diseases from unfounded fears regarding their status; and it has educated the Torah community in understanding that healthy siblings of stricken children are at absolutely no risk of producing such children of their own, provided that they make use of the *pre-shidduch* screening so that they will marry non-carriers.

Close to ten thousand proposed *shiduchim* are checked annually by Dor Yeshorim without anyone knowing his or her actual carrier status, and thus, without any reason for concern — as long as the proposed match is compatible.[1]

Dor Yeshorim's achievements have not gone unnoticed in the medical community. Its director has been invited to lecture at the National Institute of Health, as well as many schools of medicine, including New York University and Harvard. In 1996, the organization was the recipient of the Robert Wood Johnson Community Health Leadership Award.

---

1. Upon being tested, the person is given an I.D. number, which is recorded along with his or her birth date; when checking compatibility, the I.D. number along with day of month (not year) of birth are submitted; only one of the parties need be a non-carrier for the match to be deemed "compatible."

❧ Direction and Guidelines

Dor Yeshorim follows a set of guidelines formulated by *gedolei Yisroel* who continue to guide the organization in every step of its work.[1] In fact, the late Manchester *Rosh Yeshiva* Rabbi Yehuda Zev Segal was the driving force behind Dor Yeshorim's adding cystic fibrosis to its testing program. When the organization's director told the *Rosh Yeshiva* that he lacked the financial resources for such an undertaking, Rabbi Segal responded, "Do it and I will help you." True to his word, the *Rosh Yeshiva*, in the last weeks of his life, penned a letter urging support of this project.

Experience has caused the organization's rabbinic leadership to institute a strict set of rules for responding to callers who wish to check compatibility.

For example, Dor Yeshorim responds to such requests only if the young man or woman, or their parents, call. This is done to protect individuals from unscrupulous outsiders who may have their own reasons for wanting to know the compatibility of a given *shidduch*.[2] Additionally, before this policy was instituted, there was a case where a *shadchan* called to check on the compatibility of two matches. One was found to be compatible, the other was not, and the *shadchan* mixed up the results. Thankfully, the mistake was caught in time.

❧ A Timeless Lesson

When I think of Dor Yeshorim, I think of Rabbi Yaakov Yosef Herman, legendary pioneer of Torah life in America.

---

1. In a letter dated September 1997, the renowned *Rosh Yeshiva* and *poseik* Rabbi Chaim Pinchus Scheinberg of Jerusalem wrote, "I wish to strengthen the hands of those involved in a *mitzva*, namely the directors of the Dor Yeshorim organization, that they should continue to perform their testing in total confidentiality, whereby those being tested are not told the actual results (of the individual's test). This is the correct way."
2. For this reason, requests to check compatibility are responded to only if the caller is calling from the phone number that was submitted at the time he or she was tested. If the number has changed, this should be reported as soon as possible.

It should also be noted that anyone who had their blood tested before 1995 should call Dor Yeshorim to ensure that they are included in the full range of genetic testing that the organization offers (current testing includes four genetic diseases). In most cases, further testing will not be necessary.

In *All For the Boss*,[1] Ruchoma Shain's stirring biography of her father, Reb Yaakov Yosef, she describes how at age 12, he spent *Shabbos* alone on a park bench in Manhattan, with nothing but three small *challos* for sustenance. With no immediate family in America to care for him, young Yaakov Yosef had been boarding with a family who had grossly mistreated him. He had left their house late Friday afternoon, never to return. There on the park bench he promised himself that when he would get married and have a home of his own, he would see to it that others would not suffer the loneliness that he was experiencing at that moment. His house would be open to all; there would always be room for another guest.

And so it was. The home of Reb Yaakov Yosef and his devoted wife was open to all, every day of the year. On *Shabbos,* more than twenty guests would gather around their table for each meal. "Business is booming!" Reb Yaakov Yosef would exclaim in delight.

This was a man who felt tremendous personal pain and was determined to do everything possible so that no other Jew should experience similar pain.

And that is how Dor Yeshorim came into being. The organization's founder and director suffered the loss of a number of Tay-Sachs children, ר״ל.[2] He has made it his life's mission to do everything in his power to help ensure that others should not suffer as he and his family did. May *Hashem* bless him for his efforts, and may the concern and self-sacrifice that Jews show for one another be rewarded with a flow of compassion and healing from Above for all of *Klal Yisroel.*

---

1. Published by Feldheim.
2. Baruch Hashem, he has healthy children and grandchildren. He reports that his fortunes took a decided turn for the better from the time that he decided to dedicate himself to serving the *Klal.*

Every step in life deserves ample preparation – awareness of the Torah view on the matters as well as guidance in how to deal with the expected and the unanticipated… no less such a major personal advancement as marriage. The key is in the preparation.

THE JEWISH HOME: MAINSTAY OF OUR PEOPLE

RABBI AVRAHAM PAM זצ"ל

That the institution of marriage is under assault in society at large needs no elaboration. As much as we of the Orthodox community attempt to shut out the more pernicious effects of the marketplace from our homes, separation and divorce are occurring with noticeable frequency in our midst. To check its further spread, it is essential that we focus on the Torah attitude toward marriage.

The following essay is based on remarks by Rabbi Avrohom Pam זצ"ל, Rosh Yeshiva of Mesivta Torah Vodaath, at a gathering of his students. While the words are addressed to the "men of the house," with little change, they can be a source of guidance and enlightenment to women, as well.

❧ The Cornerstone

Everyone strives to be successful in life, with varying degrees of effort, depending upon how important the particular endeavor is to him. Of highest priority to most people is achievement in business or the profession of one's choice, and it is to this that he applies his utmost. The development of a happy, solid family is not often given that much effort, for it is not understood to be so notable an achievement. Yet a home, where the husband and wife are devoted to each other and live in harmony, where the spiritual growth and Torah development of the children is a dominant concern — such a house is a מקדש מעט, a sanctuary in miniature, where the *Shechina* dwells. Creation of such a house represents a true mark of success, a goal to strive for, an accomplishment in which to take justifiable pride. Since *shalom bayis* problems — problems of domestic strife — seem to abound, it would seem that unfortunately, people do not recognize the value of this achievement.

The cornerstone is mutual love and respect. תוכו רצוף אהבה, "Full of love within." And, like any aspect of a life lived according to the Torah, it would be guided by the dictum: ... דרכי, דרכי נועם, "Its ways are ways of pleasantness."

As a frame of reference, one should, from time to time, ask himself why his *neshama* was dispatched from celestial spheres to this world — certainly not to make other people miserable, or to be a thorn in his wife's side. Surely the Divine gift of life was not meant to be abused this way. To underscore the importance of mutual respect in marriage, and to understand the full import of that concept, note the admonition of the *Maggid* to the *"Beis Yosef."*

The *Maggid* — that is, the heavenly emissary that regularly visited with the *Beis Yosef* (Rabbi Yosef Caro, the author of the *Shulchan Aruch*) — once revealed to him the sacred essence of his wife's *neshama*.[1] He then explained why he did so: "So you may appreciate her and honor her accordingly." One may be certain that the *Beis Yosef* followed to the letter all the *halachos* spelled out in the *Shulchan Aruch* in regard to "Love your wife as yourself and honor her more than yourself." Yet the *Maggid* felt that with a greater awareness of the lofty nature of his wife's *neshama*, the *Beis Yosef's* respect for her would be enhanced even further.

We are not worthy of visitations by *Maggidim*, to reveal cosmic

---

1. See *Maggid Mesharim: Parashas Va'eira*

secrets to us, but in the World to Come, we may be shocked to discover who really was the gift of G-d to be our partner in life .... Imagine a person's shame when he will realize the sublime soul his wife possessed, and he will recall the careless or even abusive manner in which he treated her during their years together! But then it will be too late to do anything about it ...

One really does not have to wait for heavenly emissaries or for otherworldly revelations for an indication of the sanctity of the *neshama* of the women in today's Torah society. Thoroughly imbued with the values taught in the Bais Yaakov schools and seminaries, they are guided by a loving commitment to a life of Torah, and a desire to serve *Klal Yisrael* by raising a family loyal to Torah. The mere fact that a woman can entertain and nurture such feelings in the midst of a society that is so depraved and void of sanctity is of itself an indication of the lofty stature of her soul. Such a woman surely merits honor, for her own sake!

❧ *The Route to "Shalom Bayis"*

Shalom bayis is not to be taken for granted and left to run its own course. Like a beautiful garden it needs constant care and concern. It is interesting that in the *Kesuba* (marriage contract), the husband pledges: ואנא אפלח ואוקיר ואיזון ואפרנס יתיכי ליכי, "I will work, honor, feed, and support you." It would seem that the promise to honor is out of order, for it should have been placed first: "honor, work, feed, and support you." The fact that "work" is first would seem to indicate that just as supporting one's wife calls for a great investment of time and effort, so too must one work at properly honoring her. It is an aspect of life that does not take care of itself, but can suffer seriously if neglected.

Being considerate of one's wife calls for vigilance, especially in areas of speech. We tend to be careless with what we say, and yet a harsh word can inflict wounds that never heal. In general human relationships, the Torah prohibits אונאת דברים, causing pain with words, on which the *Sefer HaChinuch* elaborates, "One must not say anything that will pain or anguish someone, and leave him help-less." Now if this is the case in regard to strangers, imagine how much more sensitive the Torah expects one to be toward his wife. A harsh word, a demeaning expression, an insulting remark, any of these can severely strain a marriage. A derogatory name hurled out in anger can inflict a wound that continues to fester long after the reasons for the argument are forgotten.

The sensitivity of marital harmony is evident in G-d's modifica-tion of Sarah's remark about her husband, Avraham, when He had questioned them. Sarah had laughed when she heard that she was to bear a son, and said, "How is it possible that I, in my advanced stage in life, should have a son — *and my husband is old?"* In report-ing her comment to Avraham, G-d altered the last phrase, to refer to Sarah's own age instead (*Bereishis* 19:13-14). What harm would there have been if G-d had quoted her accurately? Avraham was 99 years old, had reached an extremely high spiritual level, and had even prayed for the outward signs of old age. It would thus seem absurd for Avraham to be concerned about such empty matters as his alleged lack of youthfulness.

Yet G-d deemed it important to circumvent the issue: Sarah's words were true, they reflected a fulfillment of his own prayer, and had they been uttered by anyone else, it is not likely that Avraham would have taken offense at them. But when two lives become so intertwined and mutually dependent, as do the lives of a husband and wife, then their relationship is so sensitive that a word or ex-pression uttered in innocence can cause deep hurt and actually threaten *shalom bayis* ....

It is a pity that courtship — with its carefully honed phrases so meticulously worded to avoid misunderstanding — comes to an abrupt end with marriage.

Just as an unpleasant word can have devastating effects on a marriage, a kind word can do wonders to solidify a marriage.

A *talmid* of *Hagaon* Rabbi Aaron Kotler זצ"ל recalls once driving the *Rosh Yeshiva* to Lakewood from his home in Boro Park, Reb Aaron was already seated in the car when he suddenly excused himself and asked the driver if he would mind waiting a moment while he took care of something in his house. The *talmid* followed the *Rosh Yeshiva* up to his third-floor apartment to be of assistance if necessary. They entered the apartment, and Reb Aaron went to his *Rebbitzen*, wished her *"A gutten tog,"* turned around and left. In his haste, it seems, he had left the house without bidding her goodbye. The *talmid* says that to this day, he remembers the glow of pleasure that lit up the *Rebbitzen's* face because of this simple gesture.

❧ *The Best, From the Worst*

At times it can be difficult to be appreciative and considerate, when it seems to the husband that the wife is all wrong, impossible to deal with, and so on. The rabbis of the Talmud, however, demonstrated for us how to find the resources for appreciation under all circumstances.

Rav Chiya's wife was known to cause him great anguish throughout their married life. Yet whenever Rav Chiya saw an item that he thought she might appreciate, he purchased it for her as a gift. Rav Chiya's nephew, Rav, noticed this, and asked his uncle why he went out of his way to treat her so graciously, when all he received from her was abuse. Rav Chiya replied that "the fact that she raises our children and saves me from sin is sufficient cause for gratitude. The little aggravation she gives me is insignificant in comparison to the tremendous benefits she bestows upon me."

By contrast, *Adam Harishon* is described as an ingrate by *Chazal* (the rabbis of the Talmud) for blaming his wife for having fed him the forbidden fruit ("The woman that You gave me — she offered me the fruit ..." — as if the fault lies with the *"Shadchan"*). He had forgotten how he had searched among all the creatures of the world for a mate, to no avail; and when G-d put him to sleep and created Chava and brought her to him, how his joy knew no bounds, and he exclaimed ecstatically, "This time, a bone from my bones, flesh from my flesh — this shall be called 'woman'!" The joy was forgotten in the rush of incrimination.

So, too, in many a marriage, when minor differences arise, one partner tends to magnify the problem and fault the spouse for the problem. In a moment of anger, he can deeply hurt the very person to whom he owes so much, overlooking all of the joy and happiness his spouse had brought him over the years. This is the ultimate in ingratitude.

❈ The Inevitable Differences

Since it is impossible for two people living together to agree on absolutely everything, it would be wise to anticipate the inevitable differences that are bound to arise. Is there any preferred way to iron out these differences so as not to strain their relationship?

A recently married young man sought my advice regarding a problem that had arisen in his marriage — a problem that to me seemed to be very insignificant. When I asked him why he thought it necessary to make an issue over such an unimportant thing, he replied, "That's not the idea. Sure, I can give in on this matter. But I'm afraid that if I do, she'll dominate our marriage." I explained to him that his basic premise was foolish. Any relationship is a two-way street. If he would yield on this issue, he would build up credit with his wife, and she, in turn, would be more than willing to please him on other issues that may be far more important to him. And it is not a matter of keeping score on major points but one of dividing areas of responsibility, and yielding whenever it is a matter outside of the individual's purview.

❈ The Division

How do husband and wife divide their areas of responsibility? *Chazal* have given us a practical suggestion: מילי דעלמא, mundane matters, such as those that pertain to managing the house, are primarily the woman's domain. מילי דשמיא, spiritual matters, should generally be under the husband's jurisdiction.

The husband should not concern himself excessively with the cooking, nor become overly involved with decorating the house.

He can offer his opinion, and should show interest and express appreciation in these areas and — to be sure — offer his help when it is needed. But he should bow to his wife's decision whenever there is a difference in their views.

By the same token, the husband should make the final decision in matters such as selecting the yeshiva for their children, their butcher (in terms of *kashrus*), and the customs they will observe. He should surely discuss the matter with her and take her opinions into account, but he must carry the burden of deciding. He is the *poseik acharon* — the final authority. When the husband does not have a strong religious background, the couple should consult a *rav* and follow his guidance.

☙ *The Saving Grace*

The author of *Torah Temima* (in his historical work, *Mekor Baruch*) relates a story that involved his uncle, the *Netziv* — Rabbi Naftoli Tzvi Yehuda Berlin. A distinguished and charitable businessman, who had at one time been recognized as a *lamdan* (Torah scholar), came to the *Netziv* to discuss a personal problem. While he was universally respected as a prominent citizen of his community and made an excellent livelihood, no sooner would he cross the threshold of his house that he became a non-entity. His wife completely dominated the household, and ignored him, except to berate him. He felt like a stranger in his own home, which was a source of endless anguish to him.

The *Netziv* asked him if he set aside specific times during the day for Torah study. The man replied that he had become so involved in his business that he did not have the time to establish a *seder*. The *Netziv* stated emphatically: "You must resolve to establish a regular *seder* for a few hours every day — no matter how busy you might be. You must immerse yourself in your Talmudic studies, and make it an integral, inviolable part of your life. If you heed my advice, I can assure you that your situation will improve greatly."

The *Mekor Baruch* relates that when he subsequently met his cousin, Rabbi Chaim Berlin, the son of the *Netziv*, he asked him about how this incident was resolved. Reb Chaim replied: "I am familiar with the entire story, and I know the merchant personally. As a matter of fact, whenever his business brings him to Moscow, he stops by to tell me how grateful he is to my father for his wonderful advice. His entire home life has changed ever since he began setting aside time for intensive Torah study. His wife now respects him and treats him with the utmost deference."

The advice of the *Netziv* was not some magical formula, but rather a logical suggestion. Once the woman saw that her husband had reordered his priorities and that Torah had assumed a place of prominence in his life, she realized that she was married to a truly respectable individual, and accorded him the honor such a person is entitled to.

❧ The "Frumkeit" Factor

Shalom bayis can sometimes be upset because the husband, for instance, is dismayed with his wife's carelessness in matters pertaining to *kashrus* — she accidentally mixes meat and dairy dishes, and *she'eilos* result. So he accuses her of lacking religious vigilance, and he complains to their rabbi. Often there is no basis for the *she'eila* other than the husband's ignorance of *halacha;* at other times, the *she'eila* is with good cause — but this is still no reason for anger. After all, *she'eilos* only arise among Torah-observant people. The mere fact that she presents the *she'eila* to her husband testifies to her high standards of religious concern. The non-observant never bother to ask.

Then, arguments arise when one partner has a *minhag* (custom) or *chumra* (stringent practice) that the other does not share, and the first refuses to yield on it. As worthy as the practice may be, it surely does not measure up to the *shalom bayis* that is being sacrificed in its behalf. If only both parties would consider this, they would put aside their difficulties and spare themselves much anguish.

If the point of contention is a *halacha* matter, then instead of yielding on it because of *shalom bayis* considerations, one must seek guidance from a *rav*. Generally, whether dealing with *halacha, minhag,* or *chumra* — one would be wise to consult a *rav* to determine what is the proper thing to do.

❧ *Strife Insurance*

As much as one should endeavor to avoid strife, all the more so must one try to prevent it in advance. This is best done by imbuing young people with a sensitivity for harmony in interpersonal affairs, but especially as it relates to *shalom bayis*. The burden of prevention is shared by many people. Parents must always bear in mind that they serve as models to their children, and the way they express mutual respect or sharp differences to one another makes its impression on them, even when they are small.

Teachers and *rebbeim* can also play an important role in "strife prevention" by extending friendship to their students, earning their trust, and maintaining contact with them after they have left the school, by making them feel that their doors are always open to them should the need arise. In this way, when marital problems do threaten, the former student will feel free to return and discuss them with the *teacher/rebbe*, before they mushroom into serious breaches of *shalom bayis*. Finally, and most important, every individual must increase his awareness that his purpose in life is to increase *Kavod Shamayim* — to enhance G-d's glory in the world by leading a Torah life and raising a good family דור ישרים יבורך. When one leads a life consistent with Torah, then all interpersonal dealings should conform with the ideal of "ways of pleasantness"; all the more so should this be the case in regard to all that passes between husband and wife.

GROWING INTO MARRIAGE

Rabbi Aaron Lopiansky

❧ *One Plus One Equals One*

Those who see marriage as the institutionalization of the state of "having fallen in love" suffer from a widely held fantasy, and can some day rudely discover that it is extremely easy to also "fall out of love." Those educated in our yeshivos frequently have fantasies of their own regarding marriage, although they tend to clothe them in loftier garments than do their secularized cousins. But fantasies they are, nonetheless, and they need realignment with Torah realities.

Ask a young man how he envisions the yonder side of the *chupa,* and he'll gush about the *eishes chayil* who will work all day to support him at his scholarly pursuits in the *kollel*: At the end of the day she welcomes him with a bright smile and a hot supper, then scampers off to do the laundry and dishes …. Perhaps he imagines himself as a father with a flock of angelic children, faces glistening in the glow of candles, singing sweet *zemiros* deep into Friday night.

Perhaps some are not so naive, and understand that things do not always work out so smoothly; but then, even if these thoughts are only dreams, a flawed reality can be improved by aiming for some kind of dream. Yet, these fantasies — wholesome as they may seem — can be harmful, if only for being self-serving. To build one's concept of marriage on an interpretation of the passage, "And G-d created Chava to be an *eizer kenegdo* — a helpmate," as a basis for relegating the woman to a role of physical subservience is to miss the essence of the marriage relationship. Indeed, the Talmud describes in detail how *melachim* (angels) provided Adam with all his physical needs — even broiling meat and feeding it to him (*Sanhedrin* 59a), negating any need for a physical helper.

One can suggest that Chava was created to complement Adam's more abstract qualities — to temper his "logos" with her "pathos." But this cannot be the sole reason for the creation of Chava. For the *Gemara* describes Adam as having been created with both male and female features, subsequently divided into two parts. Obviously this refers to more than his physical features.

Indeed, a closer examination of the passage indicates that the main reason for creating woman was because "It is not good for man to be *levado* — alone." Thus: "I will make for him an *eizer kenegdo* — a helper opposite him," to rid man of his *levado* status. One can even understand the emphasis of this passage as stressing the *kenegdo* (opposite him) — that "this *eizer* that I have incorporated into Adam, I will now externalize." (Perhaps a clue to the significance of this can be understood by the Midrash quoted by *Rashi*, that only G-d is meant to be *levado* — alone.)

❧ The Marriage "Yoke"

Regarding the passage, "It is good for man to bear a yoke in his youth" (*Eicha* 3,27), the Midrash defines "yoke" as applying to marriage, among other burdens (*Eicha Rabba*) ... a most unpleasant connotation, to say the least! A yoke, however, can be appreciated when viewed as a device that channels untamed energy into productive activity. Without a yoke, the strongest of forces is not only useless, but potentially damaging. A river harnessed by a dam will supply scores of communities with electricity, water, and recreation. Left to run wild, it will turn into a colossus of destruction. (Appropriately, the *passuk* uses the word *"gevver"* to denote "man," a term that usually refers to male strength — see: *Malbim* on *Yoel* 8:2 and on *Iyov* 14,10.) But what exactly is the yoke of marriage? And where does it lead?

❧ The "Kesuba"

An important part of the marriage ceremony is the reading of the *kesuba* — a complex legal document that details the husband's financial obligations toward his wife. In vain do we search for pledges of mutual love, honor, or respect. Yet, the *kesuba* is central to the Jewish wedding because it signals the assumption of responsibility for another person: "And you shall dwell in my house and your needs provided from my possessions," in some ways, the very essence of marital life. This accountability for the other person extends to the spiritual realm, as well, as is alluded to in an incident in the life of *Shlomo Hamelech*. The *Tanach* says: "Then Shlomo built an altar (to idols)" — when in fact Shlomo's wives, not he, did so. This form of expression implies that he was held responsible for his wives' actions. The *Zohar* in *Parshas Bereishis* on the *passuk*, "And G-d fashioned the side of Adam," says: *Here we are taught that parents provide for a daughter as long as she lives with them. As soon as she marries, her husband supports her and looks after her needs* (free translation). Although the *Zohar* means this as an analogy for a deeper concept, the statement is also true in its simple sense.

Similarly, a man is accountable for the actions of his children until they reach maturity, at which point he declares (in a *bracha*) "Blessed ... who freed me from responsibility for this one."

❧ The Rungs of Responsibility

Rabbi Chaim Shmulevitz זצ״ל, the late *Rosh Yeshiva* of Mir, once commented that Judaism's social-grading system is based on the measure of responsibility assumed by the "gradee." The highest rung of the social order is occupied by the king, who is responsible for the whole of *Klal Yisroel*.

Yehuda demonstrated his qualifications for Jewish royalty by expressing his responsibility for his brother Binyamin to his father: "I guarantee him, seek him from my hands."

Reflecting this same quality, Boaz assumed responsibility for a distant relative (Rus) when there was closer kin, thus meriting to be the progenitor of royalty for all time to come, beginning with his great-grandson, David. The essence of royalty, then, is the acceptance of the burden of the entirety of *Klal Yisroel*.

On the other end of the scale is the *shoteh* — sometimes incorrectly translated as a "simpleton" or "idiot" — defined in the opening chapter of the *Shulchan Aruch Yoreh De'ah* as someone not accountable for his actions. Thus, we have a full range, from *melech* to *shoteh*.

❧ To be Free and Soar?

A man's yoke of marriage has been described as consisting of the responsibilities incumbent upon him: When single, he is free to do as he wishes, when he wishes. As a married man, he is burdened by his family, worrying about his wife's comfort, happiness, and spiritual status, and concerned with his children's upbringing. He may muse: *Wouldn't it be better to be unhampered by this yoke? Wouldn't I be free to soar to the heights of intellectual and spiritual achievement?* But then he would thwart his actual growth as a person.

When a baby is born, he can barely perceive others. He lives completely within his own world, troubled only by his hunger, pain, and discomfort, happy when his needs are met. As he grows older, he realizes there is a world around him: He smiles back at people and begins to communicate with others. In time, he plays with other children and learns to become part of a group (i.e. class, club). He develops a social — and world — consciousness, following a steady progression of de-egocentrism.

This phenomena is described in *Tanach*, as pointed out by Rabbi Shlomo Wolbe, ל״צז, late *Mashgiach* of Yeshiva Be'er Yaakov, in his *sefer Alei Shur*: The passage, "Drink water from your pit (collected from other sources), flowing waters from within your well. Your wellsprings shall burst forth into the streets [forming] pools of water" (*Mishlei* 5,15, 16), traces an advance from imbibing from others to supplying others.

"When a person is born," says Rabbi Wolbe, "he possesses all his qualities in their potential; with each stage of growth, he brings them to fruition … Whether in Torah study or other areas of Divine service, a person must develop his dormant intellectual and emotional attributes.

"That period of life when a person 'finds himself' and chooses a role in life, gradually emerges as a new era of life — the era of 'your wellsprings shall burst forth': A person builds a house, fathers children, teaches students, becomes a full member of society. These extroversions of a person's *avoda* (Divine service) are stages in self-development. But instead of self-development through introversion, it is self-development through working and assuming responsibility for others …"

"A man goes up from his city — and he is elevated in his house … in his neighborhood … in his city … in all of Israel, and all the world. Yet this only came from himself" (*Midrash Shmuel* Chap. I).

"Each successive sphere of activity in which the ascending man finds himself places new burdens and responsibilities upon him. By successfully fulfilling his obligations, he elevates himself further, finding that he is given even greater responsibilities … and his 'protegerie' becomes widened" (free translation, *Alei Shur*, p. 277).

Thus, a person's growth in *avoda* parallels his natural emotional growth. From drinking waters collected from others, he graduates to self-sustenance, his own wellsprings ultimately overflowing to the benefit of others …. The period of "overflow" begins on the wedding day.

❧ The Give-and-Take of Life

A person's each and every character trait, we are told, reflects a corresponding trait of his Creator, and ideally should find expression in a loftier purpose — a sacred function. There is only one aspect of human nature that is *ex nihilo* — original with Man, without counterpart in spiritual realms: the desire to receive. A man is born as a complete "receiver," getting everything and giving nothing in return. His life purpose is to become a "giver" without taking any benefit for himself.

Before *Rebbi* (*Rabbi Yehuda Hanasi*) died, he held his hands aloft and said that he never derived any pleasure from this world. The hands are the instruments that take and give; *Rebbi* testified regarding himself that he was only a "giver."

Now one can gain more insight as to where the "yoke" of marriage is meant to lead. Marriage is the crucial turning point in the lifelong metamorphosis from being a receiver from others into a benefactor to others. Thus it is so essential that man not be a *"levado"* — that such a condition is only feasible for G-d Himself. Man must have someone upon whom to bestow goodness, or else he remains ever a receiver.

And it is also apparent how most youthful "dreams" of married life are off by 180 degrees, for they are solely based on "What will I get?" — whether in the realm of the physical and material or even spiritual ("Someone who will help me sit and learn") — while in truth one must also ask himself: "What am I capable of giving?"

❧ "Simcha" in Marriage

The Rabbis taught: "Whoever dwells without a wife is without joy."

Upon entering yeshiva, prospective *bachurim* usually are treated to a *shmuess* informing them that there is no pleasure greater than sitting and learning. It usually takes a bit of time to recognize that there are two qualifications to this assurance:

- The pleasure of learning is not similar to the pleasure of playing baseball. It is an infinitely deeper and different pleasure.
- Every person is weighted down by an inherent inertia that resists any attempts at raising one's level of spiritual attainment.
- It takes much hard work and many, many failures to achieve any growth.

These are two laws of nature that apply to all spiritual endeavors.

The *simcha* of a marriage in the light of our explanation is much deeper and of much longer duration than marital bliss in the common concept. And it is not at all easy to achieve. One of life's hardest battles is to learn to give; whether as a child of 2, or a young adult of 22.

Rabbi Yechzkiel Sarna זצ״ל, late *Rosh Yeshiva* of Chevron, explains in his commentary on *Mesillas Yesharim* why King David was punished for saying, "Your statutes are songs to me" (*Tehillim* 119, 53).

He points out that there are two basic types of *simcha*. One is represented by the joy one experiences in response to music. The band strikes up a chord and he is all a-dance. No sooner does the band stop, however, is he as sullen as before. By contrast, a person enjoys a deep, lasting joy after having built a house with his own hands. He has invested time, money, and effort, and his *simcha* upon completion is eternal.

David erred in comparing the joys of Torah to *zemiros* — music, for the pleasures of Torah study are not derived from the tantalizing *"vertel"*; rather they are the joys that grow from the investment of engaging in *"la'asok* — laboring in the words of the Torah" (from the *beracha* on Torah study).

Someone who looks forward to marriage in terms of the joys of "having a great time together" will find his happiness dissipate as the years go by, and the yoke will bear heavier. Only he who truly understands the meaning of the yoke will reap compounded interests from his investments.

Fortunate is he that achieves this, for he has realized a prime goal in life — that of "going in His ways." In its deeper sense, he has converted himself from a taker to a giver. It is a task that begins at birth and ends at death, but the fulcrum is at the day of the *chassuna*.

AN OUTLINE
FOR *HADRACHA*
(GUIDANCE) SESSIONS

*DR. MEIR WIKLER**

❧ *Some Questions Everyone Contemplating Marriage Should Be Asking, and Some Answers ...*

It has become more or less accepted that young men and women do need some preparation for marriage, beyond what they receive at home. While the standard yeshiva or Bais Yaakov chinuch (education) does help prepare for successful marriages built on foundations of Torah values, rabbonim, professionals, and laymen have recently acknowledged the need for some program to prevent the spread of marital discord.

The following article represents an outline of discussions held by the author with a group of rabbinical counselors and mashgichim associated with various yeshivos in Eretz Yisroel, who conduct marriage-preparation classes and discussion groups. This article, then,

* The author would like to acknowledge the generous assistance of Yaakov Salamon, C.S.W., in the preparation of this article, as well as the guidance of several well-known rabbinical leaders with experience in this field, who requested to remain anonymous.

describes some of the more common problems of dating, courtship and the first year of marriage. In addition, this article will suggest methods for dealing with some of these problems.

❧ Format for Hadracha

The actual format for *hadracha* is certainly not as important as the content, but as the format varies, so does the impact of such sessions. Ideally, *hadracha* should take place in the context of the one-to-one *rebbe/talmid* relationship. Young people have some very individualized needs and problems, which cannot and should not be discussed in a group setting. Another common format is the group setting, whether as an open, public lecture or a more private *va'ad, shmuess,* or discussion group. Finally, when direct contact with a mentor is unavailable, one can resort to reading material in the form of *seforim*, pamphlets, and articles.

The following outline deals with this author's suggestions for the content of *hadracha* programs for both young men and women regardless of the format. While the case illustrations presented here highlight either the role of young men or young women, all of the illustrations can be equally valid for both.

❧ What Marriage is Not

Many young people have a thoroughly distorted view of marriage, and their expectations are totally unrealistic. When people marry without correcting their misconceptions, they will probably face deep disappointment, or worse, marital conflict and discord.

These misconceptions may strike someone who is happily married for a number of years as unusual or unbelievable. To many single people, however, they may sound too familiar.

1. "Marriage is a solution for loneliness, depression and feelings of inferiority."

Certainly marriage does provide companionship, encouragement and feelings of being important to someone else. It was clearly in the design of Creation for people to have certain needs fulfilled through marriage, as the Torah states: "It is not good for Man to be alone" (*Bereishis* 2,18). A single person with many friends, for example, still experiences a void which can be filled only through marriage. This is normal and appropriate. Nevertheless, marriage cannot provide a cure for deep-seated emotional problems or social handicaps. If someone is beset with so many emotional difficulties that he or she has failed to make friends, then the complex challenges of married life will probably add only another failure to the list of earlier ones.

Should depressed or lonely people not get married? Of course they should. But they should not expect marriage to solve their problems. These young people should seek out the guidance and advice of their *rebbeim*, mentors or anyone else equipped to help them overcome these hurdles before taking on the challenges of marriage.

One respected *ben Torah*, who is now happily married to his second wife, confided to me:

> *When I was 18 years old, I and all of my friends in yeshiva honestly believed that whatever problems we had would somehow disappear after we would stand under the chupa. To tell you the truth, if I had not been such a hothead and hadn't run off to a Rav for a get (divorce) after only two weeks, my first marriage might have been saved.*

This young man was not a client of mine, nor did he ever receive any form of mental health service. He was simply sharing his personal experience with me in the hope that I pass it on and help others avoid the same mistakes.

2. "Marriage is a solution for immaturity and irresponsibility."

Anyone who has enjoyed the relative independence of being single can certainly find the increased responsibilities of marriage a maturing experience. Suddenly, money, time and other resources need to be budgeted more carefully. Another person's needs and desires must be taken into account in a new and more intense fashion than ever before. These facts of married life do help young people mature as they grow into new responsibilities and adjust to them. But marriage itself can never create maturity *yeish me'ayin* (ex nihilo) imbuing a person with a sense of responsibility where none existed before. Take, for example, the common area of going to bed and getting on time. Single people are notorious for keeping late hours — probably a time-honored custom for many generations. The demands of married life often force people into a more practical and responsible schedule. Instead of going to bed at 1:30 a.m. and getting up at 8 a.m., a young married person may retire at 11:30 p.m. and arise before 7 a.m.

If, on the other hand, someone's daily routine is so severely impaired that he or she has no schedule whatsoever, marriage per se will not be the answer. Someone who retires anytime between 9 p.m. and 4 a.m., or who can never get up in time to attend morning *minyan*, is in serious trouble. To this person, marriage can mean even greater trouble.

Unfortunately, not only young people mistakenly assume that marriage will solve chronic problems of immaturity or irresponsibility. Their parents may also share this misconception. Consider Sarah,* an attractive 21-year-old girl from a deeply religious family. Sarah does not work or attend any educational programs. She lost her last three jobs due to lateness, low productivity and absenteeism. According to Sarah's mother, however:

Sarah is such a lovely girl. She is so eidel (sweet) and frum (religious). All she needs now is to find the right shidduch (match). I'm sure that once she has her own home, she will straighten out.

The sad fact is that if Sarah does not "straighten out" *before* she gets married, the prospects for her marriage are quite bleak. She will inevitably approach her household responsibilities in the same indifferent, immature and haphazard fashion in which she approached her responsibilities at home, school and work. Since obviously her parents cannot offer Sarah proper guidance, they should direct her to someone else who can. As long as Sarah's parents ex-

---

*All names and identifying information in these case examples have been thoroughly disguised to protect the privacy of the individuals involved.

pect marriage to have a therapeutic impact on their daughter, she stands a good chance of adding to the already unacceptable statistics of divorce.

As my *chavrusa* (study partner) in our yeshiva days summed it up (we were both single at the time):

I'm fully aware that getting married will probably not solve any of my problems. But I'm just getting to the point in life that I'm tired of my old problems and I'm ready for new ones!

❖ What Marriage Is

Marriage is a *nisayon* — not in the sense of being an "ordeal" but as a "test." As one of life's greatest opportunities, marriage is a test as to how well we will take advantage of what it offers.

The opportunities, of course, are not unlimited. One's choice of spouse is certainly a factor in what can be achieved. Generally, though, those who approach marriage as an opportunity invest more into it than those who view marriage as a solution.

Marriage can also be understood as a partnership in which both spouses must try to contribute 90 percent in order to enjoy an equal share of the benefits. To paraphrase a former American president, "Ask not what your spouse can do for you, but rather ask what you can do for your spouse!"

To be sure, there is much more to say, and volumes have been written about marriage from the Torah perspective. The primary focus of this article, however, is on potential problem areas in dating, courtship and marriage. A review of Torah thoughts on marriage, therefore, would be far beyond the limitations of this article.

❖ Guidelines for Dating and Courtship

Even those singles who delude themselves into thinking that they "know all about marriage" are aware that they need guidance in the area of dating. A complacent, self-assured *bachur*, for example, will suddenly come alive and listen most attentively if his *rebbi* discusses how to select a proper mate.

The three questions raised most often regarding dating are: When to start? What to look for? How long to date the same person before deciding about marriage? Single young men and women discuss all three questions extensively, most often amongst themselves. Nevertheless, they are receptive to input on these issues from *Rebbeim* and teachers — even more so at times than they are from their own parents.

1. When to start dating?

Most young people tend to be well attuned to their own internal timetable, and are the best judges of when they are "ready." Others do need some assistance. As a general guideline, young people would do well to examine their expectations of marriage. If they are out of line with a realistic conception of marriage, they should consider themselves "not ready."

But can someone feel "not ready" when in fact he or she may not only be "ready" but "overdue?" In other words, can someone be overly cautious about waiting? The answer is a resounding "YES!" If so, how can those in doubt accurately assess their own readiness for marriage?

Questions of this nature are too individualized to be handled in groups or through published guidelines, and can only be adequately addressed in one-to-one discussions. The group session, however, can still be very effective by introducing young people to *rabbonim* to whom they can turn for private conferences on this and other subjects.

Once the decision to begin dating has been made, the next question is often raised:

2. What to look for?

The general requirements of a potential marriage partner can be discussed very effectively in the group context. Much has been written on this subject by Torah giants of previous generations. Any *hadracha* class or discussion group would benefit greatly from reviewing some of this material.

Perhaps the most succinct, general guideline was offered by the classical formula of the Talmud: *beishonim, rachmonim, vegomlei chassodim* (modest, compassionate, and generously kind). In-depth discussions on the meaning of these three qualities can provide an excellent starting point for discussing other important factors:

- First and foremost, prospective spouses need to share common values and priorities; what is important to one should be important to the other. While this may seem too obvious to mention, the area of values and priorities can become extremely problematic when the *chassanim* or *kallos* are not fully honest with themselves, or each other.

Consider, for example, a young person whose friends are **all** adopting a *kollel*-life after marriage, where the wife works to support the husband's full-time learning. This young man or woman may not know what such a life entails, nor truly aspire to that life. Not wanting to stick out from the crowd, however, he or she expresses a desire for a *kollel*-type mate. Such deception — of self and prospective partner — can have destructive consequences.

- What role should appearance and attractiveness play in selecting a mate? Most young people assume that their teachers and *rabbanim* would advise them not to consider appearance. They even feel they are cheating in some way by looking for an attractive mate. Most *rabbanim*, however, would probably advise that attractiveness is important but that it must be kept in perspective. No one should ever agree to marry someone they find unattractive. At the same time, however, no one should look only for "good looks."

    Consider Yaakov. All of his friends and relatives knew he wanted two things: looks and money. He went out with almost 50 girls until he got married. Everyone thought he got what he wanted and so did Yaakov when he married a very attractive girl from one of the wealthiest Orthodox families in the area. After three years, Yaakov learned the hard way that there is more to marriage than beauty and money. Now divorced, he is looking for a mate who may possess neither beauty nor money, but with whom he will be able to get along.

- How much importance should be placed on the relationship factor — that is, their personalities and how the two get along with each other?

With some exceptions, most yeshiva students and seminary graduates tend to pay too little attention to the relationship factor, and tend to have little background for making such assessments. Yet the need to evaluate this factor cannot be overemphasized, as a painfully clear clinical observation makes obvious! In all of my experience in working with divorcing couples and divorced individuals, I never met one person who could not recall seeing before marriage the very same traits in the ex-spouse that later led to divorce! Before marriage, these people either denied, ignored or overlooked the problems. Of course, many insignificant differences should be overlooked, and others only become critical later. But if all relationship problems are overlooked, serious marital conflict can develop.

Here, as with other fine distinctions, a private consultation with one's *rav* would be in place. Opening up the issue in a group, however, may encourage young people to consult their rabbis.

Once a single person has a clear idea as to what to look for, the next question surfaces:

3. How long to date? (And the corollary question:) **How do I know he (or she) is the ONE?**

People wonder: Does something inside tell me that this person is for me? Do I start seeing stars or hear bells ringing? How can I tell?

One experienced seminary teacher advises his students: Do you find his company pleasant? Does he possess those character traits and goals in life that you admire? Does he have any habits or attitudes that make you uneasy? If the answers to the first two questions are positive and the answer to the last is negative, he advises going ahead. He reminds them that Rabbi Samson Raphael Hirsch points out that first the Torah tells us "Yitzchok brought (Rivka) into the tent of his mother Sarah and he took her ... as his wife," and only after that "and he loved her" (*Bereishis* 24,67). In a Torah society, true love comes with marriage. When overwhelming infatuation sets in too early, caution is in order.

In spite of all the advice young people inevitably receive, no timetables can be given. Telling single people how long they should date each other before "deciding" can be destructive because people's needs vary greatly.

Some single people tend to be more nervous and anxious than others when meeting *shidduchim*, and they may need to see the same person a few times more than their friends do before making a decision. When pressured to make up their minds after seeing someone as many times "as everyone else," serious consequences can result.

At the very least, young people who are already quite tense can be made more uneasy. At worst, this pressure can contribute to an incorrect decision. How many good *shidduchim* were broken only because someone insisted, "If you can't decide by the _____th date, then it's probably not for you!" Even some unhappy marriages could have been avoided if someone had not coaxed, "If you've already gone out on _____ dates, then you must really be meant for each other!"

Another group of young people run the risk of postponing a decision almost indefinitely, and need encouragement to make up their minds. In fact, the longer they see the same *shidduch*, the harder it becomes for them to finally decide. These young people probably spend a year looking for "the right yeshiva," or a month looking for "the right dress." They found it difficult to make decisions in the past, and the decision about marriage is no exception. To be sure, marriage is a serious matter that demands careful consideration, but even "careful consideration" has limits .... Some young single people even become old single people because they carried "careful consideration" too far.

How do single people know to which group they belong? How do their parents and friends know? If someone says, "I think I need to see him (or her) some more before I know for sure," how can you tell if (s)he should be encouraged to take his/her time or to make up his/her mind?

An individual consultation with a *rav*, *rebbi*, or other mentor will be necessary to answer these questions. Many details of personality, personal and family history, age of both partners, and the specific nature of the apprehensions should be examined in a private, confidential consultation.

If individual consultations are necessary to resolve such doubts, why include the issue in *hadracha* classes? First of all, the process of resolution can certainly begin with group discussion. In addition, participants may identify the group leader as someone to turn to for individual consultation. At the very least, participants may be discouraged from trying to force themselves into anyone else's timetable. They may even come away with a greater sensitivity to their own individual needs regarding the time factor in dating and courtship.

❧ "Shana Rishona," The First Year of Marriage

No *hadracha* program would be complete without a thorough discussion of what to look out for during the first year of marriage. Even if it does take a lifetime to learn all about marriage, there are some very basic trouble spots in the first year that can be avoided if anticipated, in line with the maxim — "Who is wise, he who sees the future" (*Tamid*, 32a). Certainly, *hadracha* can not prevent all marital problems, but it can help minimize them, and possibly stem the rising tide of divorce among young, frum couples.

While there are at least as many different problems that can confront a young couple as there are young couples, three problems seem to crop up most often which can usually be traced back to *shana rishona*.

The term *shana rishona*, of course, should not be taken literally. The problems outlined here may be overcome by some couples after two months of marriage, while others may struggle with these issues for two or three years. The point is that these problems generally surface during the initial adjustment phase of marriage, which typically lasts one year.

1. Impatience and Stubbornness

Some young married men and women have a very shortsighted timetable for change, growth and adjustment. These people believe that if their spouse does not make immediate concessions to their way of thinking, they lose all hopes of negotiating the issue in the future, as though marriage were a political struggle, with wins and losses.

Most often, the issue is quite insignificant, as both partners acknowledged. It only becomes an issue because one or both spouses believe that their entire future is at stake.

> Devorah and Heschie were married three months before Pesach. As Yom Tov approached, they began discussing their holiday plans. Heschie assumed that they would spend Yom Tov with his parents, who were scheduled to move out of town right after Pesach. Devorah insisted that traditionally the first Yom Tov "belongs" 'to the wife's parents. Heschie agreed, but since his parents would thereafter be living out of town, perhaps Devorah should "give in." Devorah saw a principle here that was much larger than the question at hand. She felt that unless she stands firm on this issue her husband will "walk all over her" in the future.

Heschie and Devorah are still married and are not even considering divorce. The resentment generated by their initial intransigence, however, still surfaces today, almost five years later.

2. Protection Through Silence

The advice of *Chazal* is full of injunctions to remain silent. Some interpret *beishonim* to refer to modest reticence. In contrast, one of the popular attitudes today, which is most antithetical to Torah, can be summarized by the hackneyed cliché, "Express yourself!" We certainly do not believe that every thought and emotion must be shared openly with the entire world. To the contrary, a person should strive to internalize the external restraint and refinement that he exhibits. In secular society, people try to achieve just the opposite by "letting it all hang out."

Nevertheless, there are certain situations in which excessive silence can be destructive. Silence, like any other ideal, must be kept in perspective. In an unreasonable effort to emulate his impression of *gedolim*, a young married person may weaken the entire foundation of his or her married life.

Take Rochel and Aryeh. When they first got married, some of Rochel's
habits disturbed Aryeh. While he could accept most of these habits,
one really annoyed him. It was nothing unusual, but Aryeh's reac-
tion created a major rift that still exists today.

Often when Aryeh would be leaving the apartment, Rochel
would remember something that she wanted to tell him. Even if he
was rushing out the door, late for minyan, a shiur or just an ap-
pointment, Rochel would insist that Aryeh wait briefly until she
told him what she had just remembered.

Every time this occurred, Aryeh reminded himself of Talmudic
injunctions to remain silent, and with great self-control he sup-
pressed his impulse to criticize Rachel.

Aryeh felt very noble about his self-sacrifice. After all, he was
avoiding conflict and was sparing his wife the displeasure of being
criticized. "If I point this out to Rachel," he reasoned, "it could lead
to an argument."

In a way, Aryeh's reasoning was valid. He certainly should try
to overlook his wife's human imperfections, and unnecessary criticism and possible conflict should be avoided.

Nevertheless, Aryeh made two big mistakes. First, he assumed
that Rochel would be hurt if she knew that one of her habits offended him. Actually, she wanted nothing more than to please Aryeh.
Had she been told openly, she probably would have changed her
behavior immediately.

Aryeh's second mistake was much more serious. He thought
that he would eventually get used to this habit and come to accept
it. He was wrong. As time went on, it bothered him more and more,
until he started wondering why Rochel didn't realize on her own
that he was annoyed by her habit. At that point, the die was cast.
His annoyance quickly grew into resentment. The harder he tried to
control this resentment, the angrier Aryeh became.

Finally, after seven months, Aryeh exploded. His burst of temper
was set off by a small, irrelevant incident, but he raised his voice
and used strong language quite unbefitting a ben Torah.

The outburst did clear the air somewhat, but Aryeh felt so guilty
about it that he was more determined than ever to keep quiet.

Rachel, of course, was shocked and hurt. She felt that she had failed to please her husband and worried about their future.

> *For the next eleven years, Aryeh and Rachel's marriage was strained with occasional violent outbursts. Finally, they sat down with a counselor and began to unravel their tangled feelings. When they were through, they realized how Aryeh's overly zealous efforts "to look away" from his wife's faults had led to a disastrous chain of events, which fortunately was finally resolved.*

Certainly Aryeh's misguided effort to remain silent was not the sole cause of his marital problems. Complex marital and family problems seldom stem from one simple source. Nevertheless, if Aryeh had realized that his efforts to remain silent could do more harm than good, much of his and Rochel's unhappiness could have been prevented.

3. Passing the Tests

By far, the most pervasive and the most serious problem encountered in the first year of marriage is that of "testing."

Everyone comes to marriage with a long shopping list of expectations, hopes, and dreams. That is as it should be, for these expectations provide the incentives that help single people take the plunge into marriage. While these lists are highly personalized, there is one item at the top of many people's lists, whether or not they are aware of it: to be loved and cared for by one's spouse. No, there is nothing wrong or unusual about that expectation. Some people, however, also come to marriage with a large suitcase full of self-doubt, insecurity, and low self-esteem. Even though they desperately want to be loved and cared for, deep inside they believe that they are so unworthy and inadequate that no one could ever really love or care for them. One could assume that their spouses do care for them, or they would not have married them. Yet in spite of any expression of caring from their spouses, these people feel the need "to test" them. This may sound far fetched, but, then again, have you ever heard someone say, "If (s)he really cared about me, (s)he would _____!" Such a statement and all its variations indicate that one spouse is testing the other; that the care and concern of their spouses can only be measured by the criterion of doing this or not doing that. Sometimes these criteria are valid. No one would take issue with: "If he really cared about me, he wouldn't insult me like that in front of my friends!" By contrast, consider this criterion: "If she really cared about me, she wouldn't have put so much mustard on this sandwich!" No, not too many men would make such a statement. But many young married men and women have similar thoughts about their spouses, and such thoughts drive a wedge between husband and wife, leading to irreconcilable differences. Single people should know, before they get married, that inappropriate questions of, "Does (s)he really care about me?", whether expressed vocally or just in thought, can lead to severe marital conflict. At times, such testing can even lead to divorce. If single people are alerted to the danger of testing, especially during the first year of marriage, then they stand a better chance of steering clear of this most dangerous obstacle to success in marriage.

❧ *A Look to the Future*

Fortunately, fewer questions are being raised today about whether or not formal, structured marriage preparation is necessary. Of course, some will still remind us that their Bubbies and Zaydies never attended *hadracha* classes. Nevertheless, many yeshivos and seminaries are organizing programs of *hadracha* for their students. The outline presented here is certainly only one of many possible outlines which could be used for such *hadracha* programs. Other authors will undoubtedly present their own ideas with the result that any *rav*, *rebbi*, or teacher who wants to develop a *hadracha* program will have a wide selection of ideas and suggestions from which to choose.

Needless to say, not everyone is sufficiently qualified to lead such groups. The *Roshei Hayeshiva* and *menahelim* will undoubtedly use the same care, concern, and *daas Torah* in selecting leaders for *hadracha* classes as they use for all other matters concerning their yeshivos and seminaries.

Setting up these *hadracha* programs may not be easy. Critics will inevitably question the necessity of *hadracha* programs in their institution. In addition, demonstrating success will be impossible because we will never know exactly how many divorces are being prevented. Nevertheless, the possibility of preventing even one divorce should make it all worthwhile.

SHALOM BAYIS
THE NEED FOR FORMAL *HADRACHA*

RABBI MORDECHAI BISER

It seems that there might be a problem with shalom bayis in our community. We frequently see posters, in Brooklyn at least, announcing a shiur by yet another prominent rav on the topic of marriage and shalom bayis. Each month, in the pages of the Jewish Observer, there is an ad for a domestic-abuse hot line. We hear, here and there, of yet another young couple getting divorced, of yet another frum family breaking up. The at-risk-teen problem is growing, and without presuming to explain it, all agree that one of the probable causes is a lack of shalom bayis in many homes. The number of unmarried older singles appears also to be growing, and some suggest that attitudes toward and expectations of marriage may be contributing to the problem. I saw no firm statistics, no conclusive surveys; only the perception that something is wrong.

❧ *A Growing Problem*

I decided to investigate. I started with those domestic-abuse hotline ads, and found that the Shalom Task Force now receives several calls a day, every day, from women who need someone to talk with.[1] This translates into several hundred calls a year. The Task Force directed me to Ohel, which has a domestic-abuse project that is currently handling about twenty cases a month.[2] These are mostly women who are coming in for counseling as to how to deal with their abusive husbands. The Jewish Board of Family Services of Boro Park has a monthly caseload of about 350 individuals and families, and the Board's staff estimates that over 50 percent of these cases have *shalom bayis* problems.[3] All of these numbers represent but a small fraction of all marriages, but they are disturbing statistics nonetheless.

I then made a round of calls to some of the major *mesadrei gittin* (rabbis who administer religious divorces) in the New York area. Not a comprehensive survey, just a half-dozen phone calls in which I tallied up hundreds of *gittin* in our community in the past year alone.[4] No wonder that there are support groups for young divorced women in both Brooklyn and Monsey! Rabbi Aryeh Ralbag, *dayan* on the *Beis Din* of the Agudas HaRabonim and one of the leading *mesadrei gittin* for *yeshivishe* couples, confirms that, "in the past few years there has been a large explosion of *gittin* in the *frum* community." "And," he adds, "there is much more of a *shalom bayis* problem out there than the number of *gittin* indicate."

At this point it must be said that severe *shalom bayis* problems, domestic abuse, and divorce have *not* reached epidemic proportions in our community. Indeed, the state of *shalom bayis* in the Torah world still stands in stark contrast to that of the secular world, where it is expected that half of all marriages will end in divorce or separation.[5] We have much to be proud of. And even those

---

1. Lisa Twerski, C.S.W., Director of Training and Special Projects, Shalom Task Force.
2. Esther Katz, C.S.W., Coordinator, Ohel's Domestic Abuse Program.
3. Faye Wilbur, C.S.W., and Dr. Mark Kleinman, Director, Boro Park Jewish Board of Family and Children's Services.
4. Rabbi Aryeh Ralbag reports handling over 100 *gittin* a year; Rabbi Shlomo Herbst, Beth Din Tzedek of America, the Rabbinical Council of America, Rabbi Kurzrock of the Igud HaRabonim, Rabbi Peretz Steinberg of Queens, Rabbi Elimelech Bluth of the Beis Din of Flatbush, all report *gittin* in growing numbers. I thank Dr. Isaac Skolnick of Kayama for providing me with the list of major *mesadrin*.
5. National Center for Health Statistics, "First Marriage Dissolution, Divorce and Remarriage: United States," Advance Data No. 323, May 31, 2001.

who deal mostly with the problems – such as Dr. Shimon Russell of Lakewood, who daily receives calls dealing with *shalom bayis* – agree that the majority of us are living in at least "tolerable" marriages. But for the growing minority whose *shalom bayis* is less than tolerable, something has gone wrong. Why is this happening, and what can we do about it?

❧ *Who's to Blame*

The suggestions as to who and what are to blame for the partial breakdown in *shalom bayis* vary, and everyone can find their favorite target: unrealistic expectations of marriage fueled by misleading messages from the media; a decline in basic *derech eretz*; the financial pressures of trying to keep up with an upper-middle-class lifestyle on a lower-middle-class budget; interference from parents and in-laws; TV, the Internet, the ever-present "street"; simply living in the midst of a secular society that has accepted soaring divorce rates as commonplace.

In his booklet to *kallos*, Rabbi Shlomo Wolbe זצ"ל suggests that it is not just the secular culture around us, but the very affluence and ease of modern living that in its own way has contributed to the increase in domestic tension. As Rabbi Wolbe writes:

> *"Young people get married, never having gotten accustomed to standing up to tension and struggle, and exercising self-control, and suddenly they find themselves in a turbulent vortex of difficulties – and they imagined they would find in their homes only delight and a safe harbor from problems!"*[1]

Yes, it is easy to chalk the growing *shalom bayis* problem up to the pernicious influence of the broader society and the times in which we live. In a country in which "divorced" is the fastest growing marital status,[2] it is to be expected that some of the outlooks and attitudes of those around us would make their way into even the

---

1. קונטרס הדרכה לכלות, pp. 30-31.
2. U.S. Bureau of the Census, Current Population Reports, "Marital Status and Living Arrangements: March 1996."

most insulated homes. But blaming the problem on our *galus* does not absolve us from searching for solutions. When it comes to suggesting what could be done to alleviate the growing breakdown in *shalom bayis*, the yeshiva *mashgichim, rabbanim, mesadrei gittin*, therapists, and others interviewed for this article all speak with one voice. No need here for any intensive "studies," and yet no throwing up hands in surrender at the onslaught that this *galus* is making in our most holy institutions. Everyone I spoke with concurred that the time has come for something so simple, so very basic, that one wonders why it doesn't exist everywhere already: marriage education and *shalom bayis* classes for dating singles and engaged and newly married couples.

❧ A Solution: Formal Hadracha

In previous generations, such training and preparation came from the home. No matter how effective our *shalom bayis* curriculum, the home will remain the basic training ground for marriage and life itself. But Rabbi Chaim Friedlander ז״צל, former *Mashgiach* of Ponevezh Yeshiva, explains that in our times this is no longer sufficient, and insists that today we need formal guidance in this area:

"Our young people are not used to dealing with the difficulties that previous generations were tested with, and therefore they are less equipped to withstand difficult circumstances. In our time everything has to happen quickly – we want fast results and don't want to rely on patience. We are accustomed to a spirit of abundance, an era of easy living and simple solutions, and aren't prepared to restrain ourselves until after time a solution will be found. If a young couple receives everything on a silver platter, this only feeds their egoism and the feeling that 'everything is due and coming to me.' This diminishes each one's desire to do things for the other and their willingness to give in. *For these reasons, a lot of guidance is important before marriage, and experience has shown the great benefit of doing so.*" [1]

---

1. Rabbi Chaim Friedlander's booklet for *chassanim*, וידעת כי שלום אהלך, p. 10 (emphasis added).

Rabbi Shlomo Herbst, another *mesader gittin*, provides support for Rabbi Friedlander's observations when he reports a recent upsurge in what he calls "quick *gittin*" – couples who have been married for only a few months who mutually decide to get divorced.[1] These are young people who haven't even tried to work on themselves and their marriage, perhaps because they were simply never taught that a Torah marriage requires giving, sacrifice, and sharing.

Rabbi Friedlander thus urged that formal *hadracha* is needed for *chassanim* and *kallos* in our time. "In order to build a home ... a *chassan* needs to prepare himself, to learn well his role in building the home, and to know his obligations toward his future wife, especially to recognize her nature and her desires. He should know what difficulties are likely to arise, in order to prevent them from starting and – if they do occur – to be prepared to eliminate them while they are still fresh."[2] *Kallos* also need such *hadracha*, continues Rabbi Friedlander, and with it, the couple can begin to achieve success and fulfillment in marriage from the very first steps they take under the *chupa*.[3]

Rabbi Chaim Morgenstern, who received *hadracha* from Rabbi Moshe Aharon Stern זצ״ל, and who has been giving *chassan* classes and *shiurim* on *shalom bayis* to newly married couples in Israel for many years, echoes the call of Rabbi Friedlander:

"The first key before we start off marriage, for success, is proper *hadracha*. Both the husband and the wife, either as *chassan* and *kalla* or after they are married, must have guidance from a *bar samcha* [a reliable Torah guide]. Rabbi Wosner in Bnei Brak said 90 percent of the marriage problems would be solved if husbands and wives would have the proper *hadracha* before they are married. It is never too late. Even if we did not have the proper *hadracha* beforehand, we have to get some type of *hadracha* afterward. Marriage is so complicated, with many daily interactions, that just a mere ignorance of not knowing how to handle simple situations or what to expect when something comes up can *chas v'shalom* disrupt *shalom bayis*.

---

1. Rabbi Herbst refuses to handle such cases, but they just go elsewhere for their get.
2. וידעת כי שלום אהלך, p. 9.
3. Ibid., p. 10.

Even after marriage, couples are ignorant of the simple ABC's: what are their goals in marriage; what does it mean to be one, '*ve-hayu levassar echad*'; what is the concept of love; how to develop love; how to rebuke a spouse if you have to, how to quarrel with him or her. If you don't know these, it is like driving a car without even reading the instructions. Worse than this are the secular ideas that permeate our minds, either directly or indirectly through the media, and eventually penetrate the back door of our brains. The whole secular idea of marriage is a life of desire, of 'what's in it for me.' They enter marriage as takers, and they are immediately starting out their marriage on the wrong foot."[1]

Rabbi Shach זצ״ל recognized the "great need"[2] for dissemination of the writings of Rabbi Friedlander, and due in part to the *Rosh Yeshiva's* encouragement there are now *shiurim* for *chassanim* in Ponovezh Yeshiva and elsewhere in Israel that discuss the most intimate details of married life. But in the United States, formal *hadracha* for *chassanim* and *kallos* in the area of *shalom bayis* is hard to find. Is it any wonder we are experiencing a growing *shalom bayis* problem?

✦ Who Should Offer Shiurim?

Who should offer such *shiurim*? Some suggest that *yeshivos* and seminaries themselves should provide this *hadracha*. There are several *yeshivos* that have *shiurim* on *shalom bayis*,[3] but in most, the closest to formal *hadracha* is at best a brief "*chassan shm-*

---

1. Taped lecture, "Making Your Marriage Work" (emphasis added). Rabbi Morgenstern's excellent series of audio tapes (8 for *chassanim* and 8 for *kallos*) can be obtained by calling Rabbi Morgentstern directly at 011-8-974-1229 or 952-314-4116.
2. וידעת כי שלום אהלך, *Haskama* from Rabbi Shach.
3. A good model is Ner Yisroel in Baltimore, where the *Mashgiach* Rabbi Moshe Eisemann (and others) meets with and advises *bachurim* who have started dating, and has a weekly *vaad* for *yungeleit* in *shana rishona*. The *talmidim* raise, discuss, and get advice on issues of dating and marriage from a Torah perspective. In Lakewood, Rabbi Boruch Eli Goldschmidt זצ״ל author of an excellent *kuntres* on *shalom bayis* (שכל טוב, of which an English adaptation – *Dear Son* – has been published by ArtScroll.), and a book for women as well (*Dear Daughter*, available at most Jewish bookstores), used to conduct weekly *vaadim* (discussion groups) with *yungeleit*. Other yeshivos could learn much from these successful approaches.

uess" from the *mashgiach. Yeshivos* could consider instituting a series of special *shiurim* for *bachurim* who have begun the *shidduch* process, for *chassanim* prior to marriage, and for *kollel yungeleit* in their *shana rishona* (first year of marriage). The content of these *shiurim* could be drawn exclusively from *divrei Chazal* and the writings of *Gedolei Yisroel*, thus amply justifying their inclusion in the yeshiva "curriculum."[1]

Yet realistically, not all yeshivos and seminaries are going to institute formal *shiurim* in *shalom bayis*. How, then, do we reach our *chassanim* and *kallos*, and help them build their *bayis ne'eman* right from the start?

In this author's humble opinion, a vehicle already exists to help teach *chassanim* and *kallos* about *shalom bayis: chassan* and *kalla* classes. Every *chassan* and every *kalla* in our community attends a number of sessions — usually individually with a private instructor — for instruction in *taharas hamishpacha* and other *halachic* aspects of married life. If those teaching them were to add on to each session the essential basics for success in *shalom bayis*, the young couple would begin married life with at least an understanding of the issues they are likely to confront.

The *mesadrei gittin* underscore the importance of teaching *bachurim* the fundamentals of *shalom bayis*. For example, Rabbi Peretz Steinberg, who has been *mesader gittin* in Queens for over fifteen years – and now writes between 50 and 100 *gittin* a year – says that in his view, "In many cases the problem is that the husbands never learned how to treat their wives." Rabbi Ralbag concurs, and says that there are young men in our circles who "don't appear to have learned the basic *halachos* and *divrei Chazal* on marriage and *shalom bayis*, such as יותר מכבדה מגופו (he should honor her more than himself)."[2] The time has arrived that when a

---

1. One approach might be to offer a series of night-*seder shiurim* (e.g. once a week for six weeks or so), to *bachurim* who are about to or who have started dating. These *shiurim* could be given during winter *zeman* and then again after Pesach. *Chassanim* could also attend such *shiurim*, with follow-up *shiurim* for *kollel yungeleit* in *shana rishona*. Those recently married could also be encouraged to make *sefarim* on *shalom bayis* the focus of their daily *mussar seder*. In this way, most of our *bnei Torah* will be reached.

2. יבמות סב. See also הכלה יט פרק טו הלכות אישות רמב"ם.

bachur approaches his *Rosh Yeshiva* to be his *mesader kiddushin*, he should be required to receive *hadracha* ... if we don't want him to end up before long in front of a *mesader gittin*.

By the same token, seminaries both in Israel and in the United States should devote part of the last few months of the school year to preparing their students for dating and marriage. Ideally, properly trained *kalla* teachers should follow this up with classes on *shalom bayis* during the engagement period.

⫷ *A Shalom Bayis Curriculum*

What would be the content of such *shalom bayis shiurim*? They might start with the basics – the obligations the Torah places on husbands and wives. Here are just a few, which should be expounded upon with practical examples:

- "Her food, clothing, and conjugal rights[1] he shall not diminish."[2]
- A husband should always be careful to try to provide sufficient sustenance for his household, since lacks in this area are a major cause of *shalom bayis* problems.[3]
- A husband should be very careful about causing emotional pain to his wife, because she is more easily hurt. *Rashi* explains this as referring to using words that cause her pain.[4]
- A husband should not impose excessive fear in his home.[5]
- A husband must love his wife like himself and honor her more than himself.[6]

---

1. Good *hadracha* is often sorely lacking in this area. Many of those interviewed for this article pointed to this as a major source of *shalom bayis* problems. This is obviously not a matter for tapes and books, but for proper *hadracha* for *chassanim* and *kallos* from a proper teacher.
2. שמות כא׳ י.
3. בבא מציעא נט.
4. בבא מציעא נט.
5. גיטין ו׳. See *Rashi* and *Maharal* for a detailed explanation.
6. יבמות סב. See also רמב״ם הלכות אישות פרק טו הכלה יט.

- He should be careful with her honor because *beracha* is only found in a home because of the wife.[1]
- Speak with her gently and do not exhibit depression or anger in her presence.[2]
- "And he shall make his wife happy."[3]
- A husband should listen to his wife in matters relating to the home, and some say relating to worldly matters in general.[4]
- A wife should honor her husband greatly… he should be in her eyes like a prince or a king.[5]
- A proper wife does the will of her husband.[6]

The next step could be the excellent *kuntreisim* (booklets) of Rabbi Chaim Friedlander זצ"ל,[7] and Rabbi Shlomo Wolbe זצ"ל.[8] These contain *divrei Chazal* and advice from *Gedolei Yisroel*, including the *Chazon Ish* and the *Steipler*, on the subject of *shana rishona*, *shalom bayis*, and the goals of a Jewish marriage.[9] The topics discussed include understanding the differences between men and women, how to make each other happy, how to handle financial matters, how to properly criticize one's spouse and how to argue, intimacy and love, balancing responsibilities to home, learning, and work, and dealing with parents and in-laws. Although this is not the place to expound at length upon the ideas presented in these writings, just a few glimpses should give the reader an indication of the powerful impact they could have on the *shalom bayis* of our generation:

---

1. בבא מציעא נט.
2. גיטין ז. See also שבת לד. and רמב"ם הלכות אישות פרק טו הכלה יט.
3. דברים כד' ה. See *Rashi*. The Torah does not mean he should be happy with her (as the *Targum* of R. *Yonason ben Uziel* says), but that he should make her happy.
4. בבא מציעא נט.
5. רמב"ם הלכות אישות פרק טו הלכה יט.
6. תנא דבי אליהו רבה פרק ט.
7. וידעת כי שלום אהלך.
8. קונטרוס הדרכה לכלות and מאמרי הדרכה לחתנים.
9. Unfortunately these are not to my knowledge currently available in *sefarim* stores in the United States; for information about how to obtain them, call Rabbi Chaim Morgenstern in Israel at 011-972-8-974-1229 or 952-314-4116.

❧ *"My Dear Chassan..."*

From Rabbi Shlomo Wolbe זצ״ל:

"The *Chazon Ish* writes that 'her nature is to get pleasure from finding favor in her husband's eyes, and she always looks to him.' This requires constant attention. She puts on a dress, and hopes for a good word from her husband. She puts on a snood, and hopes she will find favor in his eyes. If he doesn't see it at all, or it doesn't matter to him if the garment is blue or green, she will be sad. She works to prepare a dish that he likes. If he swallows it down in a manner that he can barely remember what he ate, and thus can't compliment her for it, she feels cheated. Something needs to be fixed in the home and he ignores it. She hangs a picture on the wall, she places a bouquet of flowers on the table. She does it all for him, and he doesn't see it! Little by little she comes to feel that her husband isn't interested in the matters of the home that for her is the essence of her life. From these little things there develops over time a distance and a separation between them, until each is living his and her own separate life!"[1]

"The way a woman thinks is different from a man; her manner of reacting is completely different from a man's. No matter how much he tries to convince her to accept his way of thinking and to admit that his manner of dealing with things is better, he will not be successful. He needs to learn about these differences, make peace with them, and learn how to bear them .... All the things that she does that are strange or that anger us are tests for us. We must be patient and gentle and not get angry."[2]

❧ *"My Dear Kalla..."*

"How do you arrive at adapting yourselves to each other? First of all, with patience. When the differences and conflicts in your natures and views begin to reveal themselves – sometimes almost immediately after the *chasuna* – do not be afraid that your world is

---

1. מאמרי הדרכה לחתנים, pp. 2-3.
2. Ibid., p.3.

destroyed …. Know with a certainty that you have been given the ability to overcome the difficulties in your relationship."[1]

"There is a major principle that the couple needs to adopt if they want to be happy: under no circumstances to discuss matters between them to another person! This is the exclusive domain of the couple that no one else should be allowed to enter …. If there arises a question about these matters, turn to the only proper person: a *Rav* or *Gadol* from whom one can receive advice and assistance."[2]

"'The honor of the King's daughter is an inner one.'"[3] For the honor of the King's daughter, there needs to be an inner outlook! … This inner outlook doesn't see the elegant furniture in the neighbor's homes, the beautiful dresses of her friend, or the jewelry that sparkles on the teacher's neck. She has an inner happiness that is worth more than all physical wealth."[4]

❧ *More to the Young Man…*

From Rabbi Chaim Friedlander זצ"ל:

"Rabbi Dessler writes in *Michtav MeEliyahu* that love is an outcome of giving. Through giving and providing kindness, one connects to the receiver with bonds of love, and the more one gives, the more one creates a greater love. This concept should be studied well and should be a permanent guideline for one's married life."[5]

"We need to know that most of the difficulties of *shalom bayis* flow from the nature of a person, his *middos*, and his essence …. Certainly it is not easy to change. But this is the purpose of our lives. As the *Gra* explains, 'All *avodas Hashem* hangs on improving one's *middos* [and] … the essence of life is to constantly strengthen and improve one's *middos*.'… A student in yeshiva … now needs to change direction and worry about his wife, her physical and emotional needs. This re-

---

1. קונטרוס הדרכה לכלות, pp. 23-24.
2. Ibid., pp. 59-60.
3. תהילים מה' יד.
4. "It is understood that we are not against her tendency to set up the home in good taste … but all must be within the boundaries of what is reasonably affordable." הדרכה לכלות קונטרוס, pp. 39-40.
5. וידעת כי שלום אהלך, p. 35.

orientation requires him to focus on improving his *middos*, especially to abandon his narrow self-centeredness, and to acquire for himself the trait of *chessed* – of concern for another. Every improvement in our *middos* brings us an additional improvement in our shared lives, in the home we are establishing with *Hashem*'s help."[1]

"It is very difficult for a wife to manage the burdens of the home when she sees that her husband has abandoned her to her own devices, and that the housework and all of her tasks do not interest him at all, as if they are only relevant to some foreign realm. In such a case, the burden weighs on her very heavily, and she can collapse under the load, G-d forbid. On the other hand, the mere interest alone of her husband is sufficient to lighten her burden, and his offer to come to her assistance is a source of satisfaction and encouragement to her, and many times she then doesn't insist on his help at all. In the days of mourning of the *Steipler*, it was told over that one time his wife went to sleep very tired, without washing the dishes. Late that night, he entered the kitchen and washed the dishes, because he knew that his wife would be very happy in the morning to find a clean and organized kitchen. It is also told that when an *avreich*, a great *masmid*, came to him in order to ask about his learning schedule, the *Steipler* asked him if from time to time he helped his wife in time of need."[2]

❧ *Developing and Presenting the Curriculum*

Obviously, many yeshivos, seminaries, and *shuls* may wish to use these and other sources to develop their own curriculum. But I humbly suggest that providing these institutions with fully prepared *shiurim* to present to their *chassan* and *kalla* teachers would make it much easier for them to implement this proposal. For this purpose, I have therefore prepared, under the guidance of Rabbi Chaim Morgenstern, a brief outline for *chassan* teachers in English, based largely on the *kuntreisim* for *chassanim* of Rabbi Shlomo Wolbe

---

1. ibid., pp. 10-12.
2. ibid., p. 52.

and Rabbi Chaim Friedlander. Complete with sources and anecdotes, it presents the basics for *shalom bayis* in five sessions.

In addition to this "core curriculum" for *bnei Torah* in yeshivos, seminaries, and *kollelim*, there should also be two or three variants for use with other audiences, such as working singles and couples. One way to ensure maximum impact along with a consistent message to those who are not in yeshivos or seminaries, would be to prepare complete *shiurim* on video or audiotapes.[1] A good model for the success of video lectures are Agudath Israel's *Yom Iyun shiurim* and the Chofetz Chaim Heritage Foundation's Tisha B'Av presentations, which annually reach thousands of Jews in cities throughout the world. Enlisting prominent speakers to present these audio and video *shalom bayis* classes will help ensure a larger and broader audience, and will make it easier for *shuls* and community organizations to provide *hadracha* to all in need.

It must be emphasized that taped lectures and books and *sefarim* cannot and should not ever serve as a substitute for one's personal *rav* or *rebbi* for guidance in this area. It is essential for every couple to have someone they agree upon to provide them with continued *hadracha* in building their *bayis ne'eman*. Indeed, all of the *shiurim* and taped lectures should insist on this point. Each situation is different, and the general advice offered in classes may not always be the best solution for an individual couple. But the formal *shiurim* are necessary in order to teach the basics and explain to their listeners just how important such ongoing guidance is. The problem today is not that couples are only getting their marriage education from tapes and books, it is that many of them aren't getting any *hadracha* at all.

❧ Combating Chillul Hashem

In doing the background research for this article, I heard some angry voices from the left, blaming yeshivos and the Torah itself for the *shalom bayis* crisis. "They learn all day in their *Gemoras* that

---

1 See note 12 above for information on an already-existing tape series.

women are like property, and you expect them to treat their wives nicely?" "If he says *'shelo asani isha'* every morning, what do you think his view of women is going to be?" While this sort of open criticism, based on ignorance, is relatively rare, it lurks subtly and implicitly behind some of the comments that I heard from those in the "therapeutic" professions. "They learn to interrupt their *chavrusa* when they are learning, but they need to learn not to do this with their wives," was a choice quote at a meeting of *frum* mental health professionals.[1]

These and other comments point to a serious by-product of the *shalom bayis* problem: a *chillul Hashem* of great proportions. Even those in our "camp" seem to be suggesting, ever so gently, that yeshivos and seminaries are somehow part of the problem, and thus by implication that our Torah has somehow failed in this crucial area of human relations.

By not addressing the problem, we only contribute, albeit unwillingly, to the *chillul Hashem* of failed marriages among the best families in our community. Those who hear and see the results are saying to themselves,

"Woe to this one who learned Torah, woe to his father who taught him Torah, woe to his rebbi who taught him Torah. This person who learned Torah, see how destructive are his deeds, and how ugly are his ways."[2]

How ironic that the Torah, which provides the world with the Creator's instructions for happy and fulfilling marriage, should be so denigrated and mocked! The *Gemora*, replete with beautiful *divrei Chazal* about how spouses should treat each other, is seen as causing *shalom bayis* problems rather than contributing to their solution. If for no other reason than this, I would humbly suggest that it is time to start teaching our *bnei Torah* what *Chazal, Rishonim,* and *Gedolim* and *Mashgichim* of recent years, have to say about marriage.

---

1. On this point, Rabbi Friedlander writes, "*Chazal* taught us to 'honor her more than yourself.' You can't speak with your wife the way you are accustomed to speaking with your *chavrusa*. For example, you might say to him in the heat of Torah argument, 'you're speaking foolishness' or 'don't confuse me with your faulty logic,' and the like. Rather, when speaking with one's wife, he needs to be more careful — more than with himself." וידעת כי שלום אהלך, p. 22.

2. יומא פו.

❧ Additional Advantages of Formal Hadracha

A Powerful Kiruv Tool: Presenting the Torah's approach to *shalom bayis* is an extraordinarily powerful *kiruv* tool, given the failure of marriage in the modern world. Mini-*shiurim* on *shalom bayis* could thus be given by the various *kiruv* programs, leading toward classes for couples in *Taharas Hamishpacha* as an integral part of the "Manufacturer's Instructions" for a successful, happy, and fulfilling marriage.

Addressing the Singles' Crisis: *Shalom bayis shiurim* for older singles would also help address the "singles' crisis." My experience at presenting this information at singles events and in counseling older singles is that it can have a profound impact on their whole approach to dating and marriage. As one older single told me after hearing my talk on *shalom bayis* and on the differences between men and women, "You have no idea how much this will help me with my dating."

As a former older single myself, I eventually recognized the need to get *hadracha* on marriage and made a daily *seder* for myself in *sefarim* on marriage and *shalom bayis*, and found a *rebbi* to help guide me with dating. Less than a year later, I met my *eishes chayil*-to-be. In my *shana rishona*, I made a daily *seder* with a *bachur* in his late 30's in which we learned Rabbi Friedlander's booklet together. We learned about the husband's role in a Jewish marriage as a "giver," as one whose *avoda* is to strive to fulfill his wife's emotional and other needs. Despite other "strikes" against him besides his age, this *bachur* got engaged about a year later and is now happily married. If nothing else, these examples should demonstrate that learning what *Hashem* wants from us in marriage is a powerful *segula* for finding one's *bashert*!

Preventive Medicine for Teens "At Risk": While there is no consensus as to the underlying reasons for the growing number of teens "at risk," most agree that in many cases, poor *shalom bayis* in the child's home is certainly a major factor. We have begun as a community, throughout the country, to grapple with this problem and try to help these troubled youths and their families. But our most effective approach should surely be preventive – to try to create warm, loving, and supportive Torah homes at the very beginning of a couple's marriage. Formal *hadracha* in marriage and *shalom bayis* should of course be supplemented after marriage with parenting classes, but parenting classes alone will do little to help without the solid foundation of *shalom bayis*, which is a prerequisite for proper *chinuch habonnim*. As the *Steipler* used to say, success in child rearing is 50 percent *tefilla* and 50 percent *shalom bayis*.

❧ *A Time to Act*

Merely exposing about-to-be-married young men and women and newly married couples to the words and ideas contained in the sources cited above will surely have a beneficial impact on their *shalom bayis*. When complemented with memorable true stories and specific examples, these *divrei Chazal* can help transform the way a *chassan* and *kalla* approach marriage. Our Torah truly contains all we need to know to solve the growing problem of poor domestic harmony in our community; let's start teaching it!

Our goal should be that formal *hadracha* for marriage be available in every major community, and that all major yeshivos and seminaries encourage their *talmidim* and *talmidos* to receive this valuable guidance. Then, with *Hashem*'s help, both those inside our community and without will look at the *shalom bayis* that exists in the homes of our *bnei Torah*, and say of each,

"Fortunate is his father who taught him Torah, fortunate is his rebbi who taught him Torah! Woe to those people who don't learn Torah! This one who learned Torah, see how pleasant are his ways, how correct are his deeds."[1]

---

1. יומא פו.

LOVE AND MARRIAGE

Dr. David Gottlieb

One out of every two marriages in North America ends in divorce. Of those that survive, some should not: the relationships have deteriorated to the point that dissolution is the only way to relieve the misery. Thus the majority of North American marriages are failures. The explanation for this enormous human suffering is not easy to see. especially since the statistics for the best educated, most sophisticated and least inhibited segment of the population are just as bad.

For frum communities the figures are much lower. In addition. the symptoms of failed marriages that have not divorced (child abuse, wife/husband abuse, alcoholism, disappearance) are also much lower. Some take pride in our relative success at marriage; others emphasize that we still fall far short of our marital responsibilities and should regard our rate of failure as an "epidemic" or "crisis" which requires emergency measures. Without taking sides in this debate, we can all agree that we are doing something significantly better than the rest of North America. Perhaps, if we under-

stand that something, we will be able to use it even more effectively in the attempt to improve our own marriages.

✦ Biblical Marriages

When the patriarch Yitzchak met his future wife Rivka he "… took her into the tent of his mother Sarah, married her, and loved her, and was comforted from (the loss of) his mother" *(Bereishis 24,67)*. From a Western perspective, the sequence of events is puzzling: Shouldn't love come before marriage? And why is the development of their relationship bracketed by Yitzchak's concern for his mother? *Chazal* tell us *(Bereishis Rabba)* that during Sarah's lifetime, her tent — which was Yitzchak's home — experienced open manifestations of Hashem's presence. With her death, these signs disappeared. Yitzchak's criterion for a spouse was the ability to recreate the Divine environment he experienced in his mother's home. It was her proof of this ability that determined Yitzchak's decision to marry Rivka. Love for her was the outcome of the marriage commitment based on that foundation. Note that the love which grew between them is not unimportant: the fact that the Torah mentions it shows that love is one of the goals of marriage.[1] However, far from being the *prerequisite* for marriage, love *is a consequence of a marriage based upon a common vision and goal of life, and the perception that the partners are suited to achieving that goal together.* Only when Yitzchak found a partner for such a marriage and experienced the resulting love — only when the Divine environment was recreated — could Yitzchak be comforted for the loss of his mother. (Of course, some emotional bond must be created during the testing period before a commitment is made to marry. This is included in the "perception that the partners are suited to each other." How to characterize the required bond exactly requires investigation.)

The following generation gives what appears at first glance to be a contrasting paradigm for love and marriage. Yaakov meets Rachel

---

1. This gives the lie to the Fiddler on the Roof slander of Jewish marriage as a loveless relationship.

at the well and immediately kisses her. Within thirty days he loves her so completely that he is prepared to work seven years for the right to marry her. Here Yaakov's love explicitly *precedes* marriage, and in fact develops so rapidly that it appears to be almost "love at first sight" — the very antithesis of his parents' example. But this appearance is immediately dispelled by a closer look at the *pesukim* and the supplementary comments of *Chazal.* (a) When he meets Rachel at the well, Yaakov *first waters* the sheep, then kisses her, and then *weeps.* This behavior is not typical of infatuation! (b) The offer to work for her for such a long period, and the choice of seven years in particular, needs to be explained. (c) The Torah's description of the passage of the seven years "… as but a few days in his eyes due to his love of her" sounds like a beautifully romantic sentiment — until we reflect that while waiting for a longed-for event, time passes *slowly*, not quickly.[1] His love for her should have made the seven years feel like a hundred! (d) When the time is finally up, Yaakov requests the promised marriage with the words: "Give me my wife that I may go in unto her." Such a statement seems gross in the extreme.[2] How can we imagine Yaakov making it?

❧ *A Common Goal of Peoplehood*

The key to the whole story lies in the answer to the last question. *Chazal* explain that Yaakov saw his marriage to Rachel as the instrument for bringing the Jewish people into existence. Since the Jewish people is the goal and justification of the whole of creation, and the Creator made marital relations the only means of procreation. *those* marital relations achieve the pinnacle of holiness. As Adam and Chava before him, Yaakov saw no embarrassment in that process *when dedicated* to *such a goal.*[3] His statement "that I may go in unto her …" expressed the height of sanctity which he achieved.

---

1. See, for example, the discussion of *Shiras Haomer* while waiting for *Mattan Torah* in *Sefer Hachinuch.*
2. Cf. *Yalkut Shimoni.*
3. Cf. *Iggeres Hakodesh* of the *Ramban.*

Understanding that the creation of the Jewish people was Yaakov's goal in marrying Rachel, we can answer questions (a)-(c) as well. He used the seven years as a *period of preparation* for such an awesome task.[1] The choice of the time period is not arbitrary: Seven units of time connote a complete time-cycle, and a period of purification.[2] When one is preparing for a challenge which will test all one's abilities, whose outcome is of enormous importance, and which requires the meticulous strengthening and training of all one's talents and abilities, how does the time pass during the preparation period? Quickly![3] *His* love for *her* was predicated on such a challenge. *Therefore,* the seven years "... were as but a few days in his eyes." Finally, we must remember that when Yaakov first saw Rachel, he was already a prophet. A prophet by definition sees what the rest of us do not: Yaakov saw in Rachel *the mother of the Jewish people.* His love for her and all his subsequent actions were consequences of this vision. Thus we see that Yaakov and Rachel, instead of contrasting with Yitzchak and Rivka, in fact exemplify the same principle: *Love and marriage are consequences of a common vision and goal of life and the perception that the partners are suited to achieving that goal together.* This principle is one of the two pillars upon which Jewish marriages rest.

❧ *The Integration of Two Into One*

The second pillar of Jewish marriages is found in the Talmudic dictum that Adam was (or was originally designed to be) *androgynous.* i.e., a being combining male and female characteristics in all human dimensions — physical, emotional, intellectual, and

---

1. This task is what distinguishes Yaakov from Avrohom and Yitzchak, and makes him *"bechir she'b'avos"*: They each had non-Jewish children and thus were only *ancestors* of the Jewish people. Yaakov and his family *were* the Jewish people in microcosm.
2. The week, *shemita, yovel, Pesach, Shavuos* and *sefiras haomer* illustrate time periods composed of seven units of time. *Tumas mes, yoledes, zav and zava* illustrate seven units of time as a purification process. The *Zohar Hakadosh* says explicitly that Yaakov used the seven years to prepare himself for the union with Rachel.
3. Think of preparing for an exam, a performance, etc.

spiritual.[1] What are we to learn from this piece of historical information? (*Mai dehava hava*?!) We are to learn that *marriage is the context in which a man and a woman attempt to re-create or approximate the perfect male-female union represented by Adam.* Let us examine this lesson in detail.

Human relationships differ in the quality of integration they achieve. On the lowest level is the pure business relationship: Each partner enters the relationship solely for the personal gain he can achieve thereby.[2] Personal integration with the partner is nil. We may label this relationship "I-plus": Each partner is to himself a completely self-interested "I," but he recognizes that the cooperation with another "I" can profit him more than can his individual efforts.

On a higher level is the "We" relationship, in which individuals identify with the needs and goals of a group, and experience events in terms of their significance for the group. "We" replaces "I" in the thinking of the members of such a group, at least during group activities. Anyone who has played on a well-knit sports team, performed with a musical ensemble, or engaged in a similar activity, has been part of a "We" relationship. A score by the opposing team is *our* loss; my successful play is *our* success; the notes I produce is a contribution to our sound; *that is how* the *activity is experienced.* In this context a new entity is formed, namely the *group.* Individuals relating with one another in the "We" mode become members of this new entity and are integrated (partially) into it. Their individuality becomes subordinate to the group's needs and goals.

Although it is a significant improvement on the "I plus I" relationship, the "We" relationship does not embody complete integration. The group is an *association* of *individuals* each of whom retains his own identity. He merely *plays the role* of group member at certain times, and at these times accepts the group's goals as his own. This relationship does not affect his *essence.* Such a total integration, which transforms the essence of the individual to the extent that *he is no longer truly an individual,* is the highest form of human relation-

---

1. *Eruvin* 11a.
2. Of course. many business relationships become more than purely business.

ship. The new entity formed by this relationship is not a *group*, but rather an *organic whole*, of which the erstwhile individuals become *parts* (rather than members, as in a group). This relationship may be labeled "I," for two reasons. The singular pronoun indicates that the new entity does not have the multiplicity of a group, but rather is a *single* entity; and the use of "I" indicates that the new entity is a *totally integrated individual*, which supplants the individuality of those who stand in the relationship.

The husband and wife who achieve the "I" relationship do not form a two-membered group, but rather a new organically integrated whole. Compare, for example, the human body. It can be divided into head, trunk, arms and legs. Nevertheless, we do not say that each person is a group of six! The reason is that the head, trunk, etc. are *parts* of one whole, rather than individuals merely associating with one another. What makes the difference? *Integrated functioning:* Each of the parts is totally dependent upon its connection to the rest of the body for its life and ability to function. Similarly, the "I" relationship produces integrated functioning for the individuals who stand in that relationship.

❋ *Unique, and Therefore Integrated*

It must be emphasized that this integration does not compromise the *uniqueness* of those who achieve it. That x and y function together as a unit does not imply that x = y. On the contrary, integrated functioning usually presupposes crucial differences which are so related that the whole may vastly transcend its parts. Some examples: a violin and a piano playing together; forwards and guards in basketball; a surgeon and an anesthesiologist in the operating theatre; Sanhedrin, king and prophet for the leadership of the Jewish nation. The uniqueness of the individuals forming the "I" is the very foundation of the integration: It is because they are unique in precisely these ways that they can coordinate their functioning so as to form this integrated whole.

How is the "I" relationship expressed in the context of marriage? It is as if when Yitzchak says "I" and Rivka says "I," instead of each referring to his/her own self, they *both* refer to the *same new amalgam* of which each is a part. If you write "I" on one occasion and speak "I" on another, we do not understand the written "I" as referring to your arm and the spoken "I" as referring to your lungs, larynx, mouth, etc. Although produced by different *parts* of your body, each refers to the *whole*. This is because "I" refers to the smallest *whole* encompassing the part which produces it. In the case of Yitzchak and Rivka, neither of them individually is a whole any longer, thus the "I" produced by either refers to the whole of which each is a part.

The "I"-relationship marriage is experienced differently from other human relationships. Imagine that Leah is a social worker having difficulty convincing a client to get psychiatric help. Her husband Reuven encourages her and gives her advice, and the following day she succeeds. If Leah and Reuven are related as the "I plus I," the success is *hers*; he is at best an enabler, expecting her help in his projects as *quid pro quo* for his support of her. If they share a "We" relationship the success is *theirs*, but it accrues to the pair (the two membered group) through *her* action which she performs as *an individual*. If they form an "I," the very action itself is related to Reuven as well: The success was accomplished by a part of the very same whole of which he is a part.[1]

A second example: A husband and wife are together when one receives a gross insult from a third party. The spouse protests: "Your words affect me as well — I take that insult *personally*." The third party responds: "Don't talk nonsense: I didn't insult *your person*. I insulted *your spouse's person*." Is the protest nonsense? Not in the context of the "I" relationship. Just as an insult to my face is an insult to me as a whole, so an insult to my spouse is an insult to the whole of which I am a part.

This, then, is the lesson of androgynous Adam: Man and woman are created as incomplete parts of a larger organic whole which comprises both of them. Their complementary gifts and needs enable them to integrate with each other on the pattern of that origi-

---

1. When my hand imprints my name on a check, it is *I, the whole person*, who signs the check; the action accrues to the *whole* even though only a part is in motion.

nal whole. It is this which gives them the capacity to transcend the "I-plus-I" and "We" levels of human relationship, and at least approximate the integration of the single "I" of which Adam is the paradigm. The goal and challenge of marriage is to recreate Adam's wholeness to the extent possible for physically separate beings.

Love — a deep and abiding attachment to and identification with one's spouse, coupled with the joy of that attachment — is the result of forming the "I" relationship. Without this, there may be a temporary thrill, an infatuation, a mutually beneficial satisfaction of each other's needs (characteristic of even "I plus I" relationships), but not love. The "I" relationship, at once the challenge and the fulfillment of highest human integration, is the second pillar on which Jewish marriages rest.

✦ Practical Applications

The two pillars of Jewish marriage — suitability for achieving the common goal, and the "I" relationship — have many implications for practice. The *shidduch* system is designed to produce the first pillar. This subject has been discussed by others (cf. "*Shadchanim* — Matchmakers," by Chaim Shapiro) and I will not pursue it here. The second deserves very extended treatment, of which what follows is only *a few* of the *roshei perakim* (salient points).

The "I" relationship will not create itself. It must be actively pursued with intelligence and dedication. No matter how well suited husband and wife are to each other when they marry, life's experiences work to drive them apart. No man has even a vague inkling of what it is to carry, birth and suckle a child. The loss of a parent cannot be fully experienced by the mourner's spouse. Unless there is a commitment to *rebuild* lines of communication and modes of sharing, husband and wife will inevitably drift into private worlds, becoming less and less relevant to each other. Love cannot be strengthened, or even sustained, under such conditions. This means that time, effort and resources must be dedicated to constantly renewing the relationship. In my opinion, the failure to take responsibility for creating the "I" in marriage is the single most common factor in divorce. Western culture has evolved a passive attitude toward love and marriage: "Let's see if it works. If it does, fine; if not, why spend life chained to unhappiness?" "If *it* works" — not "If I will work" — and certainly not "It *will* work: I will *make* it work!" How does one relate to other difficult and important life tasks — a school exam, a musical performance, an athletic competition, a medical problem? One undertakes to practice, study, train, prepare and strive to achieve (with *Hakadosh Boruch Hu's* help) the desired result. This is the attitude one should have in marriage. A successful marriage is the personal achievement of the husband and wife who worked to create it. A failed marriage is often their personal failure.

Adopting this attitude of responsibility toward building the "I" with one's spouse provides a new understanding of typical marital occurrences. For example, it often happens that the wife (or husband) starts to tell the husband (or ...) an experience or feeling of hers which is immensely boring to him. What should he do? There are two common schools of thought. (1) Marriage is based on *chessed:* He should listen anyway as a favor to the wife. (2) Marriage is based on *honesty:* He should tell her frankly that the subject is boring to him and expect her to respect his feelings. From the vantage point of building the "I" both approaches miss the crucial point: *He should not be listening to the story, but to her.* The story is boring: If he saw it in a newspaper or heard it from an acquaintance, he might immediately put down the paper or change the subject. But this communication from his wife indicates her present state of mind, her present feelings. He wants to know where she is so that he and she can continue to build their whole together.

As a second example, consider the adage: It is easier to give than to receive. Why is this so? Because receiving often implies weakness, insufficiency, dependency and failure on the recipient's part, while giving implies strength, surplus, independence, success and also magnanimity. The ego-impact of giving is positive; of receiving, negative. If so, *one of the greatest gifts is to provide another with the opportunity to give.*[1] Often one spouse will not share problems with the other "in order not to burden her/him with my problems." The effect is to deny the other a chance to help and thereby confirm her/his own self-worth. (And the cause is often an attempt to save one's own self-image.) After a disagreement we are willing to forgive, but are we willing to ask for forgiveness? Forgiving, as a form of giving, is *easy:* It implies that we were right and the other party was guilty! Asking for forgiveness allows the *other* to be charitable in excusing *our* fault.

It is hoped that these brief examples will indicate how the goal of creating the "I" provides a new perspective on marital experiences. Consistent application of this perspective yields a new *integrative* approach which helps cement the marital bond even as life's vicissitudes assail that bond.

Klal Yisrael needs to strengthen itself against the tide of marital misery which surrounds us and threatens to undermine our marriages as well. *Shiurim, sefarim,* counseling (before and after marriage) and group discussion are needed to help us construct our marriages in the image of the Talmudic vision of Adam, and thus fulfill the destiny for which we were created.[2][3]

❧ P.S. Love and Marriage and Honor

Rabbi Yechezkiel Abramsky זצ"ל, *famed dayan of London who lived his last years in the Bayit Vegan section of Jerusalem, commented on the halacha that requires a man to "love his wife as much as he*

---

1. See *Michtav MeEliyahu.* v. 1, *Kuntres Hachessed,* Chap.12 where Rabbi Dessler distinguishes between *notail* and *m'kabel,* the taker and the giver. Much of the description of the "I" is derived from *Kuntres Hachessed.*
2. Some will worry that expenditure of time and effort will deplete our resources for other necessary goals. For example, men learning full time will regret lost hours of *talmud Torah.* This view is short-sighted: *much more time* will be lost (not to mention qualitative deterioration) from learning *in the long run* due to the consequences of lost integration and communication than is needed to prevent that loss. Compare Rashi's explanation of Rabbi Yishmael's "*minhag derech eretz*" (*Berachos* 35b): "for if you become dependent upon charity, in the end you will be prevented from (learning) Torah: *Rashi* sees a regular job as the most efficient way to maximize hours of *talmud Torah;* the same applies to investment in marriage.
3. I am deeply indebted to my wife, who introduced me to many of the ideas expressed in this article.

loves himself and honor her more than himself." The dayan ques-
tioned the necessity to so honor one's wife. After all, his love for her
should be enough of a guarantee of her honor, without requiring
"honoring her more than himself."

Dayan Abramsky's question (and his answer ultimately) becomes enhanced by Rabbi Gottlieb's description of "The husband
and wife who achieve the 'I' relationship [as] not being a two-
membered group in the 'we' mode, but rather a new organically
integrated whole." Having assumed a shared identity, there is the
ever-present danger that the husband will then behave in his wife's
presence with the same relaxed, totally undignified manner that he
may permit himself in solitude. "After all," he will reason, "it's only
I in the room — 'I' in the corporate sense, that is." And loving her
no less than he loves himself, he can be guilty of offensive behavior
that compromises his privacy and violates her sense of dignity.

Thus, says the *dayan,* the necessity of "honoring her more than
himself," even though he already "loves her as much as himself" is
to respect her dignity even when he personally senses no need for
enhanced privacy.

THE WEDDING CELEBRATION

* CHESSED, KIDDUSH HASHEM AND
SIMCHA IN CHALLENGING, AWESOME DAYS

* THE TIME FOR *TIKKUN* HAS COME:
ARE WE READY?

* THE BEST OF TIMES OR
THE WORST OF TIMES?

* OF DIFFERENCES AND UNANIMITY

* IT'S TIME TO FACE THE MUSIC

* EXCESSIVE AMPLIFICATIONS AT *SIMCHOS*

The wedding celebration can encompass everything from the most vital and crucial mitzvah rituals to exotic and frivolous trimming. Is there a way to focus on the essential and make it deeply inspiring, while avoiding the expendable externals, which can lead to tensions between chassan and kalla, and their families?

CHESSED, KIDDUSH HASHEM, AND SIMCHA IN CHALLENGING, AWESOME DAYS

BASED ON A PRESENTATION BY *RABBI YAAKOV PERLOW* שליט״א, THE NOVOMINSKER REBBE, ROSH AGUDAS YISROEL IN THE AFTERMATH OF SEPTEMBER 11, 2001

W e are living through challenging, awesome days. It can be difficult to unravel one's feelings — mourning for those who perished; expressing *tefilla vetachanunim* for those who we hope will be rescued, that they regain their health and the stability of their lives; endeavoring to bring comfort and encouragement to their families …. There is a feeling, on the one hand, of anguish; and on the other hand, of trying to understand מה זאת עשה ה' לנו — "What is this that *Hashem* has done to us?"

First of all, we should understand that the tragedy of September 11, 2001 was an attack on the entire concept of *yishuv ha'olam* — civilization. Our belief and confidence in human prowess, in man's towering abilities and financial achievements have suffered a crushing blow. Moreover, every person carries within himself *tzellem Elokim* — the Divine image — and the loss of each life is a tragedy unto itself.

In addition, we Americans are fortunate to live in a *malchus shel chessed* — under a benevolent, humanitarian system — and the members of *Klal Yisroel* in this country, in this state, and in this city have maintained a peaceful, graceful relationship with *shloma shel malchus*, full tolerance and cooperation of the government. *Chazal* counsel us to pray for the well-being of the government — הוי מתפלל בשלומה של מלכות — for without its presence, anarchy would reign (*Avos* 3:2). Beyond that, however, we have been blessed with most favorable treatment from our government. We should surely share in the pain and sorrow not only of *Acheinu Bnei Yisroel*, but also in that of the country and city at large, as well as with the families of the thousands of people who lost their lives, who are suffering as a result of the atrocity unleashed by the forces of evil that seek to undo our way of life.

✦ The Nature of the Message

We are a people who strive to learn — especially when events carry such profound messages. Our current trauma brings to mind a passage from the prophet Yona. The *passuk* relates: "Hashem cast a mighty wind on the sea and there was a great storm, and the ship threatened to break.

"But Yona descended to the ship's hold and he lay down and fell asleep.

"And the *rav hachovel* — the ship's captain — came to him and told him, מה לך נרדם — 'How can you sleep so soundly!'"

Rashi explains this to mean: "How could you sleep at this moment? The ship is about to break apart!" (see *Yona* 1,4-6).

In our times, as well, we are navigating the waters of a turbulent sea. The very world is shaking. The tallest, most imposing structures in this city collapsed. Each one of us somehow must feel an inner voice demanding: "How can you sleep so soundly!" We cannot go to sleep as easily as we did a week before the disaster, or last year! In fact, many of us have not been sleeping too well this entire past year, in view of the ongoing crisis in *Eretz Hakedosha*. But we had assumed that at least in this country, following a normal course of events, there was a sense of security. *Hashem Yisborach* has shown us that if there's a *hisorrerus* of *midas hadin* — if justice is being demanded — no one is secure anywhere.

All are familiar with the *passuk* cited in connection to the awakening call of the *shofar*: אם יתקע שופר בעיר ועם לא יחרדו, "Is a *shofar* ever sounded in a city and the people do not tremble?" The *passuk* concludes: אם תהיה רעה בעיר וה', לא עשה. "Can there be a misfortune in a city if *Hashem* had not brought it?" (*Amos* 3,6). The *navi* Amos refers explicitly to "misfortune in a city..."; precisely what we have been experiencing.

So the *Rav Hachovel*, the Master of our ship of state, is calling to us, מה לך נרדם? *How can you sleep through life peacefully, as if nothing has happened? How can you eat your breakfast, lunch and dinner, as if all were normal? "Get up! Call to your G-d! Perhaps G-d will think of us!"* (*Yona* 1,6).

It should be clear to everybody — especially to those of us in this country — that a new chapter has been opened in our lives. The status of our lives here is not the same anymore. As *ma'aminim be'nei ma'aminim* who see *Hashgachas Hakadosh Baruch Hu b'olamo* — firm believers in *Hashem's* control of events, in every detail — it is incumbent on us to internalize this conviction, not just paying it lip service.

❧ Separating the Strands

So how do we take the threads apart? First of all, the *Chumash* tells us that there will be periods during the *Ikvesa deMeshicha*, before the climax of *acharis hayamim*, of ומצאהו רעות רבות וצרות, "Many evils and distresses will befall them" (*Devarim* 31,17). We thought that we had suffered the full brunt of that prophecy 55-60 years ago, in the *churban* of *Klal Yisroel* in Europe, and that it was something of the past. But these "evils and distresses" are defined in *Chumash* as *hester panim* — the hiding of *Hashem's* countenance — an experience that is designed to shake us up and destroy our equanimity, to bring us to the realization that ואמר ביום ההוא הלא על כי אין אלקי בקרבי מצאוני הרעות האלה "Is it not because my G-d is not in my midst that these evils have come upon me?" (ibid.). We recognize our shortcomings and are ready to draw closer to *Hashem*. And yet, it says in the very next *passuk*, אנכי הסתר אסתיר את פני ביום

"ההוא על כל הרע אשר עשה כי פנה אל אלהים אחרים. "But I will surely have concealed My face on that day, because of all the evil that [the Jewish people] did, for it turned to alien gods" (ibid., verse 18).

The *Ramban* poses a question here: There has already been a *hisorrerus* (spiritual awakening) as a result of the suffering endured, and people have come to the recognition that they were inflicted with those painful experiences because *Hakadosh Baruch Hu* did not have enough of a presence in their lives. Why, then, is there need for additional *hester panim*, further concealment of His presence? The *Ramban* explains that there are *madreigos* of *teshuva* (levels of return) on the part of *Am Yisroel*. There is a *hisorrerus* (awakening) of *teshuva*, there is a *hirhur* of (an inspiration for) *teshuva*. Beyond that there is a *viduy gamur* (full confession) and, ultimately, *teshuva sheleima* (complete return).

Our recognition that we have witnessed an *etzba Elokim*, the handiwork of *Hashem* in events, means that we have experienced a *hisorrerus*. We should then be ready to advance in our closeness to *Hashem*, beyond *hirhur teshuva*, because *challila ve'challila* we do not want to be exposed to additional degrees of *hester panim*, in retribution for turning to *elohim acheirim*. — This latter expression does not only refer to idolatry. It can also mean alien forces. For *elohim* refers to any force that renders judgment, such as courts of law. To attribute events to forces in life other than *Hakadosh Baruch Hu*, at any given moment, is to be guilty of following *elohim acheirim*.

Our *teshuva* in times of crisis is not only a matter of feeling a *hisorrerus*, an awakening to improve — to *daven* better, to come closer to *Hakadosh Baruch Hu* — which, of course, is essential. We are expected to go a step beyond incremental improvement. After all, there has been a radical change in our lives, and this is because the *hanhaga* of *Hakadosh Baruch Hu* in a civilized world has also taken an awesome turn. By the same token, we must progress in our closeness to *Hashem*.

❈ Avoiding Suffering and Pain

When a person encounters *yesurim* — suffering — he must examine his actions: רואה אדם יסורים באים עליו יפשפש במעשיו.

Whether you had friends or acquaintances in the World Trade Center or not, it is incumbent on all of us to engage in introspection, aiming for self-improvement.

Rabbeinu Yona, in his classic *Shaarei Teshuva*, delineates specific requirements to achieve atonement for transgressions, in accordance with varying degrees of severity. Some sins require a complete *teshuva* to be forgiven. Others are not atoned for without some suffering, as well. One category is so grave that it has no final *kappara* until one's day of passing.

Rabbeinu Yona, however, invokes the *passuk* in *Mishlei* (16,6): בחסד ואמת יכופר עון. "By lovingkindness and truth is transgression expiated." In *Ikar* 17 of his 20 *Ikarim* (Principles) of *Teshuva* (*Shaar* I), Rabbeinu Yona explains that although some transgressions cannot be forgiven on the basis of repentance alone, and would depend on *yesurim* (suffering), involvement in *chessed* can act to exempt a person from *yesurim*. Similarly, remorse for *chillul Hashem* is normally inadequate to expunge a person of this grave transgression; complete atonement can only come with death. Nonetheless, he points out, "If a person upholds truth and supports it, and causes the light of truth to glow in the eyes of others, ... lowering factors of falsehood, in ways of *kiddush Sheim Shamayim*, he will be spared punishment."

These two elements — *chessed* and *emes* — protect a person from suffering.

We hope that as individuals we are not involved — each in his private life — in *chillul Hashem*. As a community, we must always be exceptionally vigilant to be free of *chillul Hashem*. But one thing is certain. It is incumbent upon us at this time of *eis tzara* (crisis) to seek every opportunity to fulfill the *mitzva* of being *mekadesh Sheim Shamayim*. Opportunities of *kiddush Sheim Shamayim* abound every day in our interpersonal dealings with both other Jews and non-Jews alike. Opportunities to increase *kevod Shamayim* are at our doorstep all the time — in our business affairs, in the way we speak to others, and in how we maintain an *ayin tova* — a forgiving, generous eye in regard to others.

If a Jew who believes in *Hakadosh Baruch Hu* and practices His *mitzvos* is seen to perform acts that others admire and commend, then *Hakadosh Baruch Hu* can say in regard to him ישראל אשר בך אתפאר. "Israel! In you do I find glory!" For example:

> *A recognizably Jewish man chose to terminate his taxi ride two blocks from his destination, to allow the driver an opportunity to pick up another fare more easily. The non-Jewish driver turned around and said, "Now I know why the Jews are a chosen people."*

One cannot fully assess the *kiddush Hashem* inherent in such small acts of consideration! This can happen all the time. It is incumbent on us to seek out ways in which to make positive changes in our lives, to deliberately look for occasions to be *mekadesh Sheim Shamayim* — not only to atone for past misdeeds, but to realize "And all the earth will be filled with His glory!" Through such initiatives, creation can reach its ultimate purpose of providing *Hakadosh Baruch Hu* with a dwelling place in our midst.

An exemplary case related by the Gemara deals with the sale of a donkey to Rabbi Shimon ben Shetach by a non-Jew. The rabbi discovered a large gem hidden in the saddle of the donkey, and returned it to the man who had sold the donkey to him: It was not meant to be part of the transaction. The non-Jew exclaimed, "Blessed is the G-d of Rabbi Shimon ben Shetach!" because Rabbi Shimon ben Shetach's behavior was beyond the norm of established business practices. It could only be a Divinely directed action. This gesture sanctified *Sheim Shamayim* to him.

The potential for such *kiddush Sheim Shamayim* is inherent to business; it is inherent to dealing with neighbors; it exists in family relations; and it can be the result of a life lived with careful sensitivity to all demands of *derech eretz*.

❧ *Involvement in Chessed*

"We will conclude with you." Thus did *Hashem* inform Avraham in His initial command of *"Lech Lecha"* to the first of the *Avos*, that the opening paragraph in the *Shemoneh Esrei* (*Birchas HaAvos*) would conclude with: "*Baruch atta Hashem, Magein Avraham.*" This blessing is sealed with his name.

This can also be understood as a promise to *Klal Yisroel*: History will come to its final culmination, when the world grows in *middas hachessed*, the attribute associated with Avraham.

Indeed, *gemilas chassadim* is a key to our community's ability to thrive and grow. This is certainly true of American Jewry. Not just today, and not only these past ten years. This goes back to close to a hundred years ago. But at the same time, we have much to atone for. As mentioned, *Rabbeinu Yona* underscores the message that *chessed* is indeed a source of atonement, citing the *passuk* in *Mishlei* בחסד ואמת יכופר עון. In *Sha'ar HaRevi'i*, he explains that *emes* is realized through Torah. Abaye and Rava, whose opinions are recorded throughout the Babylonian Talmud, were descendants of *Bnei Eili*, a family that was cursed to perish as young men. Abaye and Rava, however, were exempt from the curse. Their dedication to Torah study coupled with *chessed* earned them each a longer life: Rava lived 40 years, and Abaye, who practiced *chessed* in addition to Torah study, lived to be 60 (*Rosh Hashana* 18a).

Many women are deeply involved in *chessed* projects on a volunteer basis, ranging from *bikur cholim* to helping in schools and working with all sorts of charities. But there are some acts of *chessed* that everyone can do as an individual throughout the day — for example, by being *mekabel* a person *beseiver panim yafos* (greeting people with a warm welcome). In addition, many acts of *chessed* resonate with *kiddush Hashem*. This includes how, in both casual and personal relationships, one deals with others who are less gifted. It can apply in a yeshiva setting — a superior *bachur's* dealings with a weaker one … in *shul* … or simply when crossing the street; the smile one shares with someone who is in less fortunate circumstances — financially, socially, morally, emotionally. In truth, everyone can benefit from *chizuk*, a pat on the back — literal or verbal. Who is going to give it to us if not our own brothers and sisters?

In truth, there has never been a generation that needs as much *chizuk* as ours, even though we are financially far better off than our grandfathers were. Many people do not function optimally nowadays, and they need encouragement. Others are in need of *hadracha* (guidance). Offering a person encouragement and a sense of well-being is an act of incomparable value, with so much *Olam Haba* in store for those who provide it to them.

(These words should not be dismissed as just another *mussar shmuess*. Life has changed. And if one fails to recognize it, he is guilty of pure folly! It's not the same society anymore. יד ה' היתה בנו. "The Hand of G-d has been upon us." "An evil has befallen the city." Indeed, the city of New York is not the same. Are *we* going to be the same? Are *we* merely going to improve, *daven* better? Or are we ready to make radical changes in our entire way of life — with ourselves, with our family, with our *chaveirim*, in our *midas ha'emes*, our integrity?)

❧ *Areas for Active Self-Improvement*

We have all been under the impact of the volatile situation in *Eretz Yisroel*. And now we are all reeling under the shock of what has happened in this city. During an עת צרה — at a time of crisis — a person is expected to assume changes for the better. Indeed, over the past few years, we have been witness to some commendable initiatives at self-improvement. For example, people have become more sensitive about the way they talk. They eschew *lashon hara*, and have adopted regular sessions of study of *Sefer Chofetz Chaim*. We should all take advantage of this *hisorrerus* (inspiring initiative), and be much more careful as to what we say, about whom we talk, and the way we talk. It is not an easy matter, for *Chazal* recognize that all people, some time or another, become enmeshed in *avak lashon hara* — implied gossip.

In addition to referring to care in speech in his discussions on self-improvement, *Rabbeinu Yona* also includes this concept in another *Ikar*, another of his "Principles of *Teshuva*": He prescribes performing positive actions with the very limbs one has used in a transgression. For example, if someone sinned with his hand, he should do a *mitzva* with his hand. Similarly, if he sinned with his mouth, in addition to the *teshuva* process — which includes *charata* (remorse), *kaballa* (resolve), and *viduy* (confession) — he should compensate for the shortcoming and rectify it with positive actions, using his power of speech: Speak well of one another. Discuss Torah thoughts. Give people encouragement with well-chosen words.

Let us bear in mind that when facing a crisis, we would also do well to emulate *Yaakov Avinu* who was *noder* (assumed a binding obligation) in his own time of *tzara*: Should he return safely and unharmed from the years he would spend in the house of Lavan, he would create a *Beis Elokim* — a House of G-d in his life. We should be thinking along similar lines for ourselves.

❧ *Celebrating With Good Sense and Restraint*

There is yet another specific area where we must endeavor to undergo change. *Chazal* clearly call for changes of lifestyle when an individual or a family undergoes a crisis; all the more so when a *tzibbur* — the community at large — is faced with difficult times. In our current situation, it would be in place for everyone to restrain himself from *ta'anugei olam hazeh*, material pleasures and indulgences. The key word is restraint. *Perishus* — total withdrawal — is an aspect of *tzidkus* (saintliness), which is not within everyone's province. An across-the-board exercise of simple restraint, however, is something all could benefit from. We truly do not need all the comforts that we have become accustomed to.

More specifically, for the past 20 years or so, *rabbanim* have been decrying lavish *simchas*, unjustified extravagances, wasting money on all sorts of non-essential aspects of life, which are in violation of נפש שפלה, a humble spirit, which is a principal trait associated with *Avraham Avinu* (see *Avos* 5:22). While certain inroads have been made here and there, many people have dismissed most such efforts as a waste of time. For a year now, a committee of lay leaders has convened, seeking to establish guidelines for *chassunas, bar mitzvas,* among other *simchos,* adhering to specific, modest standards.

(As just one example, the *vort* people make to celebrate an engagement has come under scrutiny: What function does it perform? People borrow, and ultimately waste money on a *vort*. Why?

To keep up with their neighbors? The excuse is that everyone else does it. No one would be deprived were this custom to be discontinued.) Jews in *Eretz Yisroel* celebrate *simchos* with an abundance of enthusiasm and joy, without adopting extravagant extremes. Even those who can afford a more lavish affair would do well to follow the model of the Israeli type of celebration.

This entire reassessment is meant for the purpose of protecting *Klal Yisroel*, in the mode of *teshuvas hatzibbur, teshuvas harabbim* — community-wide reform and improvement.

The *Ribbono Shel Olam* is talking to us — here and in *Eretz Yisroel*. It is time to put an end to all of these wasteful practices as quickly as possible. Perhaps there are some courageous families who have growing children and will אי״ה be making *simchos*, and will be willing to serve as bold examples: Their *bar mitzva* celebration or *chassuna* will be on a different, more modest scale. And as for the so-called *vort*, it can be done away with completely…. This is an area where compassion, economy of resources of funds, time and energy, and good sense come together for the benefit of all.

Let us respond positively, with *rachmanus* (compassion) for one another. And *Hashem* in turn will have *rachmanus* on us.

THE TIME FOR
TIKKUN HAS COME:
ARE WE READY?

PROFESSOR AARON TWERSKI

"THE CROWN JEWEL OF OUR TORAH EXISTENCE — THE FAM-
ILY — IS UNDERGOING SERIOUS STRESS. THE TENSIONS NEED
TO BE IDENTIFIED AND STEPS HAVE TO BE TAKEN TO REDUCE
THEM TO MANAGEABLE LEVELS."

❧ *Conflict, Crisis and Confusion*

Our charge is to determine how the Jew can serve as a vehicle for *Kevod Shamayim*, i.e. how our daily lives can enhance respect for G-d and His Torah. It is often instructive to understand a concept from its negation. The clearest and most manifest expression of *chillul kevod Shamayim* arises when Jews worship idols. Of such magnitude is the sin that a Jew is required to sacrifice his life rather than commit idolatry even under coercion. When the Jewish nation first sought to violate this cardinal sin with the creation of the Golden Calf, the Torah relates that they "gathered onto Aaron and they said to him, 'Come let us make for us gods that will lead us'" *(Shemos* 32,1). *Rashi* notes that the Talmud was struck by the term *"yeilchu lefaneinu"* (lit., they will lead us*)*. The Hebrew word *"yeilchu"* is plural. The request should have been for a singular god that would replace *Moshe Rabbeinu.*The Talmud explains that the Jews sought not one, but many gods: *"Elohus harbei hevu lohem."*

Why a multiplicity of gods? Upon reflection, one can discern a profound lesson about Jews: We either worship one G-d and fulfill His will, or we are pulled in a multiplicity of directions. One source of idolatry will not suffice.

The lesson is clear. When we suffer *pizur hanefesh,* when we are torn in many different directions, it is a sign of deep and serious trouble. A Torah Jew's life must be focused. It must reflect the unity that inheres in the service of One G-d. When we sense that we owe allegiance to a multiplicity of goals, it is time to step back and ask ourselves: Are we still loyal to *Hashem* and His Torah or do our conflicted lives give evidence of a deep internal division that is inconsistent with the basic tenets of our faith? My own sense is that we are the most stressed-out generation of American Jews in recent memory. Internal stress, conflict and confusion of purpose have become staples of our daily existence. It has begun taking a serious toll on our mental health and that of our children.

I cannot claim to have conducted a scientific inquiry but anecdotal evidence provides more than a little support for my thesis. For example, discussions with those knowledgeable about the sale and dispensing of pharmaceuticals in areas of heavy *frum* population concentration in New York reveal that prescriptions for tranquilizers, anti-depressants and a whole range of soporifics are higher than they should be. Psychologists, mental health therapists and social workers confirm this observation. It is not that these drugs are being needlessly dispensed; rather, the need for them has escalated.

Perhaps even more disturbing are the observations of professional educators. I have heard from several principals and *menahalim,* as well as a random selection of *rebbis* and teachers. They all perceive a decline in performance of entering classes in the past several years. They find more children that are distracted and not able to focus as well as compared to previous years. In some schools, gross academic benchmarks confirm the learned intuition of the professionals. Most of these sources admit to being genuinely puzzled as to why the changes are occurring, but there is little disagreement that something is amiss.

I am neither a sociologist nor psychologist. My analysis need be taken with a grain of salt. I would be remiss, however, if I did not share with you insights gained from discussions over the past several years with a broad range of people from all spectra of the Torah community.

❦ *Those Who Make It, Those Who Don't, and Those Who Make It and Don't*

Earning a livelihood has been the topic of considerable discussion and concern to us. It is not merely a societal problem that is tangential to living in a Torah community. The mounting costs of yeshiva education for large families present awesome and often crushing burdens on parents. Concomitantly, inadequate salaries for *mechanchim* and burgeoning class size compromise the ability of teachers to teach with peace of mind and the potential of children to learn in an atmosphere where they are not lost in the crowd.

A sophisticated readership does not need to be told that these are not merely a desideratum which can be wished away. They are matters the *Shulchan Aruch* addresses. They are tied to inexorable *halachic* imperatives. How does our community cope with these responsibilities? For the sake of simplicity, I will break down our community into three groups. Each is faced with stress that takes its special toll in a Torah-centered community. The wealthy or the "haves," for the most part, meet their financial obligations to family and community with relative ease. Our community, however, has almost no old-line families of wealth.

We are a post-holocaust community. We have no analogs to the Rothschilds, Fords or Kennedys. Our wealth is mostly first — and at best, second — generational. It is heavily entrepreneurial. It is thin, fragile and tenuous. There is little margin for comfort.

A second category of well-to-do people are professionals who have been highly successful. Once again, these are self-made persons whose income is almost solely dependent on their outstanding individual skills and continuing performance, which is highly demanding both intellectually and emotionally.

Our "haves" are for the most part extremely stressed out. They keep long and grueling hours at work. When they return home, they cannot shuck their worries and responsibilities and park them at the door. The tension level in the home is often extraordinary. Faced with large families and community demands on their time, many of them do not cope well. What passes for communication with children is often polite banter but no real talk. The family is often an unwelcome distraction from what has become an all-consuming involvement with business and profession. Their personal commitments to Torah learning and spiritual growth are sorely tested, and they find themselves torn between unyielding demands on their time and energy. It is little wonder that they swallow tranquilizers and that their children appear more distracted and unfocused than yesteryear.

Even more distressing is the lot of our so-called "middle class." I have dubbed this group as "Those Who Make It and Don't." This hard-working middle class may be earning anywhere between $60,000-$95,000 per year (either single or two-income earners). With large families and multiple tuitions, however, these families are choking. They may be in the top 10 percent of American wage earners, but the reality is that the financial pressures are almost unbearable. As the children become older, each family begins facing the day when they will begin marrying off their children. And they often do not have the foggiest notion of how they are going to manage the expenses of a *chasuna, matanos,* let alone the desire and need to help the children in the early years of *kollel* life. They can barely make it through the month — without facing extraordinary expenses. Something has to give, and it does. The tensions of debt, feelings of inadequacy, and social pressures to earn more and work yet harder, take their toll.

> *Recently, a father who fits the above paradigm was chatting with me. He said, "Please, don't take this the wrong way. But, you know, I have days when I'm envious of my Italian neighbor who earns $500 per week. He comes home to his 1.8 children and his wife, and he is a hero. The children attend public school. He lives modestly, and he fulfills all his obligations to society. I earn three times that, and I'm a bum. I'm a bum for the tuition committee, an inadequate*

wage earner for my wife and children, and am slightly above the status of a schnorrer in the community. And now when I think of marrying off my children in the next ten years — I have nothing but nightmares."

It will not surprise you to learn that this fine *ben Torah* is on anti-depressants and tranquilizers. He has richly earned the right to them. And if the younger children of such folk begin demonstrating diminished performance in school, it is no mystery as to why.

Finally, we have those who do not make it. They are at least spared the agony of unrealizable expectations. Unless they have some special status in the community as that of an outstanding *talmid chacham*, they face the ignominy of poverty. The simple truth is that we are wont to place the "have-nots" in the *schlemazel* category. Stratification based on wealth is pernicious and sinful. It is totally foreign to Torah values. But I have heard all too many times about one or another that *"ehr iz nisht kein balabatisher yunger mahn."* Badges of shame are not worn without cost. They too contribute to the never-ending cycle of depression and feelings of worthlessness. Children whose pride as members of a family so tarnished cannot always be expected to easily don the requisite pride so necessary to a healthy ego and to strong scholastic performance.

It is not my intent to proclaim that we live in a state of disaster. The values and beauty of Torah homes provide a multitude of strengths to deal with these problems. We have a deep heritage for survival under adversity and it serves us well. If we seek to ameliorate and correct problems, however, they must be sharply stated. Overstatement is not warranted, but understatement would lull us into inaction. And act we must.

The Social Calendar

If our mental diversion and inattention at home were not sufficient, we have an added dimension that impacts upon our family life. We are all too often physically absent from home. Our social calendars have become so crowded that we have come to dread

our social obligations. Several weeks ago, I attended a funeral, ר׳ל,
one morning. A relative whom I encountered told me that after the
funeral he had to attend a *bris,* to be followed on the same day by a
tennayim, a wedding and a *sheva berachos.* Although this is unusual
for one day, it is not unusual at all to be booked solid night after
night for weddings, *bar mitzvas,* engagements, parlor meetings,
PTA's, *tzeddaka* parties, lectures, etc.

A principal of a fine yeshiva recently told me that the two months
of the year that are the most tense for students are the very months
when parents are absent from home almost every night. January
and June are examination months. They are also the prime wedding
season. For many of us, however, the phenomenon is not limited
to two months of the year. It has become a staple of our lives. We
are just way too busy and distracted. There is too much electricity
coming over the wires. If we are not careful, we shall give birth to a
new generation of latchkey children. Parents will be home for them
when they come home. But, if parents must leave night after night
to fulfill social obligations, the children will be sorely neglected.
The constant tension of having to leave by a certain time, dressing
for the event, rushing homework and supper, all exact real costs.

We need more quiet in our lives. We need it for ourselves and
we need it for our children. We need to be at home both physically
and mentally more, a lot more, than we are at present. Are there
practical steps that can be taken to reduce the psychic drain that
has become the bane of our existence? To this challenging question
I now turn our attention.

❦ Some Modest and Not-so-Modest
Proposals for Change

Before offering any suggestions for reducing the tension, a dis-
claimer is in order. My proposals will not deal with the issues of *parnassa* in general or the problems of increasing the earning power of members of our community. That is a topic worthy
of serious discussion, in and of itself. But the problems outlined
above will not be alleviated by marginal increases in wealth. And

truly significant increases in earning power are not in the offing. We cannot and should not expect to produce a middle class with an average earning power of $150,000 per year.

What *can* be done is to find ways to reduce expenditures. We have established that one area that cannot be cut is tuition. We are already operating our yeshivos on shoestring budgets. General modesty in lifestyle is certainly to be encouraged. But, to be fair to our middle class, the general lifestyle is relatively modest. The cost of housing is determined by the market. Unless we are to open up broad new neighborhoods in areas where housing costs are demonstrably less, we face fairly stable fixed costs. One area of our lifestyle must, however, undergo serious reevaluation. The cost of *simchos* of all kinds must undergo sharp and significant downsizing.

The reasons are many. First, it is the one area of our lives where we can realize significant savings without impinging on basic lifestyle. Second, with the increased size of *frum* families, the total financial and psychic burden is crushing both for those who make the *simchos* and for family and friends who participate in them. Third, we can no longer close our eyes to the opulent Jewish *simchos* that constitute such obvious conspicuous consumption that they disgrace us all.

- *Bar mitzvas* are a good place to start. There is no reason that *bar mitzvas* should not be limited to close immediate family. For the most part, they can be done at home. Where that is impossible, a small *shul* hall will do just fine. For *Kiddush* in *shul*, a *lechayim* is quite sufficient. Several *Chassidishe* communities have mandated such *takanos* (ordinances). They work beautifully. The entire cost is in the $1,000 range.
- The entire constellation of *simchos* attendant to marrying off a child needs serious restructuring. *Tennayim* should be done at home. Formal parties, from *lechayim* to *vort* to actual *tannayim*, constitute a huge financial drain. They are purely an American invention. In pre-war Europe they were unheard of.
- We must find ways to drastically cut the cost of the *chasuna* night itself. Unless tough *takanos* are put in place, we are bound

to continue the present system. We invite many friends and relatives because we are obliged to do so. They are obliged to come because they have no alternative. The inviters would be happy to forgo the formal full *seuda* invitation because they are unable to afford the cost. The invitees would be pleased to forgo attending the entire *seuda* because the cost of the present and the baby sitter amount easily to $100 for the evening. Both would be happier with an invitation to *simchas chassan v'kalla*. Without formal and binding limitations, however, sense of obligation mandates that the invitations be made and be accepted.

With burgeoning family size, *b'li ayin hara*, invitations to even immediate family can take on sizable proportions. For some families, married first and second cousins number in the hundreds. Once again, without some formal limitations, cutting costs without creating conflicts simply cannot be done.

- The cost of *Sheva Berachos* needs to be sharply diminished. Catered meals on four or five successive nights can run anywhere from $4,000 to $10,000 for the week — excluding *Shabbos*. It would be quite sufficient to have the *chassan* and *kalla* and parents for dinner and invite a small group of friends for *Birchas Hamazon*.

  Takanos with teeth could reduce expenditures enormously. Savings in the magnitude of $20,000 and more per wedding event — i.e. *tennayim, chasuna, sheva berachos* — are easily realizable. For families with eight to ten children the total amount saved is staggering. Include the debt service on borrowed money to fund these affairs, and the savings are even more impressive. Finally, consider the psychic toll on parents who are saddled with debt. And the human toll of friends and relatives who look bleary-eyed after a week of mandatory attendance at *sheva berachos*. We really must rein ourselves in.

- The need for *takanos* extends to *seudos* of *bris mila, pidyon haben* — indeed, to all *simchos* that are part of the ordinary Jewish-life cycle. Putting this entire aspect of our lifestyle in order will, when added together, have a significant impact on the quality of life for all of us. Modesty, true *tzenius*, could become fashionable.

❧ *"But I Really Can Afford It"*

Whenever the issue of *takanos* is raised we hear a hue and cry from some quarters. *"Why should we have to restrict ourselves from more lavish simchos if we can afford them? Let the rich make opulent simchos. And let the others scale down in accordance with their abilities."* Many people of substantial means strongly support the institution of *takanos;* however, the argument on part of the naysayers is stated so frequently and with such vehemence that it needs rebuttal. The primary source of the rebuttal come from *divrei Chazal.* The Talmud (*Moed Katan* 27a-b) relates:

> Formerly, it was the practice to convey food to the house of mourning, the rich in silver and gold baskets and the poor in baskets of willow twigs, and the poor felt shamed; they [Chazal] instituted that all should convey food in baskets of willow twigs to uphold the honor of the poor ... Formerly, it was the practice to bring out the rich for burial on a dargesh, i.e., an ornamental bed, and the poor in a plain box, and the poor felt shamed; they [Chazal] instituted that all should be brought out in a plain box to uphold the honor of the poor .... Formerly, the expense of taking the dead out to burial fell harder on the next of kin than his death so that the dead man's next of kin abandoned him and fled, until Rabban Gamliel came forward, disregarded his own dignity, and was brought out to his own burial dressed in simple flaxen clothes.

On a similar note, the *Mishna* (*Taanis* 26b) relates:

> Rabban Shimon ben Gamliel said: "Israel had no days as festive as the Fifteenth of Av and Yom Kippur when the maidens of Jerusalem would go out dressed in white garments that were borrowed so as not to embarrass one who had none."

As the Talmud relates, on these days, *shiduchim* were made. And *Rashi* notes that the wealthy maidens were forbidden to wear their own clothing lest they embarrass girls from poor families who had no suitable garments of their own.

Takanos of this sort have a long and honored tradition in Jewish life. The famed *Vaad Le'arba Ho'arotzos* established standards for *simchos* of all kind. The well-to-do people simply had to conform for the greater need of the *Klal*. To allow for discretion leads us where we are today. The slope is far too slippery. The pressure to conform to the more honored status is too great for mortals to resist. It is interesting that, today, when we see an elaborate non-Jewish funeral cortege, we react: "That's so goyish!" It was once very Jewish. No longer. When non-Jews look at our elaborate weddings they say: "That's so Jewish!" Enough. We need to embrace the *"hatzne'a leches im Hashem Elokecha,"* and declare it to be the norm for Jewish life.

✤ Are We Prepared to Listen?

The issue of *takanos* for *simchos* has been on the agenda of the American Torah community for many years.[*] Most recognize that they are an absolute necessity. Why have they not been mandated? Some point the finger of blame at the *gedolei Torah* for not *sua sponte* issuing a proclamation setting forth the standards. I place the blame on ourselves. Until recently, I believe we were not ready to listen. And our leaders, for good and plenty reasons, did not wish to issue decrees that would be honored mostly in the breach.

But why have we not been ready to listen? Why have the *gedolim* been so reticent to take us on? My own sense is that they sense in us a cynicism incompatible with the kind of *emunas chachamim* necessary for a true allegiance to Torah. On matters that affect our lifestyle, too many of us are quick to question every perceived inconsistency that may appear to arise, and charge hypocrisy to salve our own sense of guilt.

When I was a youngster, my father ז״ל constantly cautioned me against falling prey to cynicism. On numerous occasions he told

---

[*] See "Community Controls on Extravagance: Is It Time to Revive Them?" — JO, June '71.

me that when our matriarch Sarah banished Yishmael from the house of Avraham, her predicate for doing so was that in her view, Yishmael was the quintessential cynic. My father interpreted the *passuk, Bereishis* 21,9 "And Sarah saw Yishmael the son of *Hagar Hamitzris* who was born to Avraham *metzacheik*," to mean that she saw him scoffing. Sarah concluded that she could not raise her son Yitzchak in an atmosphere where everything sacred was subject to daily cynicism. It was destructive and antithetical to fundamental Torah values.

There is a famous Yiddish saying: *Azoi vi es kristelt zich azoi yiddilt zich.* Loosely translated, it means that Jews pick up quickly on non-Jewish attitudes and traits. The cynicism of the non-Jewish world has spilled over to the Torah world. And our generation has developed cynicism into a fine art. Ours is a generation without heroes. We are far too ready to take cheap shots at Torah leaders and to disregard their edicts. If they are on occasion silent or their words are muted, it is because they realize that we may well treat their pronouncements with disdain. The dictum of *Chazal*, "*Kesheim shemitzva lomar davar hanishma, kach mitzva shelo lomar davar she'eino nishma*" (Just as there is a *mitzva* to speak when one will be listened to, so is there a *mitzva* not to speak when one's words will be disregarded), must be taken into account. If we truly want direction from *Gedolei Yisroel* on the subject of *takanos*, we will have to communicate to them that we are prepared to put our scoffing aside and abide by their decision.

Purging ourselves of cynicism would do wonders for us all. Let me share a very moving story with you:

> *Reb Chaim Tchernovitzer, the author of the Sidduro Shel Shabbos and the Be'er Mayim Chayim, was one of the great Chassidic masters. Reb Chaim's kedusha on Shabbos was beyond human comprehension. It was said that from the time he left the mikva Erev Shabbos until the conclusion of Shabbos, he stood a head taller than he was on a regular weekday.*
>
> *In the city of Mosov lived a famous scoffer — "Hershel Mosover." He was blessed with a fine mind and an acid tongue that he used*

to heap scorn on all that was holy. He was most entertaining and whenever he would take up residence in the marketplace, he would be quickly surrounded by idle folk who would enjoy his repertoire of fun-making and cynicism. No one and no subject was off limits to him. He was prepared, if the spirit moved him, to poke fun at the greatest of the great and holiest of the holy.

Hershel Mosover was a businessman and his travels once brought him to Tchernovitz. As was his custom, he went to the marketplace and before doing business he was quickly surrounded by people seeking to enjoy themselves at the expense of others. On that day, Reb Chaim set out to collect tzeddaka from the businessmen in the marketplace.

From afar Reb Chaim noticed Hershel Mosover and decided to avoid him. Why present Hershel with yet another opportunity to scoff at the Rav of the town? But Reb Chaim came into Hershel Mosover's line of vision. Hershel called out gruffly, "Rebbe, kumt aher!" (Rebbe, come, here!) Reb Chaim disregarded the call but Hershel would have none of it. "Rebbe, kumt aher!"

Seeking to avoid a scene, Reb Chaim walked over to him. "Rebbe, what are you doing here?" Reb Chaim answered softly that he was out collecting money to redeem a family that had been thrown into prison by the poretz (nobleman) of the town for non-payment of rent for a long period of time. The family was starving and freezing in the cold, wet dungeon. Hershel Mosover asked, "Rebbe, how much money do you need?" Reb Chaim responded, "I need 1500 guilder." Hershel opened his purse and emptied it of its contents — 1500 guilder, a fortune of money. Everyone was waiting for Hershel Mosover to snatch the money back and make a joke out of the whole matter. A minute passed in silence. And then another. Finally, Reb Chaim turned to Hershel and said, "Hershel, how should I bless you? — May you henceforth taste the true flavor of Shabbos!"

Hershel returned home to Mosov penniless. At first he was ashamed to admit to his wife and children that he had squandered his fortune. Ultimately the story came out. The anger of his family knew no bounds, but what were they to do? The deed was done. Hershel returned to his place of honor in the market place of Mosov *and resorted to his old ways. Things continued normally until Thursday afternoon. Hershel began feeling unwell. He went home and tried to lie down but rest eluded him. Shortly, he was up and about dancing and clapping "Shabbos, Shabbos, Shabbos." Friday his ecstasy increased. He had to be peeled off the wall. Shabbos it-self was beyond relief. He could find no rest, dancing and singing, "Shabbos, Shabbos, Shabbos." And then Shabbos passed.*

Sunday morning, the old Hershel was back to himself. But when Thursday arrived, the scenario of the past week repeated itself. Several weeks followed this sequence. His family then learned from him of Reb Chaim's beracha. They decided that they would have to accompany their father to Tchernovitz and seek the recision of the beracha so that their father could exist as a normal human being.

When they came to Tchernovitz and made their request, Reb Chaim told them that it was not possible to rescind the beracha, but he could make it possible for Hershel to withstand the kedusha of Shabbos kodesh: "Leave him with me for a while and you will see that he will be fine."

Hershel stayed on with Reb Chaim and became his disciple. When he eventually returned to Mosov, he was no longer the same Hershel. So lofty had he grown in avodas Hashem that Chassidim who could not make the trip to Tchernovitz would travel to the Rebbe Reb Hershel of Mosov to experience the kedusha of Shabbos that one felt in the presense of Reb Chaim Tchernovitzer.

For one moment in his life, a scoffer put cynicism aside. He was able to act with compassion of a *Yid*, and became an *ish kadosh*. If we can put aside the cynical attitude that so pervades society and listen with open ears and even more open hearts, we can realize real change in our lives. If we insist on placing our own imprimatur on the *takanos* — if we first ask, "*Ma kasuv bo?*" — we shall never receive the direction we so sorely need.

The time for action and acceptance has come. We must — if we are to survive, both spiritually and physically — reorder our lives. *Takanos* are not a panacea. But they are an important start. And we must begin somewhere.

THE BEST OF TIMES OR THE WORST OF TIMES?

SHIA MARKOWITZ

"**M**azel Tov! Mazel Tov!"
How Reb Yankel and his wife Chanie have waited years to say these words! Their eldest daughter is finally engaged to a fine *bachur* from Lakewood. The phone is ringing off the hook with words of praise from relatives, neighbors and friends.

And then:

"By the way, when is the *lechayim*?"

"The *lechayim*? We're not exactly sure what we are doing. We might make a *vort*. We'll let you know."

***

After several phone calls the *mechutanim* decide to make a small *lechayim* on Wednesday evening for the immediate family and a *vort* on Sunday in a larger catering facility for everyone else. The lists are prepared; the phone calls are made. Food, drinks, flowers, tables, chairs, specialty cakes, assorted platters, music and photographer are ordered.

Somehow "the immediate family" grows to over 100 people for the *lechayim*, who are also asked to come back for the larger and more glamorous *vort*. Hundreds show up for the *vort*, many from more than 50 miles away, filing in the front door, making sure to be noticed, wishing them all the best, and leaving inconspicuously through the rear. Most of the food remains uneaten and relatives and friends are sent home with assorted goodies. The bills for the affairs add up to several thousand dollars. Reb Yankel, a computer programmer with a better-than-average salary, begins to dig into his savings — at this point, not allowing himself to be fazed with the monetary commitments to come.

***

The wedding date is set. Ten weeks to prepare, and so much to do.

Over the next few weeks, Reb Yankel and Chanie contend with the daily pressures of running a home, helping their children and attending *shiurim*. Somehow, time must be found to prepare for this most important event.

Gowns, dresses and *sheitels* need to be ordered and shopping for the trousseau begins. Reb Yankel begins searching for a new *Shas*, *talleisim* and *kittel* befitting his new son-in-law. Meeting with the caterer, invitations and furniture shopping is next on the list. *But the list seems to never end.*

On the other side, the *chassan*'s parents are dealing with the ring, assorted gifts for the *kalla*, the *aufruf*, photographer, flowers and musicians for the wedding ... and the *chassan*'s wardrobe.

The *chassan* and *kalla* spend *Shabbosos* with their new families. Gifts to be treasured — and displayed — are exchanged at every possible opportunity.

As the weeks go by the bills and pressures begin to add up, but there is no stopping now. The wedding list grows to 625 people. Reb Yankel and/or his *mechutanim* have a difficult time cutting back and reigning in the expenses. After all, everyone else is doing it, and how would it appear to family and friends if we stray from what has become the "norm"? Worse yet, what would the *mechutanim* say? Would this make a major dent in our relationship?

The wedding night finally arrives. The reception called for 6:30 finds barely a handful of people to partake in the extravagant display of delicacies ... 8 o'clock and much of the uneaten smorgasbord begins to make its way back to the kitchen, just as many of the arriving guests make their way to the *chupa* room ... .

The glass breaks, the music plays, and the beaming *chassan* and *kalla* are escorted to their *yichud* room, while the crowd enters the banquet hall. It is past 9 o'clock, and some glance at their watches hoping to have the opportunity to fulfill the *mitzva* of being *mesamayach chassan vekalla*....

It's now close to 10 o'clock. The photographer, oblivious to the anticipation of the guests, makes sure not to miss any photo opportunities....

The newly married couple finally appears, and the first dance is exhilarating. Everyone joins together in an outpouring of heartfelt *simcha* for the new couple.

Many of the guests begin making their way to the exit. *The main course is now being served.* By the time *bentching* and *Sheva Brachos* are recited, barely a handful of the large, invited crowd is in attendance.

***

The wedding has come and gone, and before either side can take a breather, the week of *Sheva Brachos* begins. New dresses, suits, and gifts, along with the catered meals and waiters, deplete the savings almost entirely. The *Shabbos Sheva Brachos* (like the past *Shabbos' aufruf*) — an ongoing mini convention of meals and speeches — is so elaborately prepared that it compares to a small wedding feast with all the trimmings.

Finally, it's over. *Or is it?* The ongoing maintenance of the new couple, by one or both of the *mechutanim*, has just begun. Of course, this is the fondest wish for both sides — the *yungerman* continues to learn in *kollel*, where he will grow into an even finer *talmid chacham*, establishing a family *al pi Torah*.

In just ten weeks, the *mechutanim* have spent tens of thousands of dollars, each marrying off their first child. Can they do less for the next one, and the one after that, and the one after that? What should be their most enjoyable memorable event is deflated by a real concern of building a mountain of debt.

✦ Welcome to the Simcha Treadmill

The scenario just painted covers a large portion of society regardless of background — *Chassidish, yeshivish* or *baalabatish.* Caught in the whirlpool of *"simcha* spending," we are often railroaded into situations we are not able to handle and bills we can not afford to pay. Many of those who are marrying off their first child do not foresee the picture at the end of the road. The reality is, it makes them feel uncomfortable. One would expect that by the next wedding a more realistic approach be used. This unfortunately is not the case.

It wasn't always this way. Years ago — from the 1960's through the mid-70's — families were smaller and therefore *simchos* were far less frequent. The guest list was also much smaller. Even the more affluent were, for the most part, not born into it. Increased wealth was usually associated with many additional hours per week of hard work mixed with a good measure of *mazel.* That kind of money was more difficult to part with, especially in the shadow of *Churban* Europe. With many people dedicated to the task of building families and new Jewish communities, money was simply too important and not available to be spent on less important items.

As the years progressed through the 80's, opportunities increased. Some of the baby boomers did not have to live through the trials and tribulations of their parents' generation and came into easy money. Many others were fortunate to turn small investments into great financial rewards. The size of families began to show remarkable increase, as did the range of acquaintances ... and so did the size of our *simchos.* 350 people grew to 400 ... to 500 ... and then to 600. The less financially able were forced to join in. *How can we not invite all those who invited us?*

❧ New Factors in the Equation

As the costs of *simchos* increase, a relatively new phenomenon is upon us. Many married couples begin their life within a *kollel* structure. A large portion of the financial obligation usually rests on both or, sometimes, one of the *mechutanim.* This stipend, which can run into the tens of thousands of dollars annually, is for many an added financial burden — on top of an already unmanageable budget. It is not unusual for a family to be supporting five or six unmarried children with tuition, camp, health, and the daily expenses typical of all families. Add to that two or three married couples whose financial wherewithall is mostly dependant upon this same set of parents. People find themselves in a spiraling debt syndrome that will take them years to recover from — if they recover at all.

While there are *yechidei segula* (exceptional individuals) whom the *Ribbono Shel Olam* blessed with an abundance of wealth, much of the Jewish world is finding it extremely difficult to cope. The cost of the entire ten-week scenario described above will average $60,000 to $70,000 combined for both families. (For those spending more, the figures can run higher than $100,000.) Multiply this by the average family of six or more children, whose *chasunos* can occur one after the other. Family members are now being asked to help. Many grandparents, who have put away savings and live on fixed income, feel obligated to do more than they can when they see the plight their children are going through. For those whose families are unable to participate, the *klal* is asked to subsidize hundreds of *hachnosas kalla* campaigns. The higher the standards of the general community, the greater the need for subsidy.

To put these numbers into perspective, consider a family whose annual gross income is somewhere around $100,000 (pretty high, right?). Saving at a rate of 6 percent per year, a family of five children would need to save more than 25 years just to pay for their five weddings! What about families whose income is considerably lower, or who have more children? It is no wonder that families are collapsing under the strain!

Imagine the dilemma of parents who are always juggling their bills, watching their children grow... and looking for ways to save for the upcoming *Bar Mitzva*. They understand that in a few short years, they will *B'ezras Hashem* begin to do *shidduchim*. Even without knowing the actual cost, they realize that a more aggressive savings plan must be implemented. Where do they look first? They can't cut back on the basic needs of the home: the rent, the mortgage, the utilities. What about the tuition bills from their sons' and daughters' schools? Do they begin to decrease their *tzeddakos*? Or, do they now consider compromising their Torah values to attain the desired results? The ripple effect from this huge disproportionate outlay of money, for basically one evening, is noticeable in all areas of our society. And as usual, it is the *Torah* and *Chessed* institutions that are on the front line, absorbing much of the impact.

✦ *Stop the Treadmill, I Want to Get Off!*

Who signed us up for this exercise program? Isn't there a way to hop off? Can't we institute basic *simcha* guidelines in line with our individual needs and resources?[1] Why do we need both a *lechayim* and a *vort*? Why must so many expensive gifts be exchanged? Must our *chasunos* really be on the scale of annual dinners of major Jewish organizations?

Steps have been taken in some circles to reduce the number of musicians in the orchestra. Why not follow the lead?

Why not popularize the exclusive use of silk flowers from a *gemach* instead of live bouquets, which will help other needy families, and spare the celebrants the difference in price?

How about an agreed upon time-limit on the post-*yichud* photography session? And for that matter, do we all really need a full-scale photography and video production?

I've picked on only a few of the items that need to be addressed. The list[1] can and should go on — but it requires serious discussion

---

[1] This partial list was compiled with the help of friends, colleagues and *mechutanim*.

and pragmatic planning by those of you who agree that our attitude toward *simchos* needs an overhaul. With enough people pooling their thoughts and proposals, a catalog of potential modifications could be drawn up. These in turn could be circulated for the purpose of creating a consensus. *Rabbanim* and community leaders have tried to address this issue over the years with little perceptible change. If anything, it is evident that the *simcha* treadmill that society has constructed has accelerated. As time passes, many more will join others in failing the stress test.

Perhaps it's time that something happen at the grassroots level, where *mispallelim* of each *shul* or *kehilla* discuss among themselves guidelines that their respective members would be willing to adhere to.

❦ *Mazel Tov, Mazel Tov!*

Reb Yankel and Chanie have just announced the engagement of their third child. It's their third *shidduch* in two years. The *chassan* and *kalla* are elated. The parents are grateful — *and petrified.*

OF DIFFERENCES AND UNANIMITY
REFLECTIONS ON "GUIDELINES FOR WEDDINGS"

PROFESSOR AARON TWERSKI

*A*fter many years of agonizing over the escalating lavishness of our *simcha* celebrations, *gedolei Yisroel* placed their imprimatur on a set of *hanhagos* (guidelines for general practice) to govern weddings in the *chareidi* community. The promulgation of those guidelines engendered a plethora of reactions. Some welcomed them with enthusiasm, others with equanimity, and still others with derision.

The truth be told, even among members of the Torah leadership, not all were in total agreement with the *hanhagos*. While some *rabbanim* and *roshei yeshiva* withheld their signatures from the guidelines simply because of their general policy of not signing their names to public pronouncements, others were motivated by more substantive concerns. Several viewed the guidelines as too tepid, others viewed them as too detailed, and yet others feared that the time was not ripe for their broad promulgation.

This much, however, is undisputed. Over the many years that *takanos* have been under discussion, there has been unanimity among <u>all</u> *gedolei Yisroel* that our lifestyles have taken on a decid-edly hedonistic and non-Jewish character, and that serious exami-nation is in order. There has been no disagreement among the *gedo-lim* that we need to downsize. The question has not been *whether*, but rather *how* to accomplish this goal. Let those cynics who point to the absence of one or another name on the list of rabbinic en-dorsements on the *hanhagos* point to even one who believes that the extravagance which has become so commonplace meets with his approval. They will search in vain. Those who continue their excesses of the past can find no support from any Torah author-ity other than in the lamentation of *Moshe Rabbeinu* when he pro-claimed: *"Vayishman Yeshurun vayivat —* and Jeshurun got fat and kicked" *(Devarim 32,15).*

❧ History of Takanos

Much has been written about the history of *takanos* in the pages of this publication.[1] All *bnei Torah* know them well. From the *takana* of Rabbi Gamliel prescribing stringent limitations on the costs of the burial of the dead; to the requirement that all maidens who had reached the age of *shidduchim* and went out to be seen by their prospective mates on *Chamisha Asar B'Av* would be dressed in borrowed clothes, so as not to shame those who were im-poverished; to the strict guidelines set by the *Va'ad L'Arba Aratzos* to govern all *simchos*, there has been a long tradition of community standards set by *gedolei Yisroel* to govern various aspects of events in the Jewish life-cycle. These are not new innovations created by zealots in 5762, but historic benchmarks in enforcing restraints when deemed necessary.

---

1. "Community Controls on Extravagance: Is It Time to Revive Them?", *Lewis Brenner*, June '71; "Notes on a Jewish Wedding," by Avi, June '82; "The Time for *Tikkun* Has Arrived. Are We Ready?" by *Aaron Twerski*, Feb '96; "Responding to the Message of Recent Events," *Rabbi Yaakov Perlow*, Oct. '01.

❧ Why Guidelines for Simchos

*G*edolei Yisroel throughout the ages have written volumes about the incompatibility of extravagance and hedonism with fundamental Jewish values. And many of the *rabbanim* who spoke so eloquently in support of the guidelines have emphasized the need for modesty as a singular virtue. If so, then, why not an outright attack on all aspects of conspicuous consumption? Why not guidelines on elaborate houses, cars, summer villas and posh vacations? And why guidelines for weddings? What about *bar mitzvas* and *seudos bris mila*?

First, let it be noted that *sifrei mussar* and *Chassidus* brim over the top with admonitions against all forms of indulgence in luxurious living. Those who wallow in materialism cannot aspire to or attain spiritual greatness. If the *chasuna hanhagos* are the first shot out of the cannon declaring an offensive on the part of *gedolei Yisroel* seeking to make a statement on one aspect of overindulgence, then it is a welcome start on a topic that will yet need to be addressed in further stages.

There is, however, a justification as to why *simchos* were chosen for *takanos* that is, in my opinion, irrefutable. There is good reason that Rabbi Gamliel made *takanos* for funerals, and that *gedolei Yisroel* throughout the ages set firm guidelines for *simchos*. For the most part, a Jew lives his life in private. What one eats for dinner, the cost of one's furniture, whether one takes a car service or the subway to work — these are not public affairs.

There are, however, events in the life cycle of the Jew that are not and cannot be private. Burial of the dead is not a private affair; *levoyas hames* is a public *mitzva*. One cannot conduct a private funeral without transgressing the *mitzva* of *kavod hames* — giving due honor to the dead. When Rabbi Gamliel saw that the impoverished had to abandon their dead because they could not bury them with the standard honors expected at the time, he mandated a single uniform funeral service for all.

Weddings are not and cannot be private affairs. The *mitzva* of *simchas chassan vekalla* forces one out of the private domain into the public arena. Once a standard is set by community custom, all conform to it or else risk being shunned. It is no answer to tell the less fortunate to make a third-rate wedding. One can no more celebrate a third-rate wedding than one could make a third-rate funeral. Marie Antoinette's injunction to the poor, "Let them eat cake," rings very hollow indeed. Rabbi Gamliel understood that when the *halacha* forces the Jew into the public domain, *chachmei Yisroel* must mandate some sense of equality so that one need not wear the badge of poverty. Very simply, there are times when one must act not as individuals, but as part of a *klal*.

In a moving address, the Novominsker *Rebbe* שליט״א related that he had been questioned by a person of considerable means as to why he should not be able to spend his money as he saw fit. The *Rebbe* answered him, "You are not only an individual, you are part of a *tzibbur*. The way in which you behave profoundly affects others who are less fortunate."

❈ *Only Weddings?*

Should there, then, not be guidelines for *bar mitzva* and *seudos bris mila*? The answer is: Of course there should be. The *Va'ad L'Arba Aratzos* included all such public events. Talk to parents who are forced to "shortchange" their 13-year-old whose classmates all have a three-day-weekend *bar mitzva* gala, or high-priced affairs in luxurious halls for several hundred couples. Contemplate the pain and shame of a youngster who feels left out because all his classmates within a period of several months have had posh celebrations and he is the class "neb." One strives that a *simcha* be full and complete — we wish our friends *"gantzeh simchos."* How complete can your *simcha* be if you know that it is driving a stake into the hearts of your children's friends? And for those who feel that they cannot impose the dishonor on their children and themselves comes the crushing cost of tens of thousands of dollars that drives them into hapless debt. The smile you see on a host's face at such a *simcha* masks the long-term pain that accompanies it.

Yes, *bar mitzva* guidelines are in order, and hopefully they will come in time. There is, however, good reason to start with weddings.

Weddings — like funerals — come at a time of overwhelming emotional stress, and the principals (the celebrants and the mourners) do not usually respond in a calculated manner. Moreover, the details of the event are often orchestrated by an imperious outsider — the caterer in one case, the funeral director in the other — at previously established arbitrary costs. These outsiders are the ones who established the norm, and as time goes on, they continue to conform to the norm, or escalate it. Only organized communal pressure can redefine that norm, and scale things down. So we focus on weddings.

❧ *The Starting Point*

There is yet another factor in the way we celebrate our weddings that forces us to begin here. The secular culture has had its impact on our view of marriage and our way of celebrating the event. The wedding has taken on the Hollywood "perfect day" mythology. The gown must be exquisite. The video and photography must be superb. Flowers must give their "Garden of Eden" effect. The tiny tots must march to the *chupa* leaving a trail of flowers. The music must be heavenly. The smorgasbord and Viennese tables must provide enough food and delectables to feed two armies, and they must be artistic to boot. Everyone who attends the same *shul* and bungalow colony must be invited. The entire class of the *chassan* and *kalla* are must-invitees. And the list grows on. It is a train without brakes descending a mountain at 150 miles per hour. It had to crash.

It has crashed.

So now we must take steps to disengage from this downward plunge and redesign our weddings. Interestingly, the starting point of these *hanhagos* is a celebration that is unanimously loathed, and yet most difficult to shake: the *vort*. Yes, the couple has just become engaged, and they want the world to know it. But convening a large celebration, with lavish displays of refreshments, floral arrangements and music is a phenomenal waste of time and money, pulling the *chassan's* friends away from their sacred studies, playing havoc with the senior generation's *shiurim* and family time, and generally imposing on friends. An impromptu *lechaim* for immediate family and intimate friends — in the *kalla's* home, if at all possible — makes so much sense; but even then one must battle convention and the couple's expectations to limit the scope of this event. It is, however, a battle worth waging.

Once this very first step in the guidelines is violated, the rest of the *hanhagos* will likely be ignored as a matter of course. We must stop and think: No one contests the superfluous nature of this gathering. All the more reason to comply with this aspect of the *hanhagos,* and begin the celebration on the right track.

❧ *The Embattled Middle Class*

The guidelines will not have a direct effect on those living at or below the poverty line. For reasons to be explained later, they would be indirect beneficiaries. These *yungeleit* do not have the option to make anything other than low-budget weddings. My discussions over the past years have been focused on our impoverished middle class who, although earning nicely by general American standards, are literally choking from their multifarious financial commitments. Families with (*b'li ayin hara*) five or more children cannot sustain themselves even on incomes of $75-to-$125,000. Between tuition, camp, medical insurance, mortgage on house and car, they live on the edge. If every second or third year, they have to finance a "*baalabatisha chasuna*," they are driven to — and often over — the brink of bankruptcy. The peer pressure to match up to expectations is enormous. They say (and I believe them) that without *takanos* they are lost.

Even the well-to-do, upper-middle class cannot afford the high cost of *simchos*.

And yet, because they are perceived as well to do, the pressure on them to make a really elaborate wedding is very great. The only solution is to start at the top and introduce some limitations. The ripple effect will be enormous. It will redound to the benefit of everyone. The gaps between the various income strata will not disappear; but they will shrink dramatically. The savings have been calculated to be in the tens of millions of dollars each year. The savings in self-respect and peace of mind are incalculable.

❧ Are We Being Consistent?

The wags and scoffers have already taken this first cheap shot. "Yes," they say, "the *rabbanim* and *rebbes* tell us to make modest weddings, but when they make a wedding they invite everyone." One could well view a wedding made by a *rebbe* as an affair of state. *Chassidim* and *talmidim* attend because it is a communal religious event — not a private *simcha*. I have attended many such *simchos*. Most often they take place in the large *beis medrash* or a large hall.

Catering is done at bargain-rate prices. Serving is on plastic dishes. All who attend share in the cost because they wish to be part of an event that is a part of their own religious and spiritual experience. The cost per couple at these events is a fraction of the cost of a regular wedding. These are no-frill *simchos*.

That should trouble no one but the naysayers. All should understand that *kehilla* events are of a different genre.

❧ An Opportunity Seized — or Lost

We need desperately to tone down our lifestyles. We need to do so for ourselves. We need to do so for our children. We need to do so for our sense of community. We need to do so out of respect for the wishes of the *roshei yeshiva* and *gedolei Torah* who have made it clear that they find extravagant *simchos* antithetical to *ruach haTorah*, to the Torah spirit. Those who know them can attest to the pain that they endure when in attendance at these events.

For those who contemplate turning a blind eye toward the guidelines, I urge you to think again. For years, many *bnei Torah* have turned to their *roshei yeshiva* for direction. The *roshei yeshiva* were hesitant to act because they feared that they would be met with a helpless shrug or — worse — with cynicism. Well, now they have spoken. If we decide to reject their counsel, we shall be making a statement loud and clear that ultimately we are not subservient to Torah authority: *Let them stick to religion and let us run our lives as we see fit!* Torah will be placed *bekeren zavis* — in an obscure corner, causing the ultimate *chillul Hashem*.

***

When *Yitzchak Avinu* was placed on the *akeida*, he asked his father: "*Abba, kefos osi yaffeh she'lo evot* — Bind me tight so that I not kick and thus render my sacrifice invalid!"

Klal Yisroel has always understood that we need to be bound so that we not render our lives unworthy. We have always understood that restraint frees us to ascend to a more noble and lofty existence.

Some predict that nothing will come of the guidelines. I disagree. I have deep faith that the overwhelming majority of *Bnei Torah* will honor them in both letter and spirit.

They are not the be-all and end-all. But they reflect an important first step on a journey that is not yet fully charted. But if the route is not defined, the destination is clear: To lead our lives within the context of הצנע לכת עם ה' אלוקיך, "Walking humbly with Hashem your G-d."

IT'S TIME TO FACE THE MUSIC

RABBI SHIMON FINKELMAN

❧ *Rock Bottom*

Recently, someone I know was offered a lift by a nice Orthodox young man. The passenger could not hide his disgust as unrefined Greek music spewed forth from the tape deck. The driver apologized, "I hope you don't mind, but I'm a composer of Jewish music and I'm searching for some ideas for my next release."

Unfortunately, it is no laughing matter.

On a visit to the Lakewood Yeshiva, the Telshe *Rosh HaYeshiva*, Rabbi Mordechai Gifter זצ״ל, was honored to deliver an address during *Shalosh Seudos*. Before Rabbi Gifter spoke, another visitor offered a heartfelt rendition of *Yedid Nefesh*. Rabbi Gifter prefaced his remarks by commenting that it was a pleasure to hear such beautiful, soul-stirring singing. As for that which has come to be known as "Jewish rock," Rabbi Gifter summed up his feelings with a play on words: *"Rak ein yiras Elokim bamakom hazeh"* (*Bereishis* 20,11) — if the song can be classified as "rock" then it is devoid of *yiras Hashem*.

To paraphrase: When words from *Tanach* or the *Siddur* are put to the tune of a contemporary love song (which, this writer has been informed, is the case with more than one popular *"nigun"*), the result is **not** Jewish music.

This article is not intended as an attack against some of today's popular Jewish singers. To the contrary, they have been blessed with an abundance of talent in a field which, as we will endeavor to show, is a most sublime form of Divine service. Nor is this article intended as a criticism of the *chassanim* and *kallos* (and their friends) who want very much for the bands to play this sort of music. Just watching the average *chassan* and *kalla* as they *daven* under the *chupa* is enough to assure us that, indeed, they are a G-d-fearing couple who yearn to build a home permeated with *Yiras Hashem*. The intent of this article is to convey some sort of understanding of what *negina* should and should not be.

❧ *Music to Awaken By*

In discussing the command that trumpets be sounded at the offering of Temple sacrifices and at times of community distress (*Bamidbar* ch. 10), *Sefer Hachinuch* writes:[1] "Among the roots of this *mitzva* is ... that a human being requires a great deal of *"hisorerus* (spiritual awakening). and nothing will awaken him like the sounds of *nigun*."

Rabbi Yisroel of Shklov quotes his teacher, the Vilna *Gaon*, as saying that in music lies the power to resurrect the dead.[2]

On a fundamental level, we can perhaps look at the structure of "Western" music, whose scale is comprised of seven notes, as being associated with *mitzva*-related groups that include: the seven-year *Shemittah* cycle and the seven cycles that culminate in the *Yovel* year; the seven (Scriptural) days of Pesach and Succos;[3] the seven weeks of *Sefiras HaOmer* which are interrelated with the seven Heavenly

---

1. *Mitzva* 384.
2. Introduction to *Pe'as Hashulchan*.
3. *Shemini Atzeres* is a festival for itself.

midos (beginning with *chessed* and culminating with *malchus*); the seven wedding blessings (*Sheva Berachos*); the seven *ushpizin* (guests) whom we welcome into our *succa*; and, of course, the seven days of the week which culminate with *Shabbos*. In the words of Rabbi Michael L. Munk: "The number seven denotes the spiritual values that were the purpose of Creation. G-d created the world in six days and rested on the seventh, as it were. As *Maharal* puts it, The physical world is represented by the number six ... but Creation was not finished until there was a seventh day ... a day of involvement with the G-dly."[1] An integral part of the *Shabbos* meals is the singing of *zemiros*. *Menoras HaMaor* (3:3) relates the word זמירות to the verb תזמר, to prune (*Vayikra* 25,4). "Just as one who prunes a vine cuts away the [dry, useless] vines, leaving behind those that are soft [and will yield produce], so do the *zemiros* that we sing remove the impediments between ourselves and the Holy One — so that our prayers will be pleasing and hearkened to."

Rabbi Yaakov Emden writes: "One who recites *zemiros* brings good to the world. He brings about an attachment between himself and G-d and causes G-d to heed his voice; his ways are pleasing and he saves the world from destruction" (*Siddur* Beis *Yaakov*).

There is no greater *mitzva* than the study of Torah. Our Sages relate that *David HaMelech's* nighttime study was preceded by song: "A harp was suspended over David's bed. At midnight, a north wind would blow, causing it to play. When David heard the music, he would arise and engage in the study of Torah" (*Berachos* 3b).

Thus, it is clear that in Judaism song is far more than a joyous pastime.

Rabbi Yitzchak Hutner זצ״ל, Rosh Yeshiva of Mesivta Rabbi Chaim Berlin, had a keen appreciation for *negina*. His sensitivity was such that in his *beis midrash*, some of the *nigunim* sung at *hakafos* on *Simchas Torah* were reserved for that occasion alone; these songs were not sung in the yeshiva the rest of the year. Similarly, he specified that certain *nigunim* be sung only at the Purim *seuda* and at no other time.

---

1. *The Wisdom in the Hebrew Alphabet*, p. 104.

At *Shabbos kiddushim* in his yeshiva, Rabbi Shlomo Freifeld זצ״ל, *Rosh Yeshiva* of Yeshiva Sh'or Yoshuv, would approve each *nigun* before it was sung. It was not that Rabbi Freifeld lacked trust in his *talmidim* to sing songs with taste; he surely relied on them. Nevertheless, he attached such importance to *negina* that he wanted to be sure the *nigun* fit the occasion.

Surely, the *nigunim* he chose bore no resemblance to the one sung recently by a Spanish worker in a catering hall, who was so taken by a particular beat, and had heard the song played so many times at weddings and *bar mitzvas*, that he knew not only the tune, but the Hebrew words as well!

❧ *Transport to Another World*

One of the great *Chassidic* masters is quoted as having said; "Song is the way to take a person from the place where he is to the place where he wants to be." As the following anecdotes illustrate, song can reach to the very depths of one's soul, and effect a complete transformation for the good.

When Aryeh[1] invited his brother Bob to spend *Shabbos* with his family on the occasion of his son's *bar mitzva*, Bob demurred, since he had long ago abandoned the religious upbringing that they had once shared.

"If I come," Bob said, "I come as is, in a T-shirt and jeans — and I don't want to embarrass you."

"You won't embarrass me," Aryeh replied. "You're my brother and I really want you to come." In the end, Bob came.

Though Aryeh is not *Chassidic*, on Friday night he took his brother to a prominent *Chassidic minyan* well known for its beautiful singing. As Providence willed it, the *sheliach tzibbur* that night was a true master of *nigun*. As *"Lecha Dodi"* was being sung, Bob suddenly burst into tears. The *nigun* had touched his soul. He ultimately returned to his roots.

---

1. The names are fictitious.

In a similar incident, a young man who had forsaken Torah and *mitzvos* as a teenager was inspired to return when attending a *Sheva Berachos* meal at which many soul-stirring *nigunim* were sung.

Children, as well, can be inspired by true *nigun*. A prominent *mechanech* related that some forty years ago he brought a young student, who was from a non-religious home, to *Shalosh Seudos* in Mesivta Torah Vodaath. The *Shalosh Seudos* was held in the dark, and slow, moving *nigunim* were sung. At one point, the *Rebbi* asked the boy, "Are you sleepy?" "No," came the soft reply, "just thinking."

Forty years later, the *Rebbi* phoned this same student and invited him to be his guest for Shabbos. "Do they still have the same kind of *Shalosh Seudos?*" the man wanted to know.

❧ *The Other Side*

J ust as song can inspire for the good, so can it excite in a very negative way. This needs no proof. There is no doubt that "hard rock" or the like awakens the most base feelings in a person and can infect a refined human being in a manner that can only be described as coarse and vulgar. There are other shades of secular music which, though not in the category of hard rock, are nonetheless harmful to the soul and have no place in the life of a *ben Torah* or *bas Yisroel*. And if we are not great enough to state unequivocally that such music stems from a source that is the antithesis of holiness and purity, the *tzaddikim* of yesteryear certainly were.

One Friday night, the *ba'al tefilla* for *Kaballas Shabbos* in Williamsburg's Modzitzer *Beis Midrash* was somewhat of a prankster. He sang *"Lecha Dodi"* to the tune of a mournful love song. When davening ended, the Modzitzer *Rebbe*, Rabbi Shaul Yedidya Taub זצ״ל, asked, "Where is that tune from?"

"Oh, it's just a song," came the evasive reply.

"Well, don't use it again," the *Rebbe* said firmly. "It smacks of *tumah* (impurity)."[1]

---

1. Related by the *baal tefilla.*

Some may contend: Did not the *Chassidic* masters of yesteryear adapt Russian marches and shepherds' croonings, transforming them into *Yiddishe nigunim*?

This writer does not consider himself qualified to respond to this question in a definitive way, but a few suggestions do come to mind. Surely, today's composers of Jewish song do not view themselves as being on the lofty level of those *tzaddikim,* whose finely tuned spiritual ears knew with certainty that the songs they sung were pure and uplifting. Furthermore, there is a vast difference between the tunes of old and the secular music of today, upon which much of contemporary Jewish music is based. Proof is the inspiration that does or does not result from a given *nigun.* The *nigunim* of old inspire *dveikus.* a feeling that one is in the midst of an intense spiritual experience. Hands join and a circle is formed; souls are bound up with one another and with their Creator. This writer can honestly say that the most beautiful weddings I have attended were those where the heart of the celebration was not the performer in the middle but the concentric circles of guests dancing in step to *nigunim* of old — or new *nigunim* with an old flavor.

This last point is particularly important. The last few years have seen the production of some beautiful tapes filled with soul-stirring tunes and tasteful music. To the surprise of some, these tapes were instant hits and their tunes are played and sung at many *simchos.* There is a difference, though, between the kind of dancing and singing they evoke and that which results from the music on which our discussion has focused. The gyrations which the latter inspires (on both sides of the *mechitza,* I've been told) have no place in *Yiddishkeit.* How sad that the holiness and purity of the *chupa* should give way to such blaring cacophony and unrefined stomping!

✦ Sublime Celebration

A friend of mine observed: There is virtually not a *shul* anywhere that would use any of these tunes in their Rosh Hashana or Yom Kippur *davening.* It seems that everyone senses that such singing has no place in these solemn and awesome days.

Yet, there are many who feel that they do have a place at a Jewish wedding.

Perhaps it would be worthwhile for us all to study the words of *Chazal* regarding the loftiness of the wedding celebration and the privilege of participating in it. While such a study is beyond the scope of this article, the following quote from *Maharal*[1] is certainly food for thought:

"Our Sages liken [gladdening the groom and bride] to building one of the ruins of Jerusalem, because the union of man and woman is itself considered the building of a home. As the Sages ordained [as part of the text of the Sheva Berachos], 'And He [G-d] prepared for him [Adam] — from himself, a building for eternity'; thus, man and woman together complete a building. This building is not a human building but a G-dly one. Therefore, when one gladdens a groom and bride and [in so doing, helps to] unite them, it is considered as if he built one of the ruins of Jerusalem, for surely, the building of one of these ruins is something G-dly and sacred. Ponder these thoughts and know that gladdening a groom and bride is a sublime mitzva."

As is well known, the day of the wedding is like Yom Kippur for the *chassan* and *kalla*, a day on which they fast, recite *"Al Cheit,"* attain atonement for their sins and pray that they merit to build a true Jewish home. They proceed from their Yom Kippur to stand under the *chupa* where *chassan* and *kalla* utilize this most auspicious moment in their lives to pray for themselves and others, after which they become husband and wife through the marriage ceremony. The wedding meal can be likened to the spiritual joy of Succos and Simchas Torah that follows the repentance and awe of Yom Kippur. Moreover, the wedding celebration is reflective of another simultaneous celebration.

It is told that at the wedding of one of his children, Rabbi Yehuda Leib of Slonim reflected: "I rejoice when my child is wed, and Ivan the Cossack rejoices when his child is wed. What is the difference? My joy is the joy of G-d, 'in Whose abode is this celebration.' "[2]

---

1. *Chiddushei Aggados* to *Berachos* 6a. For an extensive discussion of the loftiness of the wedding night and related subjects, one is directed to *Shehasimcha Bi'meono*, by Rabbi Nachman Yosef Wilhelm (Israel 1991).
2. From the *Zimun* which accompanies *Birkas Hamazon* during the week of *Sheva Berachos*.

It behooves us to ensure that the music and dancing at our weddings are, indeed, worthy of G-d's abode.

❧ All Year Round

Our discussion has focused on wedding music. In truth, it is relevant to any music we listen to, any time, any place. Some years ago, a suggestion was put forth that a committee be formed to assign ratings to Jewish books and tapes. A book or tape could be rated "excellent," "good," "fair," or "unacceptable." It seems that such a system is fraught with problems and unlikely to ever materialize. There is no reason, however, why parents cannot keep watch over what sort of music their children listen to. Given the importance of *negina,* such vigilance is basic to a parent's *chinuch* obligation. Of course, adults, both old and young, should be selective and exercise caution when choosing music for their own listening pleasure.

Most important, those who feel qualified to provide the religious community with music and song should give some thought to the responsibility which they have accepted upon themselves. It is in their power to help thousands of Jewish men and women, boys and girls, achieve a heightened closeness with *Hashem* and it is in their power to achieve the opposite.

The word מרקד can mean to dance[1] or to sift.[2] The *Chassidic* masters see a connection: When a Jew dances, the impurities within himself are sifted out, and what remains is a soul that exults as it renews its bond with *Hashem.*

But for this to occur, the song to which one dances must itself be pure. Only then can it achieve the lofty goal of true *negina.*

---

1. As in *Keitzad merakdin lifnei hakalldi?* (How does one dance before the bride? — *Kesubos* 16b).
2. As in *Mishna Shabbos* 7:2.

Excessive Amplifications
at *Simchos*

Rabbi Jeff Forsythe

*The "Amein" after the final beracha under the chupa … the chas-
san and kalla each sip wine … his foot comes smashing down on the
glass … and "Mazal Tov!"*

*The trumpets, the drums, the saxophones blast out the message:
"Od yishama be'orei Yehuda … The cities of Yehuda will once again
reverberate with joy." The friends of the chassan and kalla rush up
to congratulate the new couple, while the rest of the guests try to
read one another's lips — wondering why they left their earplugs
at home.*

Simchos are among the highlights of the year for the Torah community, but unfortunately, they are also the venue for uncomfortable, painful, and possibly damaging sound.

These celebrations are only part of the ever-increasing invasion of
noise in society at large. And — again — the effects are ubiquitous.

My cousin, 29 years old, told me he is experiencing loss of hearing …. A neighbor asks people, "What?" for failure to hear clearly
…. Another is under doctor's orders to always wear earplugs be-

cause everyday sounds are painful …. Another cannot sleep without a prescription sedative because the ringing in the ears is too
loud to let him rest or relax. These things really happen in our community — all due to loud amplification. All of these people are no
older than middle age.

Thirty-six million Americans have experienced significant hearing loss. About 50 million have ear damage. Of these, 10 million
have life-impacting suffering and two million are debilitated. Ear
damage might come slowly and imperceptibly; but one day, symptoms will be noticeable, and life will never be the same. The pity is
that much of it could have been prevented. It was artificially, un-
necessarily and prematurely caused due to exposure to damaging
levels of noise.

In the past, hearing losses started creeping up between the ages
of 40 and 50. Now, hearing loss in children is up due to noise. In
the 1980's, 3 percent of grade-school children had hearing dysfunc-
tion. It is up to about 13 percent for schoolchildren, and worse for
teenagers.

❧ How the Damage Impacts

People do not get used to noise. As long as the noise continues,
the negative effects on emotions, health and ability to function
do not subside. Noise is invisible, but nevertheless a serious threat
to the inner ear. Ear damage from exposure to noise is described by
audiologists as coming with "three p's: painless, progressive and
permanent." In the early 90's, scientists examined people living in
primitive conditions in Sudan and discovered that there existed
virtually no deterioration of hearing in elderly people! This tells us
how much our inner ears are assaulted by the proliferation of noise
in industrialized nations, where we constantly hear loud music,
machines (jackhammers, trains, airplanes, sirens), and traffic.

The more frequent, prolonged, loud, near or high pitched the
noise is, the more damaging. Hearing loss can come from one extremely loud sound, or repeated exposures to hazardous loud-

ness levels. Annoyance from noise can be sufficient to contribute to stress; to cardiovascular, psychological, digestive and other health damage and physiological disorders; and can cause negative impact on social behavior, learning ability and career achievement. Inner-ear damage from noise is increasing. The only hope is prevention.

Vertigo (dizziness) can come from ear damage. This can make the person feel like the room is spinning around or like objects are twirling around one another, often accompanied by a terrible nauseous feeling. The person must sit or lie down. He cannot function or walk and, if he tries to, he can fall and be seriously injured.

An illness (such as a virus or high blood pressure) can make an ear condition and its symptoms more severe, painful or intense. The worsening of the condition can possibly be irreversible. For example, (1) a virus can cause tinnitus (a disorder characterized by hearing disturbing sounds) to get louder and hearing to get worse in a damaged ear; (2) tinnitus can cause anxiety, and anxiety worsens tinnitus. If anxiety is not medically treated, this can become an ever-worsening "vicious cycle" of more tinnitus — more anxiety, etc.

❖ *The Jewish Dimension: Simcha Time*

Since the "culture" of deafeningly loud amplification became widespread, just about everybody in the Jewish community is vulnerable to suffering serious damage to the ear's structures and normal functions — especially through *simchos*, as mentioned. But this danger is not restricted to *simchos*. This can apply anywhere that there is loud amplification — for example: concerts, conventions, in restaurants, listening to music through headphones (close to the inner ear) above soft volume. *Simchos* — weddings, *vorts* (engagements), *Sheva Berachos* or *bar mitzvas* — however, are the most common events in contemporary Jewish life at which there is, almost predictably, dangerously loud amplification.

Compound this with the cumulative effects of repeated participation in *simchos* where dangerously loud music is played, pounding ears for several hours. Each time, a person's internal ear structures can become further weakened. Even if noticeable damage is not yet done, damage may be coming gradually, or susceptibility to serious damage can increase every time. If damage has been done, conditions can be made much worse with every exposure.

The musicians have vested interests in playing loudly. The youth consider loudness *"laibedik"* (lively) and are likely customers when they will make their own *chassunas*, if they are impressed with the noisy band.

Yet young people are every bit as at risk and subject to progressive harm and deterioration as anyone. No one who would be aware of the potential consequences would agree to subject himself to anything damaging, especially permanently. After all, by *halacha* standards, anyone who permits something damaging done to himself is considered to be out of his mind (*Choshen Mishpat* 421:12). People generally do not realize how harmful noise is until it is too late. Ear doctors interviewed for this writing report a constant flow of patients who complain of ear trouble after they had attended a *simcha* with loud amplification. Often their ears haven't been the same since.

Jewish practice should be determined by older people, not by the young. The Gemara (*Megilla* 31b) tells us: "If mature people say, 'Destroy,' and youth say, 'Build,' destroy and do not build, because destroying by the mature is constructive." Yielding to youth violates our *Mesora* (tradition) of being guided by the mature, wise and learned elders of each generation. When the youth say to "build" a celebration through loud music, this can literally destroy.

❧ *Dealing With the Threat*

If the Jewish community would recognize the intrusion of dangerously loud amplification as a serious matter, they would surely deal with it vigorously. After all, it is not a trite question. Some people might be prepared to simply leave a function if their ears start to hurt or ring. In fact, there are people who equip themselves with earplugs, available at any drugstore, for wearing at *simchos* to reduce sound by at least 22 decibels (the higher the decibel-reduction number, the better).

There's nothing wrong with hosts being pro-active when planning a *simcha*, and making a point of hiring musicians who will agree to lower the decibel count at their events. After all, they would do well to see to it that their guests suffer no harm at their affair. Incidentally, we should take note that a 30-piece symphony orchestra can be less threatening to the ear than a one-piece band that is electronically amplified, with its sound blasting forth from outsized speakers that can blow out one's eardrums.

In general, people — even those with excellent hearing — would be well advised to have their hearing periodically checked by an ear doctor or audiologist, especially if they frequent *simchos*, concerts, or other loud events.

The *Rama* (*Choshen Mishpat* 155:20) says that the *halacha's* safety criteria are to be determined by experts in their respective field. A *frum* ear doctor, who has experience with the difficulties of treatment and with patients' long-term suffering in noise-induced ear-damage cases, determined that for the sound-volume level to be safe, people in conversation ten feet apart should be able to speak in a normal tone and hear every word clearly *and* no one present at the function should have any pain or discomfort. Obviously, then, amplification should be carefully monitored at all functions — social and organizational.

Rabbi Dovid Feinstein שליט״א said that strong effort should be put into prevailing upon musicians, caterers and *baalei simcha* (hosts) to stop loudness that is at damaging levels. If all the individuals who are bothered by noise — or who recognize its dangers — would speak up, effective methods of reducing harmful noise would be possible.

It is a constant obligation to save others from harm and to warn about causes of damage. Indeed, the *Shulchan Aruch* assures us: "All who are cautious in all of these things [and avoids causing injury or damage to others] will receive wonderful blessings from Heaven" (*Choshen Mishpat* 427:10).

Maintaining Shalom Bayis

❦ A Woman of Valor

❦ *Ona'as Devarim*: The Great Threat to *Shalom Bayis*

❦ Husbands, Wives and Children

❦ It Begins With Saying "Hello"

❦ Marriages Are Made in Heaven ... People Arrange to Destroy Them

❦ Disagreement and Harmonious Growth

❦ "I'm Sorry": *Teshuva* Begins at Home

Klal Yisroel is blessed with Gedolim who teach us by word and example how to imbue every aspect of our lives with Torah values, as well as ways to honor interpersonal sensitivities. How fortunate we are that leading thinkers and mentors have instructed us – directly and through their disciples – in the ways in which a Jewish home can become a Bayis Ne'eman BeYisroel.

A WOMAN OF VALOR

THE MASTER BUILDER OF THE JEWISH HOME

RABBI SHLOMO WOLBE זצ״ל
BASED ON "A LETTER TO A KALLA" FIRST PUBLISHED IN 1976
THIS ARTICLE WAS PREPARED FOR PUBLICATION BY *PNUEL PERI*

❧ *Your Successful Choice*

My dear *kalla*, you have chosen your *chassan*, and now you are both anticipating your wedding day, when together you will begin a life of true happiness. It is natural, however, for this anticipation to be mixed with anxiety over the unknown future. Though your *chassan* has indeed found favor in your eyes, only the future will bear out whether you have chosen aptly. Only a life of partnership in your home, day by day will reveal the degree of happiness that your chassan is capable of providing you. Know, however, that *you* have the key role in preparing the foundation of your home. To a great extent, the *success* of your marriage depends upon *your* preparation and attitude.

Shlomo Hamelech said: "The wisdom of women builds her home, but folly plucks it down with her hands" (*Mishlei* 14,1). There is a particular wisdom involved in building a home. Just as an architect knows how to sketch building plans, which materials to use, and how deep to lay foundations, she too possesses "architectural" wisdom with which to construct the life of the couple after the wedding. Such wisdom was given specifically to the woman! Although the architect learns from books and from teachers, and the woman's wisdom has not been transcribed — for her wisdom is not of technology but of the heart — it is wisdom nonetheless and worthy of an attempt at defining its principles.

Commenting on *Mishlei*, the Vilna *Gaon* wrote that building a home is a construction of permanence. A marriage is not for a fleeting period, Heaven forbid, but is, with the help of *Hashem*, a *binyan adei ad*, an eternal structure. The "wisdom of women" aspires, essentially, to construct a stable, firm building.

Stability? The two of you are human beings, not angels; each possesses varying dispositions and fleeting moods. It is difficult enough for each, individually, to be stable in his actions and thoughts. Now the two of you must live *together*, and your differing needs and moods will inevitably clash. Is there not enough volatile material concealed within every home that agitates, irritates and courts despair until it could explode, Heaven forbid?

✦ A Heavenly Union

The first principle in the "wisdom of women," the wisdom of building a home, is the clear, unqualified fact that the moment that the china plate is broken during the "*tennaim*," it is confirmed that this is a union that was decreed in Heaven ("The daughter of so-and-so to so-and-so!") forty days before the embryo's formation, as the Midrash relates:

"Rabbi Pinchas said in the name of Rabbi Ivo: 'In the Torah, in the Prophets and in the Writings we find that a man's partner comes only from *Hashem*. Where in the Torah? As it is written: 'And Lavan and Besuail answered and said, 'The matter comes from *Hashem*' (*Bereishis* 24,50) …. There are those who travel to their partners and those whose partners travel to them. Yitzchak's partner came to him …. Yaakov went to his partner …" (*Bereishis Rabba, Parashas Vayetzei*).

The members of practically every union see the *hashgacha g'luya* — the revealed, careful guidance of *Hashem* — in their finding each other and then entering the covenant of marriage. We, who believe in *Hashem*, in His powerfully detailed involvement in our lives, know and trust that a man and a woman come from a single spiritual root and are matched, one to the other, from the very onset of their creation. As a result, we *are* capable of achieving mutual understanding and true peace in marriage.

❧ *First: Patience and Understanding*

Every couple, of course, must undergo a period of adjustment. After all, each party comes from a different home and from varying surroundings, and for all of the harmony in the depths of their souls, they possess differing, even opposing strengths and dispositions. How, then, do they achieve harmony?

First and foremost, there must be *patience*. When inconsonant tendencies and outlooks begin to surface — almost immediately after the wedding! — do not fear that your world has fallen apart. Be assured that it is possible to overcome the difficulties of adjustment and attain equilibrium.

"A woman recognizes guests more so than a man" (*Berachos* 10b), meaning that a woman is graced with an instinctive understanding of a man's disposition and strengths. She is specially suited, therefore, to thoroughly understand her marriage partner, and such genuine understanding removes many stumbling blocks.

For example, you may discover that your husband is not very orderly. This might shock you and even irritate you. After you've calmed down and become rational, you might consider: "Why is he so disorganized with his possessions and his clothing?" Insight should not be slow in coming. You have noted that he is immersed in learning and abstract thinking to a degree well beyond the norm and simply fails to take note of where he left his watch or dropped his clothing. You recall that he has been living in a dormitory for close to ten years, and when you inquire a bit about dorm life, you will come to see to what degree this lifestyle has made your husband accustomed to disorder; yeshiva dormitory life is a far cry from dormitory life in a Bais Yaakov. Building on this premise, you will find a way to get your husband accustomed to orderliness — drawing, of course, on an abundance of patience and good will.

There are also certain things that irritate a woman to a greater degree, such as when her husband shows indifference toward her. Sometimes, a husband fails to honor his wife's concerns, not noticing what she is wearing, whether her dress is blue or green; not taking the slightest interest in what he has eaten for lunch, though she had invested much effort in her cooking. As revelations of such indifference mount, one after the next, you may feel shattered and begin to think: "Perhaps I have chosen unwisely!" Prior to the wedding, you had found such favor in his eyes, and he had shown so much interest in you. It had never occurred to you that he could become so indifferent, a thought which could now bring you to despair.

However, there is no need to despair. The "*wisdom* of women builds her home," so accordingly, you will tell yourself that for some time your husband has lived exclusively among males and grown accustomed to dormitory life. He has been served food and has eaten well, with nobody demanding that he say "Thank you." Over the years, when his visits home to his parents were too short and far between, all of the etiquette of the home has become foreign. You must, therefore, gradually inculcate your partner with the awareness that he is not living in a "new dormitory" but in a home, *his* home, and that a home demands consideration!

❧ *Avoiding Anger*

The first step in building a home is mutual understanding. And then what? There is no doubt that in every home, and in dealing with every husband, there are factors that can irritate a woman.

The more common reaction is to become angry, which can express itself in shouting and quarreling or in silence and introversion. The first response is bad enough, for it can lead to fighting, even though in the end the husband at least may learn what is angering his wife. This is in contrast to the second sort of anger, wherein the woman, withdrawn, never reveals what has triggered her ill feeling. In the end, however, both types of anger are lethal, and it is worth bearing this in mind before you enter the *chupa*, *b'sha'a tova u'mutzlachas* (at an auspicious time). Be assured that the paths of the "wisdom of women" are not paved with anger. Anger, in any form, does not help build a home.

So what should you do when your husband irritates you? Wisdom would dictate that you speak to him on the matter, that you engage him, expressly and directly, in an issue-centered discussion and explain to him your problem with his particular habit or practice; then help him accept the conclusion that he has acted inappropriately. In the process, he may explain why he behaves as he does. If this annoying habit continues to recur, bring it up again. If you come to see that the issue stems from a long-rooted habit, the two of you should explore ways to wean him from it. Obviously, it is impossible to uproot lifelong habits in the course of a single week. This requires patience on your part and good will on his. "Anger rests in the breast of fools" (*Kohelles* 7,9). It certainly has no place in the "wisdom of women."

Beyond the habits of bachelorhood, you are bound to discover some of your husband's characteristic tendencies that are inconsistent with the ideal picture that you had formed of him. You may attempt to strive to change these, with his benefit in mind, for in your view, if he could just correct this one point, he'd be perfect. For example, he is very social and popular, and therefore does not maintain what you would consider an appropriate distance between himself and younger *bachurim*. Or he is a thinker, and while something is on his mind, he is simply incapable of conducting light conversation. Bear in mind, however, that every attempt to change his characteristics will doubtless fail, resulting in your disappointment and his bitterness. In the final analysis, just as no two people are identical, men in general are different from women. Knowing how to make peace with perceived imperfections is also part of the "wisdom of women." It should also be stressed that frequent discussion — especially during the first year of marriage — can help promote compatibility and closeness. Make a practice of discussing problems as they arise, and try finding, *together*, a design for improvement.

❧ Weathering Crisis and Stress

Our era is different from the one that preceded the Second World War. In the past, people were more capable of struggling with problems and striving to improve. Today, most young people find it difficult to withstand the slightest stress; if any formidable problem arises, they require a psychologist and even sedatives. Generally speaking, young people today are not accustomed to asserting control over themselves and overcoming challenges. One should accept that there is no home without problems, be they internal forces (involving personal adjustment) or external ones (insufficient income, etc.).

Young married people in general are simply unaccustomed to tolerating stress, and may suddenly find themselves in a whirlwind of difficulties, although they had imagined that their homes would serve as a safe harbor from problems. What should such young people do or think? How can they run their home?

Sadna d'ara chad hu, human nature is much the same the world over, and *b'nei Torah* and *b'nos* Bais Yaakov will also occasionally find themselves helpless when crisis strikes. This is a weakness that has affected our entire generation. Still, we are hopeful that a couple strengthened with faith and Torah is more apt than others to succeed in overcoming problems and crises together. After all, as stated, the foundation of a Jewish home rests on the conviction that the two are members of a union formed by He "Who created joy and gladness, groom and bride, mirth, glad song, pleasure, delight, love, brotherhood, peace and companionship." He created all of these not only for the seven days of the wedding feast, but for the length of your entire lives!

Further, the *Talmud Yerushalmi* states that "it is impossible for a man [to live] without a woman, impossible for a woman [to live] without a man, and impossible for the two of them [to exist] without the *Shechina*" (*Berachos*, Ch. 9). Coupled with the knowledge of the "impossibility of one without the other" is the awareness of the *Shechina's* presence between them, of incalculable heavenly assistance throughout their life together.

If you should ask, my dear *kalla*: "How am I capable of feeling the presence of the *Shechina* and enlisting *Hashem's* aid?" I would answer that even now, before the wedding, you should accustom yourself to *daven*, both in the morning and the evening, that *Hashem* grant the two of you success in establishing your home in accordance with His will. During *Shemoneh Esrei*, within the blessing *Shome'a Tefilla* (following the words "and from before You, our King, do not turn us away empty"), and, also, after lighting candles on *Erev Shabbos*, you should regularly pray: "Please enhance our home so that peace and harmony prevail between my husband and me." Similarly, in every situation, pray for *siyata d'Shamaya*, for heavenly aid. Also, I would suggest that you both include, within your *Shemoneh Esrei*, *tefillos* for your home and, later, G-d willing, for your children. You may be certain that there is no prayer which goes unheard and no *tefilla* without blessings flowing in its wake.

❧ Guarding Femininity

Many women seek employment to help cover a substantial portion of the family's expenses — particularly those women who have merited marrying *b'nei Torah* who will continue their studies after the wedding. A woman who holds a highly regarded position in her profession, who has extensive Torah knowledge, or whose area of employment is intellectually challenging and fulfilling, may find it difficult to devote sufficient time and effort to housekeeping and managing her home. Moreover, her taxing workload, both in and outside the home, may lead her to over-look a matter of great importance that should not be ignored. The *Midrash*, commenting on the verse from *Eishes Chayil*: "Her hands she stretches out to the distaff, and her palms support the spindle" (*Mishlei* 31,19), says that this refers to "Yael, who did not kill [Sisra] with a martial weapon but, rather, with a stake and the strength of her bare hands. Why did she not kill him with a weapon? So as to honor the verse: 'A woman should not don a man's clothing, nor should a man wear the garment of a woman; for all who do these things are an abomination to *Hashem'*" (*Mishlei Rabba 31*). Because Yael was performing a manly task — namely, killing an enemy — she was careful not to use masculine tools.

This is a basic principle in how women should conduct them-selves: Even when their social or professional status is equal to that of men, they must assiduously use the "tools" associated with women, and not resort to those usually employed by men [e.g. as-sertiveness in expression and action]. Sometimes this is not easy. Ever increasingly, a woman in the workplace is drawn toward manly practices, stifling her feminine nature. When she brings this mode of conduct home, her husband is stunned and does not know how to react; this can corrode the natural warmth between husband and wife. In fact, this is one of the causes for the deterioration of harmony in the contemporary family.

Once again, "The wisdom of women builds her home." Women naturally possess much wisdom, and they must draw on it to build a home. One aspect of this wisdom that the modern woman in par-ticular must exercise is the guarding of her femininity, even while her hands "support the spindle."

ONA'AS DEVARIM:
THE GREAT THREAT TO SHALOM BAYIS

RABBI MATIS BLUM

The material in this article is drawn from a lecture delivered by
Rabbi Avraham Hakohein Pam זצ"ל *to bnei Torah. Although the*
ideas appear to be addressed specifically to men, they apply equally
to women. Many of these insights have been published in Hebrew
in Rabbi Pam's sefer, Atara LaMelech.

"הוי עלוב ואהוב לכל איש. ולאנשי ביתך יותר מכלי" (מס' דרך ארץ זוטא
פ"ג כדי גירסת הגר"א)

Our Rabbis prescribe that a person should be humble, patient
and beloved to all people, but especially to his family members — to his wife and children. Unfortunately, in some situations,
it is these people — the ones closest to him — who are neglected
and not treated properly. While a person may have a wonderful
reputation in the community for his accomplishments and acts of
chessed, his own family members may view him from an entirely
different perspective — one that is not nearly as favorable.

In the recent past there has been a great deal of emphasis on avoiding *lashon hara*, and the devastating effect that it can have on people's lives. However, I feel that there is another area of speech that has not been stressed enough, which is equally harmful and which can undermine the very foundation of family life. It is also a prohibition explicitly mentioned in the Torah — *Ona'as devarim*. The Torah commands, "*V'lo sonu ish es amiso* (*Vayikra* 25, 17) — You shall not cause pain to your fellow man."

The *Chinuch* (*Mitzva* 338) explains:

"שלא יאמר לישראל דברים שיכאיבוהו ויצערוהו ואין בו כח להעזר מהם"

We are prohibited to utter words that hurt and cause pain especially when the subject is helpless to protect himself. This is true even when dealing with strangers. How much more so when dealing with one's own spouse and family members.

Chazal (quoted in the *Chinuch, Mitzva* 65) note: בן קובל לאביו אשה לבעלה וכו' — When a child is hurt, he runs to his father for protection and comfort. When a woman is offended, she turns to her husband for solace and compassion. When the pain comes *from* her spouse, however, she has no place to go for help and understanding. The hurt is more intense because it comes from the one she loves and trusts most, and who is supposed to love her. By causing his wife pain, the husband is violating the basic contract of the marriage — the *kesuba* — in which he accepts the responsibility to honor and take care of his wife in the manner in which a Jewish husband is expected to treat her.

Harsh words — words spoken in anger or just carelessly without considering what the effect will be on one's spouse — can cause deep wounds. The pain that is inflicted lingers and festers until the foundations of the marriage begin to erode to the point in which there is abuse, and this can eventually lead to a *get*.

❖ Care Before Marriage

When a young man and woman are seeing each other for *shidduchim* purposes, they put a great deal of thought into *what* they say to each other, and *how* they say it. After each date, they analyze the conversations and evaluate whether they spoke properly or not, and whether or not it will affect the *shidduch*. After marriage, however, people talk and say things without giving a thought as to how it will affect their spouse — whether it will impact on their *shalom bayis*. People would be well advised to be as careful with their words after marriage as they were when they were dating. If one is in doubt about whether or not to say something, he should ask himself, "Would I have said this while I was dating her?"

When speaking to a group about *shalom bayis*, I presented the following anecdote: When a husband and wife sat down to breakfast one fine morning, the wife remarked, "I woke up this morning at 6 o'clock and I feel as though I've already put in a day's work."

The husband replied, "You woke up at 6 o'clock? When I left for *shul* at 7 o'clock you were still sleeping!"

"So what? So you're calling me a liar?!"

"I didn't say that!"

"But you implied it!"

"You're always distorting my words. You turn them around. I can't talk to you!"

"*I'm* distorting *your* words! *You* can't talk to *me*?!"

And so the conversation continued. The breakfast lost its taste. The husband left without saying "good-bye," and the wife had a miserable day.

Fortunately, this scenario didn't actually play out as described; but it could very well have happened. The husband, however, had enough sense not to say anything. When he heard his wife say that she woke up at 6 o'clock and felt as though she had done a day's work, he didn't feel that he had to comment on this. Had he responded, the original story would likely have been the script.

It is not necessary to have the last word. Problems develop when each side wants to have the last word and win the argument. Nobody wins arguments — they merely cause tensions to escalate. Restraint in speech is the basis for *shalom bayis*.

❦ Avoiding Labels and Names

An important part of *shalom bayis* as well as *chinuch* is to know how to express oneself in the event that one is upset with his spouse or children.

The *Chazon Ish* זצ"ל once pointed out to a person who used the expression, "It's a lie," that it would have been more appropriate to say, "It's not the truth." Although the two expressions seem to be very similar, nevertheless, to a sensitive person there is a great difference — the same as the distinction between *"temei'a* — defiled" and *"lo tehora* — not pure."

Even worse than exclaiming, "It's a lie!" however, is to say, "You are a liar!" for in the latter situation he is attacking the essence of the person. Just as *Chazal* (*Bava Metzia* 33) distinguish between a *roveitz* ("who is crouching") and a *ravtzan* (an animal that is constantly crouching, so that he is described as a "croucher"), so too, a *shakran* (liar) implies that falsehood and lies are part of the person's very nature. Calling someone a liar is an insult that goes to the core of his identity.

I once heard a mother telling her 3-year-old child, "You're a bad boy!" The child began crying uncontrollably, and only with great difficulty was the mother able to calm him down. Had the mother simply said, "Stop that! What you are doing is very bad!" the child would not have taken the insult so much to heart. But by using an insulting label, the child felt worthless and his feelings were greatly hurt. If parents use derogatory names when they become angry at their children, they are doing them great harm. Such verbal abuse can cause feelings of inferiority in the children and can have a long-term deleterious effect on them. The same is true in regard to marriage: When one spouse becomes angry at the other and hurls insulting epithets at him or her, it can undermine the foundations of their *shalom bayis*.

Frequently, long after the reasons for the quarrel are forgotten, the unkind names that one spouse called the other are remembered, and it is very difficult to undo the harm that was caused.

Shlomo Hamelech wrote in *Mishlei* (12, 18): "There are some whose speech is [as harmful] as the piercing of a sword, but the tongue of the wise heals."

✦ Complaining

An important component of *shalom bayis* is to keep things in proper perspective and to realize that many things that people complain about come from the greatest *berachos* that *Hashem* bestows upon them.

When *Bnei Yisroel* complained about the *mon* (manna) in the wilderness, the Torah proceeded to describe its wonderful qualities. And *Rashi* (*Bamidbar* 11,7) notes that the verse wishes to teach us an important lesson: "Behold, you who come into the world, what My children are complaining about. Yet the *mon* is so valued."

A simple application of this: The husband comes home from work and finds the house in complete disarray — toys are strewn about, shoes are scattered all over, the children are running wild, and supper is not ready. The husband complains to his wife about her lack of housekeeping abilities and uses unpleasant terms to describe his feelings.

At that point the words of the heavenly voice ring out, "Behold, you who come into the world, what are My children complaining about!?" How many people pray and yearn for normal healthy children who will be able to run and play and make a mess in the house! How many people wish that they had a wife to come home to!

(In the *Baruch She'amar* prayer we say, ״ברוך מרחם על הארץ ברוך מרחם על הבריות״ — "Blessed is the One Who has compassion on the earth. Blessed is the One Who has compassion on the creatures." Some explain this in a humorous vein: There are some people who have compassion on the earth — they are more concerned that the floor be spotless, that it constantly be swept, and that toys be put away. There are others who are more concerned about the family members and "have compassion on the creatures." If the children are healthy and happy — even if they make a mess — this is their greatest joy, and they thank *Hashem* for this blessing constantly.)

Before complaining, one would be well advised to think about the underlying source of the complaint and determine whether he should in actuality be eternally grateful for the situation — a caring wife and healthy, active children.

❧ A Sensitive Relationship

The relationship between a husband and wife is a very sensitive one and can easily be upset. We can observe this from the fact that *Hashem* found it necessary to change the words of Sarah — when relating them to Avraham — from *"Va'adoni zakein"* ("and my master is old") to *"Va'ani zakanti"* ("and I have become old"). Why was it necessary to do this? Sarah had merely made her comment privately. Additionally, saying that Avraham was old was not a derogatory statement. To the contrary, Avraham was the one who had beseeched *Hashem* to make him look old (*Bava Metzia* 87a). If so, why did *Hashem* deem it necessary to modify Sarah's words?

Apparently, the relationship between a man and his wife is so delicate, that the same words that would be considered innocuous — or even complimentary — if said by an outsider, could be misconstrued and thought to be insulting if said by a spouse.

Chazal (*Bava Metzia* 59b) tell us that a man must be very careful not to cause pain to his wife because her tears come easily, and therefore *ona'asa kerova*. *Rashi* explains that a husband must be very careful not to cause pain to his wife with insulting words, because punishment for his harsh words is swift in coming.

The *Beis Yoseif* relates in the *sefer, Maggid Meisharim* (*Parshas Va'eira*), that the *Maggid* (the angel who would learn with him and admonish him) revealed to him the lofty nature of his wife's soul. Now, we can be certain that the *Beis Yoseif* conformed to the words of *Chazal* (*Bava Metzia* 59) that a man should always be careful to properly honor his wife, and that he should place her honor before his own. Nevertheless, the *Maggid* felt it imperative to inspire him to honor her even more by revealing the ethereal nature of her *neshama* (soul).

Unfortunately, we do not have *maggidim* to reveal to us the sublime nature of our spouses' souls. Most likely, however, it will become known to us in *Olam Haba* (the World to Come), and if we do not respect them properly and cause them pain while they live with us, the shame that we will experience will be unbearable.

✦ The Constant Challenge

Shalom bayis needs constant strengthening and vigilance. We find that when the angels came to inform Avraham and Sarah that they would have a child, they asked, "Where is Sarah, your wife?" (*Bereishis* 18, 9). *Rashi* comments: The angels knew where our Matriarch, Sarah, was. Rather, [they asked the question] to point out her great modesty to Avraham [that she was in the tent] in order to make her more beloved to him.

What is fascinating is that the couple involved — Avraham and Sarah — were elderly people who had lived together in harmony for many decades. But in spite of all this, the angels deemed it worthwhile to point out Sarah's special qualities so as to make her even more beloved to Avraham.

Maintaining *shalom bayis* in the most fragile of relationships is the great challenge that all married people face. One must continuously work on improving it, and appreciating and honoring the unique qualities of his spouse, and the many blessings that *Hashem* has bestowed upon him. One must be constantly vigilant to avoid harsh, critical, insulting or sarcastic comments to one's spouse, and not insist on getting the last word in. By following this formula, one can be assured of making his home into a suitable place for the *Shechina* (Divine Presence), where he will be able to raise holy and emotionally healthy children who will be a source of pride to *Klal Yisroel*.

HUSBANDS, WIVES AND CHILDREN

RAV CHAIM PINCHAS SCHEINBERG

*Based on an address to a gathering of young married yeshiva men by Rabbi Chaim Pinchas Scheinberg שליט״א, Rosh Hayeshiva of Yeshiva Torah Ore in Jerusalem, and a senior member of the Moetzes Gedolei Hatorah (Council of Torah Sages). This article was prepared for publication by **Rabbi Shlomo Furst**.*

❧ *What Goes Wrong in Contemporary Families?*

I am frequently asked to help people deal with problems of *shalom bayis.* Tensions between husbands and wives are very common throughout modern society, even within our religious families. If unchecked, a sequence of events begins that can unfortunately result in divorce.

I am not always able to determine the true initial cause of the problem. When I question the couple, however, the mutual answer that they usually give is incompatibility and lack of communication. I ask them what happened to break up their relationship; the couple was not always estranged. Originally, the couple had felt that they were compatible and there was communication between them. The many hours that they spent dating must have been filled with conversation. During the course of their courtship, they must have compared their views about life and their expectations regarding marriage.

Weeks, perhaps months were spent evaluating all the possibilities of a Torah life together. There must have been broad agreement about a variety of important life issues for them to both agree to marry each other. They looked at the situation from all angles until they finally decided that, in fact, this was the person whom they wanted to be their mate — their partner for life.

After such efforts and careful consideration, what happened to change everything? Why did their marriage bring them further apart rather than closer together?

❧ Courtship and Marriage: A Study in Contrasts

The usual answer — which I believe to be a true one — is that it is easy for a couple to enjoy casual meetings, spending a pleasant evening talking about topics that they enjoy. After the date, they return to their homes to lead their separate lives.

By contrast, life together as husband and wife can result in a clash of personalities. Everyone has his or her particular pattern of behavior and way of thinking, and this can lead, at least temporally, to disharmony. When faced with the many challenges of life, spouses will not, at first, always agree with each other because, until their marriage, they were two separate individuals. Getting the two different personalities to merge and to live together in harmony is the essence of marriage. Married life consists of many growth experiences — sometimes, difficult situations — which are really opportunities for the new couple to adjust to each other; to compromise and learn to live together.

Marriage is not a matter of spending an hour or two together.

When dating, both the man and the woman seek to find favor in the eyes of the other person. They will exert themselves, to the limit, to make as nice a showing as possible. They will each act graciously, hoping to be seen as the perfect choice. People, however, cannot keep up a show all the time; yes, it is possible for an hour or two, but marriage is a lifetime experience.

❧ The Crux of the Matter: Being Cautious and Caring

The crux of the matter, which is in fact the solution to many of our problems, lies in the amount of interest and motivation we devote to being cautious and caring enough to remain in control of ourselves to maintain our best behavior when trouble threatens. Marriage challenges us to strive and, therefore, rise above natural, unthinking responses. Disagreements and difficulties will always arise, but the test — and the success of our efforts — is determined by how we react.

The same rule applies to our children. Some children behave better than others, some worse. Nonetheless, the father and mother must take them in stride. Patiently, parents must raise and educate their offspring in a gentle, kindhearted way.

Parents try to correct areas of stress and difficulty with their children as much as possible. Whatever they can do will be done, for parents will persevere, and not give up on their child. As difficult as the child may be, parents still nurture hopes for their child. Unfortunately, husband and wife do not always feel that way about their marriage. Sometimes they do give up. They may feel that it does not pay to go on together. The opposite, however, is true, for divorce is not a solution. In fact, it creates more problems. There are new issues of child custody, visitation and alimony ... and loneliness. In many cases, the attitude that spouses are expendable is not *daas Torah*.

Chazal teach us that one's wife is equivalent to the husband's own body — "*ishto ke'gufo*." The husband and wife form a complete unit. The *Zohar HaKadosh* refers to the woman as *"plag guf "* — that is, half of the person. Until marriage, there is separation — one physical half here, the other physical half there.

Forging a bond of love, respect, and kindness between a man and wife calls for special effort because there was no previous natural bond between them. Living together, a joyful fusion of man and wife — and consequently, providing a conducive atmosphere for raising children — is the great challenge that *Hakadosh Baruch Hu* expects us to live up to.

❦ *Where Chessed Begins*

The Gemora (*Sota* 14a) teaches us that the Torah begins with chessed and ends with *chessed*. The Torah starts with an act of kindness — for, after the sin of *Adam Harishon*, *Hakadosh Baruch Hu* prepared special garments for Adam and Chava. Furthermore, the act of kindness was complete in its every aspect, for the *passuk* in *Bereishis* 3,21 states that *Hashem* even dressed them.

The *chachmei hamussar* (Torah ethicists), however, ask: Was this act the true beginning of *chessed*? The very creation of *Adam Harishon* in was an unmatched act of perfect kindness!

Hakadash Baruch Hu created *Adam Harishon* with His Divinely fashioned *guf* (body) and *neshama* united and vibrant in *Gan Eden*. Our highest spiritual aspiration is for our *neshamos* to reside there. Obviously, the creation of *Adam Harishon* was an act of kindness. Why does the *Gemora* overlook this as the first instance of *Hashem*'s kindness to man, and instead choose to cite the making of clothes and dressing *Adam Harishon* as *Hashem*'s first act of kindness?

The answer that is given is that to do *chessed* with *Adam Harishon* would be very easy — in fact, effortless. Anyone would feel honored — and it would be our greatest pleasure — if, for example, one were able to do *chessed* for the *Chofetz Chaim* ל״צז. We would vie with one another to be of some service to such a great and blessed individual, and we would feel no hardship or difficulty in doing it. So much more so for *Adam Harishon*, who was far holier and infinitely close to perfection. There is then nothing exceptional in the act it-self, because recognizing the greatness of the recipient automati-cally spurs us on to perform acts of kindness toward him.

By contrast, what would common sense tell us about *Adam Harishon* after his sin? Through his act, he brought death and de-struction to the world. We would be convinced that such an in-dividual is not deserving of our *chessed*. What had been the easi-est, most desirable thing to do is now difficult, even impossible to imagine. Therefore, precisely after the sin is when the Torah reveals to us what true *chessed* is. Not *chessed* defined by common sense and intellect, but *chessed* based on Torah.

Thus, when *Chazal* say that the Torah begins with *chessed*, it re-fers to kindness that *Hashem* did with Adam and Chava after their sin. Obviously, *Hashem* infinitely exceeds our mortal limitations of mind and heart. We do see, however, that *Adam Harishon* acted to-ward Chava after the sin in a special way, and we can certainly relate to that.

❦ Chava After the Sin — "Mother of All Life"?

*A*dam Harishon named Chava — *"Eim Kol Chai,* The Mother of All Life" — only after the sin. Logic would say to name her "the mother of all death"! Eating from the *Eitz Hadaas* (The Tree of Knowledge) brought death to the world. How does the name *Eim Kol Chai* befit Chava after her sin?

In spite of what had happened, Adam recognized Chava's great-ness and potential, especially her potential for life. Before the sin, no name was appropriate. A name must reflect the essence of its bearer. Before the sin, words could not truly depict the full extent of what Chava was. After the sin, the tragedy and its consequences did not numb Adam. It is *chessed* to forgive and move on. He did not lose himself. Life could and would continue. Chava would help him bring life to the world.

Similarly, the *chessed* of the Torah begins only after Adam's sin, to teach us that *Hashem* did not forsake Adam even when he disobeyed His command. His *Tzellem Elokim* was not destroyed, and so Adam was still able to see Chava's greatness — even after her mistake. Accordingly, Adam called her "The Mother of All Life" because this was her true essence and potential. She did bring death, but bearing in mind the significance of the *Tzellem Elokim* within her allowed Adam to deal kindly with her.

The Torah tells us all of this to let us know that we, too, must have compassion, regardless of our emotions or our logical justification to act harshly. This is especially important in our relationships with our spouses and our children.

❦ *Rising Above Narrow Perspectives*

Many of our family problems would be solved if we would give thought to the basic goodness of those people who are closest to us. *Shalom bayis* problems are a result of narrowness of spirit. The time for *chessed*, real *chessed*, is when our spouses need our forgiveness and our hearts … hearts that are willing to look beyond the mistakes and frustrations of daily life and see the spouse's true virtues and greatness; hearts that are big enough to forgive.

This is especially important now, for our current lifestyle — even amid our bounty of luxuries — still contains many tensions and pressures. Our grandparents did not enjoy the many conveniences of today's world. There were no refrigerators or canned foods in their days. Meals had to be prepared from scratch. It was hard work, and there was poverty.

Nonetheless, they led a harmonious life. Luxuries do not guarantee *menuchas hanefesh* — tranquility and peace of mind. Neither does poverty decree a sad life. Our attitude is the controlling factor, and not the material benefits. Work does not weaken and break a person, but pressures and tension do. Together, the husband and wife can plan and seek out ways to reduce the pressure within the home. They will have more *menuchas hanefesh* and at the same time, as a team, deal more effectively with their concerns.

We have been blessed with spiritual greatness, so we must not lose our tempers and allow our emotions to rule over us. We have to live up to the *Tzellem Elokim* within us, which means to think beyond the normal response, and rise above the moment's disappointment. So many times petty considerations taint our perceptions. In turn, this can lead to frustrations that only worsen the situation.

We must remember that our spouses — just like ourselves — have *Tzellem Elokim* within them. This should lift our thoughts above the daily difficulties of married life. In addition, since we possess an element of *Tzellem Elokim*, we have infinite potential to overcome any situation, and maintain patience with our spouses and understand them and their needs.

❖ Discussions: Later ... On the Same Day

The *chessed* of the Torah begins when there is a problem. When everything is fine, doing *chessed* is simple. Real *chessed* starts when something did go wrong — during times of stress and trouble — for this is the exact moment when we are tested and are expected to live up to our potential. In the midst of our disappointments and frustrations, we must all strive, for the sake of *shalom bayis*, to remain gracious and understanding — to summon forth the spiritual greatness within us. This is the key to *shalom bayis*. Then, later, the matter can be discussed without tension and frustration. Having the patience to wait is greatness ... and *chessed*. It will solve many of the problems that crop up in the home.

In general, our concerns should be discussed the same day. If left until the next day, the problem will fester with additional frustrations. Bottled-up emotions will inevitably spill over into outbursts, which are counterproductive. Then, in the chaotic aftermath, the couple must seek to renew their mutual trust and respect. Friendly behavior builds respect, while the opposite has terrible repercussions. It is always best to clear up the issue — calmly and with consideration — on the same day. Look for the first chance to talk over the problem, preferably, if possible, before retiring.

The husband and wife should be comfortable discussing their mutual and personal problems. In this way, they both feel that they are a part of each other's lives. This builds self-esteem and mutual respect, for it is an acknowledgment that the spouse's feelings and opinions are valid and useful. When we express our concerns, we feel relieved and are encouraged. Husband and wife are meant to be partners in marriage and best of friends in life.

❊ Consultation and Seeking Advice

Consulting a third party can be essential in making major decisions, helping keep families together. In general we often need to rely on other people to cope properly with our problems. We must have a positive outlet for our frustrations in life. Feelings can become bottled up if we do not share difficulties with someone we can trust. It is important to have a good friend, a confidant with whom to share what is bothering us. We will then be equipped to cope positively with life's difficulties, and depression will not creep into our lives. Disappointments will not sour into ill feelings.

Unless there is an issue of mental health, most problems in *shalom bayis* can be resolved. Normal, sound and sensible individuals can, with proper guidance, solve their family difficulties — provided that the problems and their frustrations have not become too unbearable. This is when depression can occur. Their relationship weakens and communication breaks down. Long before the marriage gets out of control, couples need to seek sound advice. This advice must be based on the Torah's teachings and principles, bearing in mind that the Torah has a solution for all situations.

When we compare our relationships with our spouses to our relationships with our children, we see that there is often a different standard of behavior. Parents are naturally much more patient and understanding with their offspring. They will make great sacrifices for their children. Many parents come to me for advice about how they can save their child. Parents do not throw their children away. There is no option of divorce — a parent cannot separate from his or her child. Therefore, parents look for advice to improve the situation.

Many times, I ask spouses why, when it comes to doing *chessed* with other people, we are quick to help. We seem to have so much sympathy and compassion for strangers. *Klal Yisroel* is famous for its excellence in helping those who are poor, sick and helpless. Our great forefather Avraham *Avinu* excelled in this *midda*, and bestowed it on his offspring. We all try to emulate his great example, but unfortunately, we do not work as hard on it at home as we do in the public domain.

What seems to be such a burden at home is a pleasure in public. We must work faithfully to remove all barriers that hinder us from doing *chessed* in our homes. As difficult as it may be, the home is not a place for misbehavior or cruelty. Fear is destructive to our relationships, especially with children, for they look to their parents for love and security.

Our children require sympathy and understanding, patience and love. Fear will only cause emotional scars and psychological complexes — sometimes for life. Our moods and reactions — sadness, anger and dissatisfaction — cause unwanted negative influences in our families. We can win over our spouses and children — gain their respect and cooperation — just by being gracious to them.

❦ Confronting Problems With Joy

We need to keep our senses and see situations clearly. Everyone has problems. Normal people cope, and in the end are successful. We can have *simchas hachaim* in spite of our problems. If we persist and maintain a good attitude, knowing that there are solutions, we will not aggravate the difficulties. This is greatness. Small-mindedness, however, makes us shortsighted. We do not see clearly and we can lose hope.

True, many times a situation may call for greatness, for there may be a very severe problem in the home, but that is when the *chessed* of the Torah begins. When our logic says *No*, the Torah says *Yes*. Yes, this person — my wife, my husband, my child — needs my *chessed*, my compassion, my smile. We have the spiritual capacity within us to overcome the moment's tragedy. We can rise above it and *Hashem* will help us. We were created *bTzellem Elokim*, and it remains within us, and so we can transcend difficult conditions.

This excellence — the splendor of the Divine Presence within us — obligates us even in the face of the worst problems, to know and believe that any problem can be solved in a good way. Through their sin, Adam and Chava brought death to the world, but they made a comeback. They did *teshuva*. We have the same greatness as they had — *Tzellem Elokim* — and so we too should never give up. The denial of this greatness within us results in an attitude that is limited to human logic and common sense. It leads to hopelessness and depression, and ends in failure.

Hashem expects us to do *chessed*, the true *chessed* of the Torah. We must act with sympathy and understanding within our homes and be *besimcha*. *Simcha* creates a healthy home environment that children, today more than ever, need so much. If they are to grow up to be well adjusted and sound individuals, they require a happy home life. Giving our spouses and our children a pleasant household — this is *chessed*! Our obligation to them is so much greater than with strangers. If we run to do *chessed* outside the home with strangers, why not do it at home as well?

It Begins With Saying "Hello"

❧ From Woman To Woman —
With a Message for Men as Well

W e are all familiar with Reb Zusha's account of nervously anticipating his facing the *Beis Din shel Ma'ala* — the Heavenly Court. As he put it:

> *The interrogation would begin: "Reb Zusha, why aren't you on the spiritual level of Avraham Avinu?"*
>
> *I won't worry. I'll tell the Beis Din, "I am not on Avraham Avinu's level because I was not blessed with the attributes of Avraham Avinu."*
>
> *Then the Beis Din will ask me, "Reb Zusha, why aren't you on the spiritual level of Moshe Rabbeinu?" Here, too, I won't have to worry. I can answer them, "I don't have the traits or characteristics that Moshe Rabbeinu was blessed with, so I cannot be on his level."*

Then will come the question, "Reb Zusha, why aren't you on the spiritual level of Reb Zusha?" Reb Zusha sighed. When asked why didn't I utilize my traits, my attributes, to the best of my ability, ... then I won't have an answer.

When we face that awesome day before the *Beis Din shel Ma'ala,* and they ask us: Why didn't we make our marriage the best we could with the attributes each one of us was blessed with? Why didn't we build the greatest *bayis ne'eman* we could, each according to his or her own capabilities? What are we going to say? Are we going to have an answer?

❧ Will "The Real Me" Speak Up?

A few years ago, I dealt with a married woman; this couple had been experiencing marital problems for quite a few years before the wife came to me. Without going into detail, their problems were not one-sided. During the course of counseling, I gave her a very specific work assignment. I told her that, until the next session, I expected her to send off her husband with a pleasant comment — "Goodbye, have a nice day" — in the morning when he leaves. The point was for her to begin the day positively — *regardless* of the husband's response, or whether he even bothers to acknowledge her efforts. I told her that I don't care what happens the rest of the day — they can do as they please. If they want to "fight and punch" — fine, they can behave "naturally." (At the time, I was only addressing one specific point.)

We were attempting to introduce change, altering the family dynamics with minimal effort in the morning. And I am 100 percent convinced that had she put forth even this minuscule effort, it would have helped them. Like a pebble thrown into a pond, the small ripple spreads, causing a bigger ripple, then a bigger one ... until you effect a big change in your attitude. It just has to start somewhere, by someone.

This woman, looking me in the eye, said, "I can't. It's just not me. I have to be honest."

I tried to explain to her, "You're both adults. Even though it may be a bit forced and uncomfortable in the beginning, it's for the good of your marriage. You must introduce change. You must stop your destructive cycle and begin a new positive one. In this case, it must come from you."

She still absolutely refused, saying, "I've got to be me."

I finally asked, "You say, 'I've got to be me.' Who is this 'me' you have to be? A mature woman who can't say 'hello' or 'goodbye' to her husband? We're talking about your partner in marriage! Is this the real you?

"Let's work through an example. Be honest. It's 3:30 in the afternoon; you are worn out from your children. Finally, you're able to put your feet up on the couch; your little ones are strewn around you, one or two have fallen asleep on the couch, one is reading quietly — belly down on the floor, your baby has finally dozed off in your hands, and you are breathing deeply and are just about to drift into slumber. Suddenly, someone is buzzing at the doorbell ... totally without compassion. You pull yourself up, mumbling under your breath about it being between 2 and 4 o'clock (considered to be rest hours in Israel), hoping the children don't wake up ... fix your *sheitel* as you open the door and find one of your not-so-favorite neighbors ...., 'Hi, hope you weren't sleeping. I'm right in the middle of my cake and I am missing some sugar .... I need only one cup .... Can you help me?'

"How do you react? Of course, you will answer politely with a smile, 'Oh no, it's not a bother, I never sleep in the afternoon .... Here, I'll get you a cup of sugar.'

"Is this the real you? Shouldn't the real 'you' sound more like: 'What do you think I am doing at 3:30 in the afternoon? Don't you have the decency not to worry about your cake but let me sleep? And now you woke up my baby with that loud ring ....' But we don't talk like that .... We overcome our natural tendencies and play the gracious hostess. What happened to the 'I've got to be me'?

"You know what? The true 'you' is whatever you want it to be. 'I've got to be me' really means: I am what I want when I want. It's an excuse not to do what I really should do."

Why do we put up such a "phony front" for our neighbors and friends, who may help us very much, but don't compare to our husbands, who are our lifelong partners in marriage? Sure, we are overworked, underpaid, moody, sometimes hormonal, tired out, frazzled, but we are capable of doing for our husbands what we do so naturally for others. We can and must make that effort to be the "me" we really should be.

Rabbi Amnon Yitzchak often says, "The *Shechina* or the *shecheina* — the One Above or the neighbor — who affects our way of acting? Is our foremost concern what the neighbors think about us, or is it focused on doing *Hashem*'s will? The difference between the two words is only a tiny *Yud* — but the *Yud* symbolizes the power of the *pintele Yid*, the inherent strength we all have within us to realize our task in this world and to focus on it. Real *tzeniyus* is focusing upward and not sideways; concerned with what *Hashem* thinks of us, and not necessarily seeking approval from others."

❧ *Clear Goals, Devoted Efforts*

There is a "men's story" that can be retold for everyone's benefit.

A *yeshiva bachur* told his *Mashgiach* that he had heard that a person who goes through life married to a horrible wife merits instant *Gan Eden*. He asked the *Mashgiach* if this is true. "Yes," the *Mashgiach* said, "but I strongly suggest not tempting fate by marrying a woman like that."

The *bachur* was adamant that the *Mashgiach* find him such a wife. Though the *Mashgiach* tried to dissuade him, the *bachur* insisted — he wanted *Gan Eden*. So, the *bachur* got his dream. The *Mashgiach* found the absolute worst female human being on the planet. The morning after the *chassuna* he awoke to "Good morning" whispered in a very sweet voice. "Dear, I prepared breakfast for you." There she was with a fancy tray with delectable food. Surprised, he thought: Well, it's only the first morning; the next day she's sure to act the way I want — like a *klavta* (shrew). The next day was a repeat; sweet, smiling wife, doing his will. As the days passed, the newly married *bachur* was becoming apprehensive and upset. Absolutely frustrated, worried about his *Gan Eden*, he confronted his *klavta*, "What is going on? I married you because you are supposed to be the worst!"

Glaring at him with a wicked smile, she exclaimed, "If you think I'm your ticket to *Gan Eden*, you've got another thought coming."

We are capable of displaying any behavior we want; even a *klavta* can behave like a *tzaddeikes* if it suits her purposes. We, who are really *nashim tzidkaniyos*, and want our marriages to flourish, are surely capable of putting forth the necessary effort to assure our success.

❧ More Than a Glass of Milk

*P*irkei Avos enlightens us on how to endear ourselves to others and make people appreciate us: "Initiate greetings with everyone."[1] If it works for strangers, imagine how effective it can be with our spouse and children — especially since we have the opportunity to apply it to them several times a day. But we must be the initiator.

Regarding the phrase from Yaakov's blessing to Yehuda, "[You will be] white toothed from milk,"[2] the Gemara says, "The person who displays the white of his teeth to his friend [with a smile] is superior to one who quenches his friend's thirst with a drink of milk."[3] There is an illuminating interpretation of this remark: Imagine being thirsty on a hot day, and someone offers you a drink of cool water — how refreshing! But *Chazal* are exact in their selection of beverage; they chose milk.

Yes, water is special — it offers a wonderful, thirst-quenching feeling to whoever drinks it. But milk has even greater powers, for it contains vitamins and minerals, it has substance, it gives strength

---

1. Rabbi Masya ben Charash, *Pirkei Avos* IV, 20.
2. *Bereishis* 49, 12.
3. *Kesubos* 111b.

to the body. Yet, *Chazal* tell us, someone who smiles at his friend does even more, offering him emotional nutrients.

In his discussion of this concept, Rabbi Shimson Pinkus זצ״ל concludes, "A proper relationship and a pleasant atmosphere between husband and wife strengthen and encourage their physical and mental status, enhancing a feeling of love that gives the couple the energy they need to deal with daily challenges."[1] Smiling at others gives them the strength to handle the vicissitudes of life. When we use our influence to create a warm and positive atmosphere in our home, we endow the entire household with emotional strength. (It cannot be emphasized sufficiently how absolutely essential this is in today's environment.)

As water can act as a mirror — it reflects the person looking into it — so, too, do people tend to reflect our attitude toward them.[2] The way others act toward us can be an indicator of how we feel toward them — a response in kind. Note, then, that our husbands and children may be responding to us in the very manner in which we relate to them. We thus possess the ability to influence their attitude and change their behavior toward us. That is, we possess the ability to improve our marriage. (No matter how good your marriage is at present, every marriage can always be better.) A good start is by acknowledging one's husband with a warm and friendly send-off and a similar greeting on his return.

⚜ *Far-Reaching Effects*

Note how *Moshe Rabbeinu* is called *eved Hashem* (servant of G-d), even after his death. How can someone be called an "*eved*" even after he is no longer in this world? The *mefarshim* explain that in actuality, *Moshe Rabbeinu* is *Hashem's eved* even now. Since he was the *Rav* and teacher of all *Bnei Yisroel*, and his teachings are being put to practice — and will continue to be so until

---

1 See *Tiferres Avos*, by Rabbi Shimshon Pinkus.
2 See *Mishlei* 27,19.

the end of all generations — he is as if alive, teaching all Jews even today, and beyond.

We can apply this concept to ourselves. When our actions have a positive influence on others and teach others, we gain merit. If we succeed in inspiring our husbands and children to be engaged in their *avodas Hashem* with joy, then we, too, will be worthy of the title *avdei Hashem*, even after we leave this world.

When the Heavenly Court asks us why we weren't like *Rebbetzin* so-and-so, we won't worry; we'll answer just like Reb Zusha answered: "*Hashem,* You didn't give me the capabilities of *Rebbetzin* so-and-so." But when the question is raised, "Did you put forth your maximum effort so your marriage would be the *beracha* it was meant to be?" — will we have an answer? If, as *nashim tzidkaniyos,* we dedicate ourselves to the success of our marriages, we'll have a positive answer.

And it all begins with a smile.

MARRIAGES ARE MADE IN HEAVEN ....
PEOPLE ARRANGE TO DESTROY THEM

Yosef S. Rosenshein, Ph.D.

❧ *Marriage and the Pleasure Principle*

Jews traditionally expect to enter marriage "for life," and view divorce as acceptable only when there is complete incompatibility and there is no chance for the couple to live together in harmony. This is in total opposition to the contemporary concept of: "If I'm not fully pleased with my mate, it's time for us to separate."

There are many statements and anecdotes by *Chazal* (the rabbis of the Talmud) that back up the Jewish view of marriage.

A most striking example of this view may well be the story of Rabbi Akiva, who, with the consent of his wife, spent twenty-four years of their marriage away from home, studying until he became the great *Tanna*. Clearly, she viewed this period crucial to making theirs more than just another successful marriage, because she obviously did not see her marriage as a union entered for the purpose of providing her with life's earthly pleasures. To her, marriage was a means for her and her husband to realize lofty, transcendent goals unattainable to either of them alone.

In dramatic contrast, one sees numerous couples today fighting over the most trivial types of rewards that the husband or wife feel should be forthcoming to them from the other partner — a situation that results from their expectations of maximum pleasure and their feelings of entitlement. In referring to Rabbi Akiva, we are not advocating that husbands take twenty-four-year leaves of absence. Rather, we are simply offering his situation as a contrast to contemporary cases where members of a marriage react to the pleasure principle on a daily basis, and use it as a moment-to-moment happiness-barometer to measure the success of their marriage.

✦ *The Difference That Counts*

In addition to an unrealistic attitude toward happiness and pleasure, contemporary society is responsible for yet another problem affecting the stability of marriages. In their drive for equality in the job market, the professions and the academe, women have been stressing similarities in talents and abilities that they share with men. In the process, many people have come to believe that men and women are basically the same and this in itself has been the cause of much misunderstanding and marital strife.

There is a need for a reawakening of the concept that man and woman are indeed two separate biological and social entities; in many significant respects they are even more different than alike. This concept is important throughout married life. At the very outset, during their first two or three years of marriage, a husband and wife will find themselves engaging in many activities separately, and they may wonder if they truly were "made for each other." In actuality there is nothing inherently wrong with this. Indeed, scientific studies have shown definite, undeniable differences between men and women in abilities, strengths, and interests.

An application of this concept is the need for each partner to accept the other's exclusive domain with regard to home-making and earning a livelihood. Many couples actively argue or fight about their roles and jockey for dominance in these two domains. Would they but accept that husband and wife are indeed separate, distinct, and entitled to exclusivity, and that each one should carry major responsibility for his/her own domain, much controversy would be averted. On the other hand, decisions regarding family affairs must be a shared responsibility, with the active participation of both parties. Husbands who leave the home completely to their wives and use their daily schedule as an excuse for avoiding joint participation in family decisions are abdicating their role as family (co-)head, and certainly are not improving the possibilities of their marriage's success.

❧ Abandoning the Gold Standard

Another problem area quite common today grows from pursuit of a high standard of living, which puts tremendous pressures on a husband and creates great difficulties in the marital situation. Too often, newlyweds base their expectations for their new home on the life-style they had experienced in their parents' home. Even though they are starting out life anew, these high, often unrealistic, goals can generate a situation where a husband's minor insecurities become major problems in a marriage. Newlyweds must see themselves as launching a new life in all respects, including their style of living, and not enter marriage as if they are wealthy.

Parents regaling their children with all types of goodies often unwittingly exacerbate the problems, and do not allow the newlyweds to grow and struggle together, starting off on their own life. Just as too much softness spoils children, so too can it spoil a good marriage. In this respect, the overly expensive wedding and all the trimmings that go with it only add further fuel to this flame of outsized demands and expectations, which often begin during the engagement period. Thus, it becomes most important to concentrate on setting priorities in the spiritual aspects of life and to permit the material side to be low keyed — and allow married life to flow from this source. (This advice may strike the reader like a tired platitude.

Be that as it may, following it still makes for a healthier, less stressful marriage.)

❈ *Generational Independence*

Marriage represents the creation of a new household, independent of the families the members come from. Too strong a personal dependence on parents can lead to marital difficulties. When couples marry, their parents should help them realize that they have to make their own way in life, that their decisions should be made together with their mates and that their primary responsibilities are to their mates, as is stated unequivocally in *halacha*. Most problems in this area arise when one or both of the partners are totally dependent on their parents who, as well meaning as they may be, can only cause difficulties in the marriage, since as parents they often see their own child's interests overriding those of the mate.

Most commonly, when difficulties begin, children turn to their parents for help — a most tragic mistake — instead of seeking outside help from a *rebbi*, rabbi, or under certain circumstances, a marriage counselor. The key to helping a couple through a problem or a conflict is objectivity, and this can never be provided by parents, who feel closer to their own child than to a son-in-law or a daughter-in-law. The wise parent, when approached by a child, advises him to work out his problems with the spouse or to seek outside help.

❈ *Coming to Grips With Counseling*

While it can be very difficult for couples to enter marriage counseling, they should recognize that counseling has helped preserve many a marriage on the verge of breaking up. Being forced to express one's inner feelings to a third party often allows a person to pull back a bit and look at things in a more objective fashion.

Although all professionals in this field must be well trained and highly capable of handling the strong and sensitive feelings expressed in marital disputes, these requirements take on additional dimensions when dealing with an Orthodox Jewish couple. Issues relating to childrearing, *taharas hamishpacha*, personal matters and general problems of Jewish law as it relates to the roles of the male and female in the family cannot be approached in an intellectual fashion by a therapist who lives outside the realm of *halacha*. Counseling must come from a background of experience and from a sense of commitment. In addition, many areas of life have come under assault today — the tendency of women to assume increasingly active roles outside of the home, for instance, is creating marital difficulties, as are problems relating to birth control, abortion and other popular tomes of the day. It is thus all the more hazardous for an Orthodox Jewish couple to consult a non-religious counselor.

❧ *Meet the Krauses*

To illustrate some of the points we have discussed, the following real-life situation in marital counseling can serve to show how various complicating factors may work together to make the first years in married life difficult ones.

Madeline and Joel Krause (fictitious names) had been married for six years when they sought counseling help. Madeline complained that her husband had little time for her or the family. His only interest in life was "being successful in business," she claimed. Joel, a professional, was very difficult to reach because he considered himself a person with insights and understanding, and in certain situations, counseled people himself. For example, when Madeline complained that he did not spend enough time studying with their son Zevi, he replied that through the tuition he was paying the *rebbi* to teach Zevi, it was as though he were learning with the boy. In this way, Joel used his superior Torah knowledge, drawing on its authority, to deal with a childrearing issue.

Madeline also complained that Joel often traveled on business for weeks at a time and demonstrated little interest in her. Here his response was that since she had always wanted him to be successful in business and knew he had to be traveling, she, in effect, had consented to such long stretches away from home at the outset of their marriage and had no grounds for complaint. Furthermore, when the husband chose to be lenient in halachically prohibited areas, and she would point this out to him, he would dismiss her challenges saying that she did not truly understand the *halacha* or that she was unfamiliar with the spirit of the law. It should be noted that Madeline was a compliant type of person who generally avoided confrontation. In addition, she had but a smattering of Jewish knowledge, and as a result was very hesitant in her responses.

The greatest *halacha* problem arose in the clash between the wife's obligation to respect her parents and her husband at the same time. While Madeline was ready to admit that her husband and parents did not get along, and that she often felt that her parents were wrong, she could not accept his approach to her parents, which alternated from completely cutting them out of their lives to throwing tantrums on the occasions that they did visit them. Joel, avoiding the emotional issue of how this bitterness between the parents and the son-in-law developed, instead expounded on her Torah-directed responsibility to obey her husband. His defenses barred any response from her, and she was caught in a situation which eventually had caused her to become ill because of the conflict between her love for her husband and her devotion to her parents.

This couple had been to a Jewish family service before coming to the Orthodox therapist who is reporting this case. The therapist's first step was to put the halachic issues into their proper context, referring them to an outside rabbinical authority to clarify the *halacha* in each case. From there he proceeded to the interpersonal realm.

When the husband had to deal with the *halacha* issues more openly, he was forced to recognize his own problems and defense mechanisms. Once he was able to see through his defense systems and how he used them to negate his spouse, the counseling flowed easily. This in turn led to changes in their relationship. After a few weeks, Joel was left in therapy alone, with his wife only participating as a support person when needed. In three months of working together, the marriage changed totally for the better.

Joel's problem is not an isolated case, but one that is commonly found among men. The male ego, at times, feels a need to act out in denial rather than deal with his own problems within his own structure.

* * *

In closing, may I say that marital counseling is a pressing need, and the Orthodox Jewish community should endeavor to make it available. It would also be helpful if *kalla* and *chassan* classes would also include pre-marital counseling as well as post-marital discussions in interpersonal relationships. Hopefully, couples will take the message of this article to heart and seek help when necessary so as to avoid the destructiveness of divorce, if at all possible.

DISAGREEMENT AND HARMONIOUS GROWTH

RABBI YISROEL REISMAN

Even couples married for many years should keep themselves focused on *shalom bayis*. Everyone can benefit from an occasional reminder, and it pays to always be alert for advice to stay on the right track.

A lesson that the *Chasam Sofer* derives from *Parshas Chayei Sarah* stands out as crucial appreciation of the difficulties that normal people can encounter in this area. His words are both simple and profound; intellectual, yet practical; they offer sound advice for all couples to whom *shalom bayis* is sacred.

Eliezer proposes that Rivka marry Yitzchok. In response, Lavan says, "*Mei'Hashem yatza hadavar* — this marriage is Divinely ordained. *Lo nuchal dabeir eilecha ra oh tov* — there is nothing we can say, neither bad nor good."

Chasam Sofer asks: It was understood that Rivka would marry Yitzchak. Certainly, no person would say anything bad about a *shidduch* once he realized that it was a sealed agreement. But, why not say something good? After all, if the *shidduch* was going to happen anyway, why not offer a positive assessment of the *shidduch*?

Chasam Sofer answers that the Torah (through Lavan) is teaching us a lesson regarding marriage. We often harbor the misconception that to make a good marriage, it is crucial that both partners be similar, that they be as identical as possible. But this is not true. In a successful marriage, it is important that there be differences between the two partners, as well. If two people are exactly the same, what benefit is there in marriage? Instead of one six-foot person, marriage would give you eleven-and-a-half feet of that person. He is the same; nothing has changed. Marriage would not bring any fundamental improvement to a human being.

On the other hand, if the two are different, there is a great advantage. When two people with differences join together to form a single home, there are going to be disagreements. How wonderful! They will disagree, they will argue, they will discuss ... and ultimately, they will come to a decision regarding their course in life. The decision will be well thought out. It will be the result of much analysis and deliberation. And it will result in a well-planned life.

"*Lo nuchal dabeir eilecha ra oh tov* — there is nothing we can say, neither bad nor good." The *tov*, says the *Chasam Sofer*, is not always *tov*, and the *ra* is not always *ra*. Differences between husband and wife may seem to be *ra*, but it is not actually so. These differences may in fact be the greatest *tov* in the life of the couple.

Chasam Sofer gives one example of this idea, an example with which many couples would easily identify. Often (*very* often), one partner in marriage is a *pazran*, a person who is quick to spend money, while the other is a *kamtzan*, reluctant to incur expenses. They often disagree on how their finances should be run. How fortunate they are! Imagine if they were both *pazranim*, impulsive spenders; the house would come to economic ruin. No money would be saved. If both would be *kamtzanim*, reluctant to part with their money, the house could not be a happy place. It is because they are different — one is a *kamtzan* and the other a *pazran* — that they will disagree and their constructive dialogue will bring them to a proper, happy medium.

❧ A Funny Thing Happens on the Way
Back From the Chupa

I am fortunate enough to be in yeshiva, where I come into contact with young *chassanim*. They are full of enthusiasm as they tell me, "You know, it's amazing. We're the same. Could you believe it! I loved it in *Eretz Yisroel* and she loved it! We like similar foods; we have similar hobbies; we even use the same brand of toothpaste!"

Then they get married. They find that they are not so alike after all. They like the same foods, but one likes to eat out while the other likes to stay home. They both use the same brand of toothpaste, but one replaces the cap, while the other loses it. (It seems that the *Ribbono Shel Olam* uses this crucial factor in determining *shidduchim*; pairing one cap-loser with a cap-replacer.)

Suddenly, things are not so rosy. There are disagreements, then arguments, and the happy couple is not so happy. There are problems and the match made in heaven is a mismatch!

The *Chasam Sofer* says: "Problems? Not at all. This *is* a match made in heaven, a perfect *shidduch*! That's precisely the benefit of marriage!"

❧ Afraid of Disagreements?

Perhaps we can better appreciate this by referring to the *chavrusa* relationship. Two young men are studying together, trying to appreciate the depth of a *sugya* (topic in the Talmud). The Gemora introduces a concept, which can be understood two ways. Each *chavrusa* pauses to mull over the two possibilities.

Occasionally, you have *chavrusos* who will generally agree. They understand the Gemora in a similar manner. They read the Gemora, express their understanding, and move on. Across the study hall, there are two other young men who are studying together. They come to same *sugya*. One expresses his understanding. The other disagrees. They begin arguing. One cites a source, to support his approach; the other presents a logical counter-argument. Look — they're fighting!

Which pair of *chavrusos* is ideal? Which will have a better chance of fully appreciating the *sugya*? The pair that agree? Or the pair that disagree? Which will pursue the truth? Which is more likely to become complacent and move on without much thought or depth?

You get the picture. We know that the best *chavrusa* is the one that disagrees, providing that he disagrees on the issue with intellectual honesty, and with the willingness to yield when disproven, realizing that he in truth is a winner. Now he has arrived at the truth. This is what a good *chavrusa* is all about.

The *sugyos* of life deserve the same scrutiny. Disagreements are important tools in a good, constructive dialogue. They are an integral part of marriage. No wonder couples so often disagree!

I had often heard that in-laws sometimes do damage to a marriage. It's something I could never understand. Which parents would destroy a marriage?

Over time, I've observed that problems often stem from parents' insecurity. When their child and his/her wife/husband have disagreements, the parents suffer from their failure to learn this *Chasam Sofer*. They fail to realize that disagreements, when engaged with willingness to listen and mutual respect, are a part of marriage. Yes, your *tatelle* can learn to work things out without you!

After yeshiva, I often walk around the block to catch a bus home. One evening, as I turned the corner, I saw a member of our kollel standing at the edge of the street, looking toward Boro Park, where he lives. I realize that he's waiting for someone. I see that he is repeatedly looking at his watch... then down the street... looking... stepping out... he looks angry. I realize that he is waiting for his wife. I sympathize.

As I walked by, I commented to him, "Yehuda, don't blame her. Blame the Ribbono Shel Olam. He created wives that way."

The following day, Yehuda approached me to thank me for my comment the evening before. "We were headed to an important appointment. My wife was late. When she finally arrived, she was ready for a fight. I was ready for a fight. Instead, I got into the car and said, 'Reb Yisroel said it's not your fault! I'll take up my complaints with the *Ribbono Shel Olam.'*"

Accept differences; that's the lesson of the *Chasam Sofer.* It's a lesson for *shana rishona,* the first year of marriage, and a lesson for all subsequent years of marriage.

❦ *A Deeper Appreciation*

Rabbi Chaim Shmulevitz takes this lesson a step further. In *Sichos Mussar* (5732:20), he refers to a "*sod gadol be'yetzira,*" what he calls a great secret of creation. "A woman is created to be helpful to her husband, and as a result of this responsibility, she is endowed with the ability (*chush ha'rei'ach*) to sense the truth regarding the manner in which her husband conducts himself, in relation to his spiritual status."

He explains that a woman's ability to disagree with her husband regarding his conduct — and to be correct in her contention — is a gift to the husband from the *Ribbono Shel Olam.*

The Gemora relates that Rav Chanina ben Tradyon, one of the ten *harugei malchus* (Torah giants martyred by the Romans), was punished because he pronounced *Hashem*'s Name as it is spelled, something that is normally done only in the *Beis Hamikdash.* When the Romans took him to be killed, his wife was defiled as well. The Gemora relates that he was punished for pronouncing *Hashem*'s Name, while she was punished for not preventing him from doing so. How incredible! Rav Chanina was a *gadol hador* (leader of his generation), a *poseik* (authority) for his people. He held that he was permitted to pronounce *Hashem*'s Name. Wouldn't it be expected that his wife accept his *p'sak* (ruling)? How could she be faulted for failing to correct him?

Rabbi Chaim Shmulevitz presents this question, and concludes that even if a man is a *gadol hador,* his wife's ability to sense his failings rises to correspond to his level. Thus, his wife did indeed have the ability to correct him.

What men often see as a hindrance, as a burden, is actually a gift of the highest order!

How tragic it is when people turn the great gifts of marriage into problems. The very potential for disagreement and constructive criticism that marriage offers should be appreciated and utilized with great joy.

If we understand that it is inherent in marriage to have disagreements, to build from differences — and yes, to accept criticism — then we can build in our marriage.

❧ Ishto Mosheles Alav

The Gemora (*Beitza* 32) teaches "There are three whose lives are not lives." One of the three is *mi she'ishto mosheles alav*, a man whose wife rules over him.

Using the *Chasam Sofer*'s idea, we can understand this Gemora in a new light. The *Gaon* of Vilna teaches that there are two Hebrew words for a monarch: *melech*, king, and *moshel*, ruler. There is a fundamental difference between the two.

A *melech* is a king who is willingly accepted by his subjects as their leader. His commands are followed happily. A *moshel* rules by force, against the desire of his subjects.

Ki lashem hamelucha u'moshel ba'goyim, the Jewish people have accepted *Hashem*'s rule willingly, but the idolater does not accept *Hashem*'s dictates. To him, *Hashem* is a *moshel*.

Only when *Mashiach* comes will all accept *Hashem*'s rule willingly: *"V'hayah Hashem l'melech al kol ha'aretz*. On that day will G-d be King over all the Earth."

Returning to our subject, *mi she'ishto mosheles alav*, a man whose wife rules over him, lives a tough life, indeed. This is because his wife's opinions cause him anger and aggravation; he feels threatened by her. She has become a *moshel*. Sad, indeed. A couple should never have a *memshala* relationship. The home should have an atmosphere of *malchus*, where the royal couple rules jointly, and disagreements that arise are cause for fruitful discussion and joyful growth.

We need to internalize the *Chasam Sofer*'s message. Having a disagreement does not mean that a marriage is a failure. It makes growth possible. It can make a home better than it was before. Yes, intelligent people can have different opinions.

And so, the next time you and your wife view a matter differently, declare with appreciation, "*Baruch Hashem*, this is a marriage made in heaven!"

"I'M SORRY"

TESHUVA BEGINS AT HOME

DR. MEIR WIKLER

✦ I. The Elements of Atonement

Not all sins are absolved on Yom Kippur. As the *Mishna* states, "Yom Kippur does not atone for transgressions between man and man unless one [first] appeases his friend" (*Yoma* 8:9). The Gemora explains the extent of our obligation to ask others for forgiveness. "Rabbi Yitzchok said, 'Whoever annoys his friend — even if only with words — is obligated to appease him'" (*Yoma* 87a).

The Shulchan Aruch also includes this requirement and goes one step further. "Transgressions between man and man are not atoned for by Yom Kippur unless he [the transgressor] appeases him [the victim]. Even if he only provoked him verbally, he must still appease him. *And if he is not appeased with the first [attempt], he should return and go [to him] a second time and a third time*" (*Orach Chaim, Hilchos Yom Hakippurim* 600:1). [Emphasis added.]

Clearly, then, we are halachically obligated to apologize whenever we have hurt someone in any way. And the ones we are most likely to hurt are those with whom we live — our spouses. *Teshuva* for *aveiros bein adam l'chaveiro* — interpersonal sins — must therefore begin at home.

What is the best method to "appease" your spouse? Why are some apologies accepted, allowing couples "to move on," while other apologies tend to provoke even more hostility than they were originally designed to diffuse? This article will address these and other practical questions about healing wounds inflicted in marriage.

⁂ The Three Most Important Words in Marriage

Often, when speaking publicly on husband/wife relationships, I pose the following question to the audience: "What are the three most important words in marriage?"

After a brief pause, I continue. "Now, I know what you are thinking. The first word is 'I,' but the third word is not 'you.'"

Puzzled, even worried looks appear. Then I relieve the suspense. "The three most important words in marriage are, 'I was wrong.'"

Invariably, many members of the audience nod their heads in knowing approval. It is almost impossible to live with someone, anyone — roommate or relative — without offending him once in a while. To heal the wound that you inflicted, whether willfully or not, you must apologize. Your spouse's acceptance depends in large measure on how well you apologized. A successful apology will clear the air, diffuse your spouse's angry feelings and soothe the injury. A failed attempt, on the other hand, will generate more pain, disappointment and resentment.

To properly elucidate this aspect of marital communication, I will present two thoroughly disguised case examples from my practice, one of failure and one of success. While the apologizers in both of these cases happen to have been the husbands, in general, wives need to ask forgiveness no less than their husbands.

For Mutty, the most important goal in life was to be respected and honored by others. And for Mutty, the quickest and most direct route was to amass as much wealth as possible.

Although Mutty was making a comfortable living as an executive in a real estate management firm, he was not earning a salary close to what he hoped to be earning after seventeen years of marriage. As many of his friends and neighbors were purchasing or building new homes, Mutty felt pressure "to keep up with the Cohens," but could not even redecorate his modest home.

Mutty then withdrew all his family's savings to invest in "high tech" stocks which were soaring at the time. To increase his potential profits, he purchased the stocks "on margin," which meant that he was actually buying on credit. When the stock market crashed, Mutty's entire house of cards collapsed and Mutty was forced to declare personal bankruptcy. Mutty and Lieba's home and cars were seized and they moved into a small apartment.

Lieba was openly angry: "How could you have taken such a risk? Why didn't you tell me about this before we lost our home?"

"You were not interested," Mutty shot back defensively. "You never asked about our finances."

Fast forward four years. Mutty and Lieba are now living in a new neighborhood in a private, but simple home. Mutty is working as the Chief Financial Officer of a junior college and reestablished their credit rating. Mutty would like to cash in his life insurance to invest in real estate, but needs Lieba's approval to cancel the insurance policy.

"Do you think I'm crazy?" Lieba explodes. "I'm not ready to lose our assets again on another get-rich-quick scheme!"

"But, Lieba, this is different. I am not hiding anything from you. The real estate market is booming now. Trust me."

"How can I trust you? You kept me completely in the dark last time."

"I was different four years ago. Can't you forgive me?"

"You want me to forgive you? In the past four years, you have never once apologized."

"O.K., Lieba, you're right. I should apologize for what happened. I'm sorry I got into that mess. But I was under a lost of pressure at the time. Could you please forgive me now and let me cash in the insurance? This is a great opportunity now for both of us."

Even though Mutty was brought to tears by her refusal, Lieba remained steadfast.

❧ III. What Went Wrong?

Why was Lieba so unforgiving? Where did Mutty go wrong? And was there another way Mutty could have apologized, which might have been more effective?

Mutty did not understand that the purpose of any apology is to heal the wound inflicted by the perpetrator on the victim. The victim is emotionally hurt, and is frightened that (s)he may be hurt again. The apology, therefore, is supposed to provide the victim with reassurance that the same injury will not be repeated.

Mutty viewed an apology as a means to escape punishment or other negative consequences of his misdeeds, and as a tactic to get Lieba to agree to release his life insurance policy for him to invest. Failing to understand the purpose of an apology, he delivered his in a most ineffective manner.

Many people share Mutty's misunderstanding of asking for forgiveness, and their apologies are as ineffective as Mutty's was.

For an apology to be effective, the following guidelines should be followed:

1. Do Not End Any Apology With "But ..."

If you follow your apology with a long list of excuses, rationalizations or justifications — valid as they may be — you will severely water down its effectiveness.

Mutty included a "but" in his apology, inflaming Lieba's anger at him. It signaled that he was more interested in defending himself and escaping her wrath than he was in accepting responsibility for the consequences of his behavior.

2. Acknowledge Your Wrongdoing.

To be effective, your apology must include a statement of exactly what you are apologizing for. Saying only "I'm sorry" leaves it doubtful in your spouse's mind as to what you are regretting. Are you sorry you got caught? Are you sorry your spouse is angry at you? Or are you sorry for what you did?

Usually, a hurtful episode includes multiple statements and/or actions. Not all of them were equally offensive to your spouse. You must, therefore, spell out exactly which statements and/or which actions you now regret.

Had Mutty apologized for using poor judgment in taking such a huge risk, his apology would have been more effective. More importantly, however, Mutty should have included his deceiving Lieba, violating her trust in him, as well.

3. Acknowledge the Damage.

A complete apology should include a list of the damages that the victim suffered. It is not enough to say you were at fault for going through the red light, for example. You must also mention to the owner of the car you hit that you are responsible for bending his fender and cracking his headlight.

If you do not realize on your own, then by all means ask your spouse how you hurt him or her. If you already know, however, then definitely inform your spouse that you comprehend exactly how (s)he was inconvenienced, insulted or worse.

Mutty should have said, "I know I was responsible for our house and cars being repossessed. I caused you and the children to be embarrassed and forced out of our home. And I gave you good reason to be distrustful of me for a long time afterward."

4. Acknowledge Your Spouse's Feelings.

The purpose of your apology is to convince your spouse that you fully understand the gravity of your error. If you have any idea how your spouse felt about what you did or said, then mention it.

This will communicate your full appreciation of the consequences of your actions. The purpose of your apology is to convince your spouse that you fully comprehend the severity of your offense. Clear reference to the negative feelings your words and/or deeds triggered in your spouse will increase the effectiveness of your apology.

If you are not clear about how your spouse felt, then certainly ask. At least that way, you will demonstrate concern for his or her feelings.

Mutty could have told Lieba that he understands now how shocked she had been. He could have acknowledged how disappointed and angry she must have felt toward him. Finally, he could have indicated that he recognized how much the financial debacle must have made her feel alienated and distant from him.

5. Spell Out Your Resolution.

You are convinced that you will never repeat the same mistake again. But your spouse is not as certain about this as you are. To reassure him or her, disclose the steps you will take or have already taken to prevent a recurrence.

If you have made a personal promise to yourself, let your spouse know about it. If you have a plan that will prevent you from making the same mistake again, spell it out. If you have resolved to handle similar circumstances in a more constructive fashion in the future, then, by all means, let your spouse in on it.

Had Mutty decided that he would make full financial disclosures to Lieba in the future, or that he would never take high financial risks at all, sharing these commitments with Lieba would have gone a long way toward reassuring her that the previous catastrophe would not be repeated.

6. Ask for Forgiveness.

Only *after* you have completed steps 1-5 are you ready to say you are sorry and ask your spouse to pardon your wrongdoing. To seek absolution *before* you complete steps 1-5 makes it appear as if you are only seeking to avoid suffering any consequences. Your goal in apologizing should be to make restitution for your offense and to reassure your spouse that the misdeed will not be repeated.

For four years, Mutty never apologized to Lieba for his misconduct. He did not acknowledge his error or the damage he caused. When, after four years, he did ask Lieba to forgive him, the reason was transparently clear. He wanted Lieba to give him permission to cash in his life insurance policy.

You might wonder whether it really mattered how Mutty worded his apology. After all, Lieba was so hurt by his deceit and high risk taking that no apology would have earned him a complete pardon. Nevertheless, it would have gone a long way toward healing the wound inflicted by his actions.

❧ IV. Label and Blima

Longstanding open wounds can be healed. The healing, however, is not an event, but a process which only begins with an effective apology. To enable the reader to fully appreciate the dynamics of this healing process, I present another in-depth case example:

Before Label and Blima got married, they discussed every detail of their *chassuna*. Label, for example, wanted his rabbi, who would officiate as *mesader kiddushin*, to address the couple under the *chupa*, as was the *minhag* in his family. Blima was not too thrilled about this, for her relatives and friends are not accustomed to this practice. As a concession to Label, however, she consented.

The rabbi enthusiastically accepted Label's invitation, adding that he would like to speak, briefly, during the *seuda* (meal) as well. Label took it as a matter of course that Blima would not object to a short *d'var Torah* at the dinner. He was mistaken.

"Speak twice? Is he serious?" Blima was incredulous. "People want to socialize at a *chassuna*, not listen to speeches. Once is pushing it. But twice is out of the question."

At Blima's insistence, Label agreed to go back to his rabbi and ask if the dinner speech could be eliminated in deference to Blima.

"No speech at the *seuda*?" The rabbi took umbrage. "It is our *minhag* to speak at the *seuda*. This is not a matter of *kavod*. It is a matter of principle."

Blima, however, would not give in. As the special day approached, Label assumed it would all work out. He was wrong again. The rabbi sent messages to Blima that she would be pleasantly surprised with the brevity and warmth of his dinner speech. In the end, Blima relented. The rabbi's *d'var Torah* was brief and extremely well received, but Blima was left with a huge reservoir of resentment. She felt that Label did not live up to his commitment.

After the *chassuna*, Label tried to minimize the incident. "We're married now. That's the main thing. Everyone had a wonderful time at our wedding."

This only poured salt on Blima's wound. "So what if everyone had a wonderful time?" Blima shot back. "Not only did you disregard my feelings, you also reneged on an agreement we had made."

Label decided to avoid the issue entirely. In time, he reasoned, Blima would let go of her resentment and forget about the entire episode. And indeed, she would have done well to take into account Label's loyalty to his rabbi, and simply forget about the incident. But that did not happen.

Over time, whenever Label would mention the name of his rabbi, Blima expressed a disparaging remark. Fourteen months after they were married, Label felt he could no longer tolerate Blima's sniping comments whenever his rabbi came up in conversation. Although he had pleaded with Blima to forgive him, he never succeeded in receiving a full pardon from her.

If he ever hoped to put this issue behind them, I advised Label, he would have to offer an apology that covered all of the bases outlined above. Label was convinced that even a full apology would be useless. Once again, he was wrong.

Label brought up the subject on his own: "Blima, I want to apologize to you for something."

"What did you do now?"

"It isn't something recent. It took place fourteen months ago."

"What are you talking about?"

"Our *chassuna* and the fact that the rabbi spoke at the *seuda*. I'm sorry it disturbed you so much. And I'm sorry it put such a damper on our wedding for you. I know you had told me that you were opposed to any speeches at weddings and you felt embarrassed to have two. And I know that I had promised you that I would speak to the rabbi about it before the *chassuna*. I did try to dissuade him from speaking at the dinner, but I was not successful. I realize now that you were hurt by that. And you felt betrayed by me. I really am very sorry. I'm asking you not only to forgive me, but also to tell me what I can do now that will demonstrate to you that I do realize how much I hurt you and that I am determined not to hurt you again."

"For one thing," Blima replied after catching her breath, "you have just proven to me how sincerely sorry you are. I believe your remorse is genuine. You don't need to do anything to prove it. And secondly, — I accept your apology."

During the past year, to Label's surprise, Blima has finally let go of her anger toward him and even dropped her resentment towards his rabbi, demonstrating that wounds that festered for fourteen months can be healed if apologies are complete, sincere and non-defensive.

Yes, Blima had been holding on too long to her grudge and she certainly could have made life easier for Label by accepting one of his earlier apologies. But sometimes you need to apologize even when your spouse is making it difficult for you.

* * *

Remember, that to be absolved for the sin of hurting others, you must ask whomever you hurt for forgiveness. You must apologize.

A good place to start that *teshuva* process is at home with your spouse. Following the guidelines above can increase the chances that any apology you make will achieve your goal of appeasing your spouse and healing whatever wounds you may have inflicted.

DEALING WITH EXTRAORDINARY CIRCUMSTANCES

❧ A DIFFERENT KIND OF BABY

❧ A FUSION OF GIFTS

❧ HEADING A LARGE FAMILY

❧ *SHALOM BAYIS*: A VIEW FROM YOUR CHILD'S EYES

❧ PREPARATION FOR MARRIAGE: PREVENTION FOR DIVORCE

❧ SOLOMON'S NIGHTMARE

Just as no two individuals are alike, neither are any two marriages. While some surprises are delightful, others can be daunting. It is always healthier if one can establish some kind of approach for dealing with the unanticipated, should it take place — for better… or the best.

A DIFFERENT KIND OF BABY
COPING WITH THE CHALLENGE OF INFERTILITY

ARIELLA DAVIDSON

T he history of the world is often divided by its professional practitioners into Ages: the Middle Ages, the Age of Exploration,
the Age of Industry, the Age of Democracy. If, as political theorist
Francis Fukuyama posits, we have reached the End of History, if all
the great deeds have been done, and all the heroic epics written, our
technocratic, clerical time might be dubbed the Age of Acronym.

Deerstalkers have the NRA, seven-footers the NBA, Golden
Agers the AARP, witch-hunters the IRS; there's CNN for news
junkies, JFK for conspiracy theorists or aviation buffs, WWW for
web surfers.

And so, like most Americans, I, too, belong to a special-interest
group. We have our issues, our particular focus, and a magazine
that gives us our very own acronym: A T.I.M.E.

Never heard of it? Probably not. That's because many of you are
bustling, busy mothers and fathers. A T.I.M.E. stands for *A Torah
Infertility Medium of Exchange.*[1] It's a magazine, with an attendant
website, created for the purpose of allowing those suffering the

---

1. This is an organization that supports and educates those in the Jewish community experiencing infertility by offering a telephone help line, peer support network, support groups,
educational symposia and the A T.I.M.E. Reader.

searing pain of infertility in the hyper-fertile Orthodox world to air their concerns, discuss their fears, share words of encouragement, and exchange all sorts of information, medical and halachic.

❖ *It Wasn't Supposed to Be This Way*

We all had our dream weddings, the perfect bride and groom on the three-tier cake. And then, if our society was any indicator at all, the next step was producing five or eight or ten or twenty-five kids sometime in the span of the next three years. Along the way, the cake would get destroyed, of course, but that was just part of the fun.

But a strange thing happened. Two years passed, and then four, and then seven. And the cake stayed perfect. Bride and groom, frozen in endless, glossy adulthood, with nary a runny nose or dirty diaper in sight.

Many couples experience difficulties of one sort or another as their marriages progress, whether it be illness of a family member, financial concerns, or problems in child raising. The problem rears its head, it is dealt with and resolved in one way or another, and they move on.

But *Hashem* handed the A T.I.M.E. crowd a very unique sort of challenge. For those of us in the infertility community, this is not a test that builds up to a point of crisis, and then reaches resolution. It's more like Chinese water torture: drip, drip, drip, the unremitting pressure of the same thing happening. It questions the fundamental assumptions upon which our identities rest. Who am I, when that basic cornerstone of my being, my physical body, does not play its appointed role, and make me a father or mother? Who are we, this couple who are not parents? Infertility becomes the baby, the catalyst that affects and colors and challenges and changes every couple to whom it is born.

⋇ Obsessive or Overreacting?

I leaf through the Winter 2000 issue of A T.I.M.E., and come upon the following in "Daunting Dilemmas," an advice column:

When I try to discuss our infertility with my very understanding and caring husband, he gets upset and tells me to stop obsessing about it. I think he is underreacting; he thinks that I am overreacting. I can't think rationally about how to handle this because it is a male factor problem. Perhaps subconsciously I resent it. How can we discuss this constructively without either one of us becoming upset?

Boy, does this question pack a punch. She hits all the buttons: obsessive thinking, different styles of communication, fear of rejection, questions in *emuna*, the ubiquitous Jewish disease of guilt.

I'm not much of an astronomer, but one of the first lessons I learned, early on, was that Men are from Mars, and Women are indeed from Venus. What my husband sees as obsessive rehashing with my friend of my experiences that morning at the doctor, I see as therapeutic and cathartic. A number of times he's expressed the concern that my constant discussion of infertility with this friend is only drawing me deeper into the coils of depression. I counter that she is my escape valve, that without her shoulder to lean on, I would be infinitely lonelier and sadder. And who does he talk to? He just doesn't have the same need. When sadness overwhelms him, he seeks out dear friends whose company he enjoys, but the conversation centers on the *yeshivish* equivalent of the Super Bowl and the World Series (what *masechta*, what *daf*, what *chavrusa*, what's the *"reyd,"* etc.). Heaven forfend that it should get any more personal than that.

In the same vein, my Mars-dwelling husband has often amazed me with his ability to rejoice in the *simchos* of other. I can see that he really means it when he seeks out a new father, gives him a hearty handshake, and wishes him a sincere *mazal tov*. My Venusian response, on the other hand, to news of a new birth on planet Earth, is more likely to be a shoe thrown at the nearest window, along with a flood of tears. Of course, it doesn't help that my body is a veritable factory of mood-altering hormones, the production of which is often enhanced and augmented by powerful fertility drugs.

❦ Ravings of a Human Pincushion

It is a common misconception that the source of fertility problems lies in the female half of the equation. Research indicates, however, that forces preventing conception are equally divided between men and women. And yet, all the research in the world does nothing to assuage the feelings of guilt and resentment that worm their way into an infertile marriage.

Guilt. Completely illogical. It makes absolutely no sense to assume blame for something over which you have no control. However, early on in this game, those of us lucky enough to have been chosen as players learn that logic isn't on the game board. In the ever-seething emotional cauldron of infertility, the partner diagnosed with the problem often carries a heavy weight around his or her heart. *I've failed him ... I've failed her. If she were married to someone else, she'd be a mother. I'm holding him back from being a father.* And even more insidious, a fainter whisper: *I'm not fully a woman ... I'm less than a man.*

Resentment. In the vast majority of instances, it is the wife who has to bear the brunt of treatment. Shots, pills, invasive procedures — all exacerbated by the pre-rooster hours at which these procedures often take place (to allow working people to get on with their day) — are generally her burden. *It's not fair,* many women find themselves thinking. *All he has to do is and look sympathetic, while I've become a hormone-crazed human pincushion.*

❦ From Alienation to Connection

And yet, with the passage of time, the very same experience that can alienate so powerfully can also provide incredible opportunities for connection; on one level, between husband and wife, and on a deeper level, between the couple and *Hashem*.

Because when all the howling is done, and the denial overcome, one begins to intuit that there must be more to this experience than banging heads against stone walls. The ticking of the dreaded biological clock infuses the phenomenon of time with amazing clarity. One becomes intensely cognizant of every passing day, because every dawn is another chance at hope, every night shadowed with sadness. We are so aware, so intently aware, of our limits, of our finiteness, of our powerlessness. And that awareness brings in its wake a desire to grasp at the Infinite source of all power, the Father Who loves even as He chastises, Who caresses as He challenges. Infertility forces us to hear that ageless question: *Ma Hashem Elokecha sho'el me'imcha?* What does *Hashem* want me to do with this? Who am I expected to become?

And so we talk to Him, not only at times of formal prayer, but throughout the day, through the constant cycles of hope and death. We learn humility, as we see the ineffectiveness of man's most strenuous efforts. And inevitably, the *mikdash me'at* — the little sanctuary — that we carve out for *Hashem* in our hearts affects the bond between us as well.

For we have become partners in raising Infertility, this baby of ours. And in this partnership, we must draw upon many of the same resources that our friends who are parents use in the upbringing of their children. *Emuna*, patience, humbleness, humor, an overriding sense of purpose and mission. True, the *nachas* may be a bit more elusive than that derived from a *bar mitzva* boy saying his *pshetl*, or a daughter starring in a school concert; but we can take great pride in being chosen for, and meeting, the challenge of this very unique sort of *tzaar gidul banim*.

✦ *Through the Back Door of Our Minds*

I remember when the sensation struck me, about five years into our marriage, of being in suspended animation. I looked around at our dear friends who had been at our wedding. Many of the singles had married and begun families, and those with one or two kids now had four or five. And then there was us, Yehuda and Ariella, eternally the "young couple." It seemed to me that I had my nose pressed up against the glass, gazing longingly into the tantalizing window of a shop I could not enter.

And yet, if it's immortality that one seeks through his children, by bequeathing to them the heritage of Sinai, it seems to me that there is indeed room for us in the shop. We just have to enter in through the back door of our minds and hearts, instead of by the front door of DNA. There is so such to be done — in *kiruv*, in *chinuch*, in *chessed* — and we possess that most precious of resources. We have the time to get involved.

We also have time to enjoy each other, to travel and see the world, to have fun together. Incidentally, the experience of travel has often provided a few of the lighter moments of this trial. Because whenever we would board a plane, and see parents struggling with numerous offspring, and even more pieces of luggage, shlepping crying babies, leaking toddlers, and whining kids through the narrow aisles, we would turn to each other and say, "Maybe this isn't so bad after all!" (Not that we weren't yearning to be in some form of their situation, of course, but there is something to be said for traveling with someone who can put on his own oxygen mask, and go to the restroom alone.)

Yamim Tovim, when families assemble, each sporting their latest addition, can be extremely painful for us; but at least we can enjoy an afternoon nap undisturbed, and learn something together when we get up. (A sight that a niece found somewhat disconcerting: "Tanta Ariella, girls don't learn Torah!" Well, honey, this one does. And with rather a good *rebbi*, I might add.)

We've learned how to talk, and how to listen; how to laugh together, how to feel each other's pain, not as the hurt of another person, but as the ache of the other half of ourselves. Together we have grown, as spouses and as Jews.

Ultimately, infertility has given both of us our best friend.

A Fusion of Gifts
When the Strength of a Frum Family
Merges With the *Baal Teshuva's* Resolve

Chana Levin

❧ *How Could it Happen?*

*T*he *Jewish Observer* featured an article, "*Lehavdil*," by Aviva
Minsk (May '97), in which the author writes with justifiable
pain that for many F.F.B. (*Frum* From Birth) families the idea of a
B.T. (*Baal Teshuva*) marrying their daughters or sons is "beyond the
pale." I would like to reassure her along with other B.T.'s that not
all F.F.B.'s feel that way. I think I am uniquely qualified to comment. Twenty-five years ago, I, from an F.F.B. family, whose father
ז״ל received *semicha* from Rabbi Yosef Kahaneman at the esteemed
Ponovezher Yeshiva in Europe, married a *baal teshuva* — and a relatively new one, at that.

Why did I do something that was almost unheard of then, and
even today? I suppose the simplest — and best — answer is that
we were *bashert* for each other. *Hashem* — the greatest *Shadchan* of
all — had it all arranged. We needed each other to become the people we are now. Had I married one of the nice, complacent, inter

changeable young F.F.B. men with whom I had met on *shidduchim*, I probably would have remained on the same religious level all my life, doing everything by rote, never growing.

As soon as I met the man who was to become my husband, I knew he was different. At first, I was most impressed with his obvious intelligence. One snowy winter afternoon we went for a long walk, and he told me his story — how after a totally secular upbringing, he had decided to lead a Torah life. He explained all the difficulties that decision had brought.

Twenty-five years ago, the *baal teshuva* movement was just starting. My husband did not have an instant support group, special programs, *Shabbatonim* or even the trusty ArtScroll *Siddur* to help him. He was basically a pioneer, struggling along on his own, trying to make sense of the strange world of Orthodoxy he had chosen — or felt compelled — to become part of. Everything was new to him and could be achieved only with difficulty. When a family invited him for Shabbos, he was handed a *bentcher* but held it upside down! He had to struggle to learn *Alef-Beis* from a child's *sefer*. For someone who had always known academic success in the secular world and was in fact attending a prestigious law school at the time, it was definitely not an easy transformation.

Another obstacle he had to face was alienation from his parents, as they had felt he was rejecting them and their values. Somehow he had the strength and courage to maintain his newfound beliefs and eventually succeeded in repairing the rift between him and his family.

I was so moved by his story, I knew then he was my *bashert* for whom I'd been searching for so long, and that our futures were to be inevitably intertwined.

So we were married. My husband continued on his spiritual journey, and by so doing took me along with him, away from my F.F.B. complacency. I learned to see the world of Torah through new eyes, giving me a different perspective on things I had always taken for granted. The experience was like a fresh breeze blowing into a musty room, which had been sealed up for too long.

❧ From Generation to Generation

Several months after our wedding, we went for a short visit to his family in New Jersey. They were friendly and welcoming, going out of their way to accommodate us with specially bought kosher food and paper plates. Somehow, they even found two candles for me to light on Friday evening. But as I did so, I reflected that it was probably the first time that Shabbos candles had ever been lit in that house.

I began to wonder how my husband, having grown up in such a secular environment, had ever managed to move so far away from it. In *shul* on Shabbos morning, I watched from the *Ezras Nashim* as my husband *davened*. He prayed with such *kavana* that I could only thank *Hashem* for this *neis*, the strength he had been given to leave his former life and claim his Jewish heritage.

Then his mother told us a quaint family story of the strange old lady — her grandmother — who was so "old fashioned" that she never removed her headscarf. Even when she wanted to wash her hair, she had her daughters hold a towel over her so that the "beams of her house" should never see her uncovered head. "Just like Kimchi," I exclaimed in wonder, recalling that story.

So my husband did have *yichus*, after all! The chain had nearly been severed, but he had reconnected it now. Surely it must be in the *zechus* of his great-grandmother, the *tzaddekes*, that the next generation of the family is now *frum* again.

When our oldest son was 3, we carefully explained to him that *Abba* was a *baal teshuva* and discussed what it meant. We told him that when *Abba* was a little boy he had never known the beauty of Shabbos, the fun of Purim, the excitement of finding the *afikomen* on Pesach, building a *sukka* or lighting Chanuka candles. On Rosh Hashana and Yom Kippur, he didn't go to school, as in New York City even the public schools were closed then. But his family didn't go to *shul* either. He had always felt that he was missing something. But now, through our children, he could experience all the joys he'd been denied in his own childhood. We explained that a *baal teshuva* was someone who had chosen to become *frum*, and that was very special. Our son then insisted, "I want to be a *baal teshuva*, too."

At first we tried to rationalize with him and he started to cry. Then we realized that all of us can be — and should be, in a very real sense — "*baalei teshuva*." We should all continue to grow — spiritually, in *mitzvos* and learning — never being satisfied, always striving for more, perfecting ourselves into becoming the Jews we have the potential to be.

Now my husband is teaching in a yeshiva here in Israel, writing *sefarim*, and doing *kiruv* (outreach) work with new *baalei teshuva*. For who can empathize better than one who has gone through the experience personally? This past Shavuos, we had the privilege of having a new *baalas teshuva* stay with us. Having grown up in a secular, left-wing kibbutz, she recently discarded its emptiness and, like Ruth, found inner strength and a new meaningful life for herself as a *frum* woman. She was thrilled with the whole concept of Shavuos as *Mattan Torah*, having only experienced it before as a secular "harvest festival." As we walked together to a midnight *shiur* for women, she looked up at the starry sky as if truly expecting it to open at any moment.

"*Hashem* is giving us the Torah tonight," she said with such joy in her voice, it was contagious. I told her that her enthusiasm was a real inspiration to me.

Then she thanked me for being a positive role model for her, as the woman she was striving to become.

❦ Continuing the Journey

If one of our sons should one day want to marry such a dedicated young woman, I would certainly give them my blessing and be proud to have her as my daughter-in-law.

HEADING A LARGE FAMILY

FAIGA KOENIG

Rabbi Neiman and family took close to two minutes to get on the bus. Nine kids scrambled for seats as he bought a youth ticket with twenty punches that would be finished before the sun set. The median age on the 33 bus was mid-40's, the day was hot and the looks were disapproving. One passenger said what a significant number of her fellow passengers were no doubt thinking: "Why don't you leave half of them at home?"

"I did," he answered.

This story is true. So is the one my neighbor told me about her attempts to rent an apartment in one of Brooklyn's heimishe neighborhoods. "Just how many children do you have?" asked the owner.

"Four lovely girls," she replied smiling sweetly. She didn't mention the ten lovely boys ….

Reb Nachman would say that if you want to know the soul of a nation, listen to their jokes. The jokes that people tell about families such as mine (14 lovely children and two shop-worn,

middle-aged parents, thank you) tell the truth. We are a belea-
guered species.

❧ Mother of Fourteen Tribes

The people making these jokes weren't with us in Meron the beautiful afternoon we sat outside the tomb of Rabbi Shimon Bar Yochai. It was Eliezer's big day. His third birthday was marked by his introduction to his identity as a Jew. The little person he would see in the mirror with a *kipa* and *peyos* is definitely a member of the chosen people. The entire family came for the occasion: five married siblings and their spouses and 10 tiny nieces and nephews. This is, of course, besides the eight brothers and sisters who share his life daily.

We were, indeed, a tribe. Like our patriarch Yaakov, I had crossed into Israel with almost nothing (and certainly no one). G-d in His mercy has given me all that I could have imagined, and more. We sang, took pictures, visited the holy places in Tzefas and ended the day at the shores of the Kinneret.

Eliezer is our youngest. He is treasured and beloved, the sunlight and joy of our household. He is far richer than I was at his age. I slept in splendid isolation in my own room. I had far more clothing (and far more fashionable outfits). I said goodnight to my doll collection nightly and entered a fantasy world in which there was sound, action, color, and most of all, drama. Eliezer lives in a room that he shares with four others. His days are rich and full. He is a fourteenth child. They do not have any idea of how precious he is, not only to me, but also to us all. They do not know that the light that he sheds was never shed by anyone quite like him.

They weren't with us when we left our tiny home on the arrestingly breathtaking hill on the *moshav* and rented an apartment in the heart of the city. There were two children's rooms. One was small. I thought that one or two children could have their quiet spot. Nobody wanted it. I relented, and allowed all five of the children to sleep together.

❧ Not Just a Secular Attitude

I am often asked how we ended up with more kids than fit on one side of my Israeli identity card. I find myself in the peculiar position of defending being the recipient of what is the greatest of blessings that G-d offers humans. It would be comforting to pretend that only secularists look askance at large families. The underlying assumption that we are martyred for having chosen a lifestyle in which both parents sacrifice the quality of their lives for the sake of living up to a religious principle is alive and well in the most surprising places. The spirit of the times has seeped into our attitudes toward children far more insidiously than we can even begin to calculate.

A young bride, the daughter of a *kollel* family, confided in her best friend's mother that she would be happy if she had no children during the first year or two of her marriage. "So many of my friends are divorced, I would want to be sure that my marriage is stable first." She teaches in one of the most prestigious elementary schools in the Torah community.

"I don't want to live like my mother," was the conclusion voiced by a minority (but still significant) number of young girls who were talking with surprising frankness in a class on marriage.

I sometimes find it hard to believe that these are the daughters of Rachel, who equated childlessness with death, and indeed was comforted in her final agony with the realization that she had brought a child to the world.

Rachel realized that each child that she brought into the world was unique. Each one of the Twelve Tribes was a building block in what later would be the Chosen People. She understood not only that having the merit to dedicate her heart and soul to forming a tribe of Israel was the most significant contribution that she could possibly make; it was for her the ultimate statement of her self-expression. Everything about her would live forever in her children. She is the bow and they are the arrows.

❋ *Feeling Like a Failure*

Kids are different than tribes. We all know that the Twelve Tribes have something to do with eternity, something to do with G-d's plan for the world. Kids, on the other hand, are seen by a lens that sees only the absolute present. They are dirty, noisy, and frequently disobedient. They stubbornly refuse to become what we envisioned for them. Only one tenth of them are in the upper tenth percentile in school. There are (surprisingly?) just as many in the lowest tenth percentile. The worst of all is that we feel like failures.

Until you get your first note home from kindergarten about the importance of combing the little *tzaddik*'s hair with a fine-toothed comb, you never even began to understand the hymn "You'll never walk alone." They are picky eaters, and dislike the whole-grain vegetable quiche that you saw in the cookbook. We feel like failures.

They are not like the children in the trendy Frovels (*frum* novels, which are a species of their own). They can break your façade of civility, and erode your self-esteem. And of course, at the end of a frustrating highly forgettable bedtime, the worst blow of all is the nagging voice of the Little Critic that tells you, still again, "You are a failure." We give the Voice credence. We have come to accept a definition of success and failure that is superficial, materialistic, and status oriented.

❋ *"My Child Isn't Mine ..."*

My second oldest daughter is the educational director of an unusual kindergarten. It services children who have physical and intellectual disabilities as well as healthy children. They learn together, play together in an atmosphere of mutual acceptance and harmony. She told me of an astonishing incident. The neighborhood mothers come to pick up their children at closing time. Efrat, Ronit's mother, is among the regulars who sit on the sunny stoop waiting for the kids to be escorted out. She was at the end of a pregnancy, and no doubt finds Ronit, who has multiple disabilities, quite a handful. One of the other regulars is Chavi. While she no doubt is a good person at heart, she often speaks first and thinks second. Her faux pas are usually somewhat amusing (What? You're only 41?). Today it could have led to murder-by-humiliation. After they had run out of remarks on the weather et a.l., she turned to Ronit's mother and said, "You must be nervous. After all, you may have another child with the same syndrome."

There was a second of silence so thick that it could be cut with a knife. It felt eternal. In that split second, my daughter, who heard the remark, would have paid a fortune for a credible distraction. Before she could speak, Efrat answered. In her usual sweet and deliberate style, she said. "My child isn't mine, he belongs to G-d. I'll be happy with whatever child He gives me."

Her measure of success and failure is real. It isn't colored by shallow standards of status, appearance, or expectation. She will never either be, or feel, like a failure.

⤜ *Growth Without Guilt*

The most important step in raising a large family joyously and successfully is trusting *Hashem*. He wants you to give no more than your maximum, nor to stunt you by wanting less from you. Once you have given what you can, accept that you are serving Him, and that the results ultimately are in His Hand. Once guilt, compulsion and anger are not your constant companions, you can begin to enjoy your family. Are there stresses? Of course. Does the same Torah that promises us that earning our bread will be a challenge tell us that raising children will be one as well? Aren't we told that neither the Future World nor Torah nor *Eretz Yisroel* can be acquired with ease? Isn't "striving" the source of any meaningful achievement, whether it is for a degree or a painting? The *Maharal* tells us that the reason that we struggle to achieve life's greatest goals is to force us into entering a state of self-transcendence. This is true in no area more than it is in child raising.

Rebbetzin Z. brought up her family of 18 children in a two-room apartment in Yerushalayim. They are now adults. Each one has grown to be an extraordinary member of the community. My eldest daughter sat next to her at a wedding. She couldn't resist asking her for her secret. She answered by telling a story: When her children were young, her 11-year-old (who is now a Rosh Yeshiva) was bored one afternoon. He went up to the roof of the building, and began to play with the solar heaters. He discovered that they move. Shortly after this discovery was made, one of them "somehow" was dislodged and crashed down to the street below. By G-d's mercy, no one was in the road where it smashed sending metal shards in every direction. His mother heard the noise, looked out and then up. She saw him trembling and pale, too terrified even to cry. At that point, the Rebbetzin said, she knew that she had a choice to make. "I asked myself, would he do this when he is 30? Of course, the answer is that he won't. I decided that this is not worth an emotional investment. We spoke. A repayment schedule was arranged, and the tragedy that was averted was discussed. I saved my emotional impact for things that could leave an imprint. When the children hurt each other, when they lied as children do, it was then that I invested myself."

Without questioning the powerful effect that Rebbetzin Z. had on her children, let us focus on how they affected her. They were the building blocks of her character! Our sense of success must include this part of our own evolution as well. This takes us to the crux of the issue. Everything that is permanent and real is invisible. The people who emerge from the tiny bodies are invisible. The self-transcendence is imperceptible, because we are myopic. What is visible can be so overwhelming that it eclipses everything else.

What Can We Do When We Are Overwhelmed?

Lisa stood on the porch and looked at the cloudless blue sky. She wanted to be anywhere else. The apartment felt like a prison. She rose mechanically in the morning, and "serviced" one child after another. Getting dressed seemed redundant. The clothes that she selected with such care were stained and faded from frequent laundering. The house was always half clean. She wanted beauty, ideas, information, and companionship. She looked once more at the sky, opened her mouth and screamed silently.

The easiest answer is to let the kids grow up a bit, and pray to never, never, never have any more. The problem is that a crucial fact is not discussed — a trade off is being made. No Eliezer. Maybe no Rikki or Yankel. Their songs will not be heard. The person you may have become as their mother is stunted.

Sometimes the trade off must be made. There are times when emotional or physical incapacity leaves little leeway for choices. A *rav* must be consulted. But whether he says yes or no, this, when made with open eyes, is a heartbreaker. When life is in danger we eat on Yom Kippur or break Shabbos. The Halachists tell us that, when possible, the act of desecration (e.g. calling the ambulance) should not be relegated to a child or an ignoramus. It should be done by a respected adult, since this is G-d's will for this situation, and we don't "second guess" Him. Great *rabbanim* of the previous generation were known to have encouraged and strengthened people who were forced into transgressions of this sort to do so with the *simcha* with which they would do anything else that *Hashem* wanted of them. However they didn't enjoin them to enjoy the view from the ambulance, or to put ketchup on food that is eaten on Yom Kippur in a situation of duress. It is far easier to imagine them comforting the person involved by pointing out that there will be many other opportunities to experience the delight of a halachic Shabbos or the awesome sanctity of Yom Kippur. When *bi'di'eved* becomes *lechat'chila*, we sentence ourselves to walking in darkness.

❧ Shuttling From the Crushing to the Ecstatic

How can we walk in light day to day, when the immediate can be crushing at one moment and ecstatic at the next? Having spent the last 34 years as a mother (as I write this, I cannot believe that this is really true; my image of myself is far younger than the 34 years of my parenthood), I will share a few observations.

1. Be good to yourself. Find the time to do what you need to in order to maintain a positive outlook. For some women this can mean a workout, for others a *shiur* or a part-time job. Give yourself social contact by making full use of Alexander Graham Bell's invention to broaden your horizons. Nourish your body with healthful foods. However, since the angst that many women feel isn't only physical, the most important thing of all is that you don't neglect your spirit. The wisest investment that I have ever made is investing 20 minutes a morning for *tefilla* when my children were still young, after having rushed through minimalist *davening* for years. It required my getting up (even) before the kids, but my sense of reality was grounded. I knew why I was here, I could look at myself and my family and feel *Hashem's* love for us. Everything was different. Don't cheat yourself by drying out your spirit!

The silence of dawn was the perfect backdrop for the words that I had been saying by rote. "*Baruch She'amar* — Blessed is He Who spoke and brought the world into being ... *Ezras Avoseinu* — You have helped our ancestors through their travails ... *Mechayei Hameisim* — Your revive life constantly." Nothing is dead or doomed! We must thank You for the miracles that You do morning, evening, and noon."

I had not seen the miracles. I was too absorbed by the ebb and flow of daily life. When I reentered the world of the ordinary, it was different. It was beautiful. Even crying sounded different. It is the sound of life.

2. Don't be "good" to yourself by escaping. You have to come back. There is an enormous difference between self-nurture and escape. One enhances the moment. The other avoids it. Don't "service" your children so that you can get on with "getting anything done." Don't deny yourself the scent of baby shampoo. As you spoon oatmeal in, and the rivulets of the fashionably colored liquid drip down the baby's chin, give yourself the time to make eye contact with her. Enjoy her wakefulness and wonder. Enjoy kindergarten theatrics and toddler art. Enjoy the process of their learning how to find their place in the world.

Our Shabbos guest no doubt thought that I was running a group home. She had never seen so many children under one roof in a non-institutional setting. She began by introducing herself. I prodded them into answering her. In a pre-school effort to make our guest feel at home, Aharon introduced himself as Closet. ["*Aron*" is the Hebrew word for closet.]

Reuven looked doleful as he entered the kitchen straight from school. He held my hand, and asked if I knew Lemech, Noach's father. I asked why he wanted to know. "He died," he told me gently. He had assumed that I was at least 5000 or so years old.

3. There will be tough times. Illnesses, teething, sleepless nights are all part of the package. There will be days when you don't cope, and interviews with teachers that you wish didn't happen. Your role is neither to be perfect, nor to have a perfect child. Your role is to give and to let the act of giving transform you. It is not always easy to know how to give. There will be times that the greatest gift is structure or disapproval, and far more times where the greatest gift is unconditional love and acceptance. Don't walk the road alone. Adam and Chava were the first parents; you do not have to start where they did. Read the books. Find a mentor. For some of us, the most natural mentor of all is our own parents. For far more of us, we must use our powers of observation to find the people who we can turn to for guidance. Never be ashamed to move beyond what you see doesn't work. Be open to new ideas.

4. Most of all, learn to turn to the One Who is the ultimate possessor of both our children and us. Be open to Him and turn to Him not only during *tefilla*, but moment by moment. He entrusted you with your children and knows both you and them.

Enjoy!

SHALOM BAYIS
A VIEW FROM YOUR CHILD'S EYES

RABBI SHMUEL GLUCK

❈ *Parents: The Most Effective Teachers*

What does it take to make a marriage successful? A successful marriage requires trust, commitment and sacrifice. It is not a coincidence that these same requirements are needed to make a good parent. Once we recognize this fact, we can succeed in both achieving a happy marriage and raising good children.

This following article is a compilation of discussions I had with troubled children, many of whom have become disillusioned with *Yiddishkeit*. The common theme is the correlation between homes blessed with *shalom bayis* and well-behaved children, and homes where arguments and friction are the norm and rebellious children. Although it would be inaccurate to say that good families do not sometimes find themselves with difficult children, the friendship within a close family slows a child's downfall and hastens his return back. Those in the *kiruv kerovim* (bringing religious Jews closer) field can often tell you which parents have a successful marriage and which do not, simply by speaking to their children.

What is the connection between being a good spouse and good parent? Our lives are complex, and throughout the day we play many roles. We are employees and employers, *rabbanim* and *shul* members. At home we are father, mother, and/or grandparent. One role that we all play is teacher — we teach others by example. It is this form of teaching that the *Tanna* was referring to when he said in *Avos*: From *all* I have learnt and have come to understand.

This acknowledgment places an enormous burden on the parent. Our actions are often public. How much do we affect others? How much of a responsibility do we have toward our children? As a parent, we have the greatest opportunity to teach our children. Our children instinctively come to look upon us as their leader and mentor.

Our greatest impact on our children is in regard to the *mitzvos bein adam lechaveiro* — interpersonal commands. And the greatest opportunity we have to demonstrate our care and concern in this area is by the way we interact with our spouses. As such, we must recognize *shalom bayis* as being the cornerstone of *chinuch banim ubanos* — educating our sons and daughters.

⟡ *Respect — The Necessary Ingredient*

Maximizing our ability to teach our children depends on one key ingredient: respect. In order to earn our children's respect, we must present ourselves as being worthy of emulating. We should be well rounded: successful in Torah, successful in supporting a family, and successful in interacting with family and friends. If children perceive their parent as failures, we cannot expect them to respect them.

Often children's only examples of "other" parents are at their friend's house, when the adults are generally on their best behavior. As a result, our children are deceived into thinking that their home is the only one with any arguments or difficulties. Specifically, in a home marked by lack of harmony, the child sees a lack of personal respect between his parents. Can a parent who cannot earn the respect of his — or her — own spouse become a positive role model for his child?

Nor can a parent who does not show respect for his wife expect his child to respect her. Demanding it conveys the message: Do as I say, not as I do. A wife who interrupts her husband in public has taught her children that one can follow their impulses, even at the expense of someone who is important to them.

Children are sensitive to the mood that prevails between spouses. A home that is permeated with stress makes them extremely uncomfortable. Children, girls in particular, will seek the solitude of their bedrooms and shut themselves off from their family. They will also eventually seek other circles of friends to compensate for the family they believe they lack. Unhappily, the alternatives may not always be desirable.

❖ Our Children — The Sum Total of Their Parents

There are several reasons children behave like their parents. The first is that they naturally follow the path that they have seen their entire life. Let me relate one particular story.

"Moshe" was brought up in what appeared to be a fine, typical home. His father, however, had a temper, constantly finding fault with his wife. Many of these arguments took place in front of the children, and they became accustomed to their parents' constant arguments. It was never clear to the children who was right or even who began the confrontations. Moshe obviously resented being brought up in such a home, but he was not aware of the deep anger that grew within him. He left his home at 14, and has hardly spoken to his family since.

My conversations with Moshe have always concluded with his repeating his strong resentment toward his father. Yet he continues to act more and more like the father from whom he is trying to distance himself. Part genes and part upbringing, a child cannot break away from the behavior he so dislikes by virtue of resentment alone. It takes a sincere commitment to change from the familiar, something most of us are unwilling to do. Moshe continues to subjectively distinguish between his temper and that of his father. He cannot, or is unwilling, to see the similarity between them. The terrible cycle begun by his parents continues.

Another student once confided to me, " My father lies in front of me. He does it to avoid confrontations. If he's late, he'll say there was traffic. I, too, have learnt to get my way." The father, though, laments to me why his son cannot talk straight. I can only wonder at the irony of the situation.

As parents, we forget that our home is our child's window to the outside world. If we act fairly to others, they will assume that all adults act fairly, especially those in the *frum* community. If not, they will assume that all adults are unfair, and again, particularly the *frum* community. The child will draw on these experiences when deciding whether or not he wants to remain *frum*.

Often, children decide that all adults are insincere or selfish. The source of this information is limited to one family: their own. With their biased, limited view, they confirm their belief. It is always important to bear in mind that your home is your child's model of the world.

✦ An Allegiance to Family

To a child, parents who argue appear as strangers living together. It seems to the child that there is no bond or commitment to each other. Family commitment is something that cannot be taught, but must be felt. The protection and caring of one for the other is an important lesson that can only be seen in the home.

A teenage friend of mine suggested the following insight: He has long disliked his father's treatment of his mother. He recently noticed that when he visited families for *Shabbos* he gravitates to the wife during conversation, feeling uncomfortable with the husband's presence. He added that another mutual friend gravitates toward the men because of his resentment over his mother's treatment of his father.

I have seen many young couples who are intuitively caring and receptive spouses. Without direct lessons from their parents, they seem to naturally follow what they have seen in the home. Couples who work out issues smoothly are often the offspring of a happy and respectful upbringing. They have noticed many subtle gestures. A parent will offer small talk to break the ice after a fight. Another parent will always compliment the spouse's appearance. These subtleties become ingrained in their children and are repeated during their own marriage.

It is worth mentioning that to our children, we are larger than life. What is actually a small argument may appear to our children to be much more significant. Children with little self-esteem, in particular, interpret these incidents as being of greater importance than they truly are. Often, without any clear reason, they blame themselves for their parents' arguments.

In addition, we often argue in front of our family, yet apologize privately. Our children are only seeing half the story, missing the happy ending. Often, the true cause of friction is never revealed to them: a bad day at work, or a sick grandparent. The younger our children are, the less are they able to interpret what they witness.

❧ *Quarreling Parents — Dealing With the Problem*

*C*hinuch under ideal situations is difficult; when parents disagree, it is almost impossible. While no two people agree on everything, what can parents do when they disagree on everything? First, they must recognize that children are masters of interpreting the unspoken word. They intuitively recognize signs of uncertainty, dishonesty, and a lack of unity. They may interpret the passivity of one parent as a sign of disagreement. They will then move to take advantage of this, believing that this conflict will not allow parents to effectively monitor them. In general, one of the main weaknesses of parents is failure to recognize the depth of their children's understanding of the nuances of body language. Children will often manipulate parents into internal conflicts, distracting them from their mutual goal: *Chinuch*.

Parents who disagree should honor the following guidelines: Ideally, parents should have someone experienced and accessible to speak with, someone with whom both parents feel comfortable. He must know and understand their child, as well as the general relationship of the parents and their ability to be *mechanech* (educate) their children. Honesty is of the utmost importance when seeking advice.

❧ *Differences in Dealing With Discipline*

When there is no one available, I suggest the following rules: The parent who believes in the method being promoted should be the one implementing it. The same parent must "clean up" from any problems. For instance, if one parent wants to strongly criticize a child during an already tense moment, that parent must deal with the ensuing tantrum. If a child constantly runs toward one parent, that parent has a strong say in the method of discipline, as he is the one dealing with the crying child.

What should you do when a child, after having had an argument with your spouse, asks for your support, and you feel your spouse was unjustified? You can neither agree nor argue with your spouse. Yet you must convey to your child his responsibility for the encounter. The proper response should sound like this: "You know your father/mother gets upset when you do that. You should have expected he/she will punish/scream at you for that."

How should a parent respond when his or her spouse constantly overreacts? Here, a more dramatic approach is needed. Don't wait for the next confrontation: Show your conviction toward the issue. (Conviction is not anger or resentment, simply a strong belief in his mistake, conveying that you will not back down until this issue is settled.) If his or her methods are as extreme as you believe they are, take him or her to someone both respect.

Remember to deal with policy, and not individual cases. Individual cases are personal. General rules are broader and can be accepted more readily. Be prepared. By being forceful, you might have to undertake the bulk of the *chinuch*, oversee recreation time, and supervise most of their homework, as well.

In extreme cases it might be necessary to calmly, and privately, confirm to the child that you feel the other parent is being too harsh, and that you will work with him (the child) if, he in turn, will work with you. Do not legitimize angry or impulsive behavior as ever being justified. You must, without anger, convey, "Nobody's perfect, not even parents. But it is still your responsibility to avoid behavior that causes anger." In general, I believe children do not have to believe parents are perfect, just that despite their mistakes they mean well.

❦ *In Conclusion*

Marriage is a deceptive relationship. The idealistic optimism of the new *chassan* and *kalla* gives way to the realization that they have committed themselves to a responsibility that will take all the energy and resources they can muster. A strong marriage is a worthy and necessary project, as it becomes a role model for our children, grandchildren, and our community.

I would like to conclude with the *Maharal*'s statement in the Gemora: "A proper match is as difficult as the splitting of the Sea." The *Maharal* adds that the miracle is not in finding the match, but in keeping the couple happily together for the rest of their lives. Let us work on this daily miracle, proving us worthy of a home where the *Shechina* resides within our walls.

PREPARATION FOR MARRIAGE: PREVENTION FOR DIVORCE

DR. MEIR WIKLER

"Dovid, if you don't chazer the Gemara more often, they will never accept you in the Mesivta!"

"You'd better study your Chumash, Esta, if you're serious about attending Seminary next year!"

These are familiar sounds in any Torah home. Preparation for all levels of Torah study is taken seriously by many of today's parents. These parents are not professional educators, only *shomrei mitzvos*, following the teachings of the *Gemara* (*Kiddushin* 29a), that preparing a child (and providing) for Torah study is a major parental responsibility.

The *Gemara* also includes preparation for other of life's necessities, such as having a trade and being able to swim, in this list of parental responsibilities. With equal zeal, then, parents also plan for their children's vocational training. Finding the proper *shidduch*, the *Gemara* explains, is another top priority.

Unfortunately, the preparation often stops there. Certainly *finding* the proper *shidduch* for a child is extremely important, but do parents look to the finding of a *shidduch* as the entirety of their assignment, or perhaps part of a more complex chapter in parental responsibility?

Today, marriage (and parenthood) are taken too much for granted. At 19, 20, or 22, 23, a seminary graduate and a *yeshiva bachur* are automatically considered ready for marriage, without any preparation. To be proper spouses and parents are probably the greatest challenges they will ever face, and yet they are expected to face these challenges totally without preparation. Why should immature members of our community be permitted to flounder in the sea of family life without adequate swimming lessons?

No, our *Bobbes* and *Zaydes* never had preparation for marriage beyond what they saw at home. But, then again, their generation also did not witness the epidemic of divorces plaguing the Torah community today, and required no additional pointers.

Needless to say, many complex factors contribute to the tragic breakdowns of today's young families, but certainly, with proper preparation, at least some of them could have been prevented. A brief case history will illustrate one type of marital breakdown which perhaps could have been prevented.

✦ The Case of Rivka*

Rivka was always a good student and her parents heard only praises from her teachers. Although quiet, she kept up with a small circle of close friends all during her elementary school years.

Shortly after beginning high school, however, Rivka seemed to become even more quiet than before. Her contacts with friends decreased and the occasional smile was now seldom seen on her face.

Rivka's parents attributed her seriousness to the increased academic demands of high school. "Surely by next year," they reasoned, "Rivka will outgrow this."

---

*While the cases cited here are drawn from this author's professional practice. it must be stressed that all identifying information has been thoroughly disguised to protect the confidentiality of the individuals involved. Any similarities between these cases and any actual situation known to the reader should be attributed only to the widespread nature of this problem.

By her senior year, Rivka had no friends, went out of the house only for errands and school, and spent most of her time in her room.

Her parents received positive reports of Rivka's academic progress, and they continued to assume that she would "outgrow" her withdrawn nature. Student teaching in seminary, they concluded, would help to "bring her out."

Two years later, the picture remained the same. By now, many of Rivka's classmates were becoming engaged. Her parents speculated that she was envious of the other girls, yearning for her own *chassan*. They inquired about *shidduchim* and after several meetings with Chaim, a well-recommended *talmid* from a high caliber yeshiva, they encouraged Rivka to accept his marriage proposal.

Before the end of her first year of marriage, Rivka became so upset with marital problems that she wanted to leave Chaim and move back to her parents' home. Both sets of parents encouraged the couple to consult a Rav, who eventually referred them for professional help.

Chaim refused to meet with the professional and preferred to speak with another Rav. Two years later, after many frustrated efforts to resolve the marital conflicts, Rivka and Chaim were divorced. Chaim remained in the couple's apartment and Rivka returned to her parents' home with her baby.

Rivka's parents knew of the first Rav's efforts to refer Rivka and Chaim for professional help, so they encouraged her to meet with the family counselor.

Chaim was never seen by the counselor. From Rivka's reports of his behavior, however, it was clear that he also brought his own "*peckel'eh*" of emotional difficulties to the marriage.

In time, with professional help, Rivka unraveled the mysteries of her own feelings. She was able to trace her emotional problems back, as the reader has undoubtedly already done, well before her marriage, to her high school days. A detailed record of the treatment process is not relevant to the purpose of article. Suffice it to say that Rivka has since gotten a job, established her own home, and has begun to build meaningful and satisfying friendships.

The crucial aspect of this case was the relationship between Rivka and her parents. Although they were deeply concerned and loving parents, they felt more comfortable consulting Rivka's teachers and a Rav than consulting Rivka herself. It was never easy for them to sit down and talk with any of their four children. Rivka, however, was the hardest to talk with because she was the youngest. As a result, she was the first to be overlooked by her parents.

No one can say just what would have happened if Rivka's parents had made greater efforts to really get to know her. It is, of course, quite possible that their initiatives might have been rebuffed by Rivka, anyway. In other words, just because her parents would have tried to learn from Rivka what was bothering her does not mean that she would have been able to tell them. Nevertheless, greater direct involvement by Rivka's parents could have resulted, at the very least, in seeking professional help while she was still in high school. Had she done so, it is very possible that her trip to the *chupa* would have been only "one way."

❖ What Can Be Done?

Case illustrations are as dangerous as they are helpful. Defensive, frightened parents can read Rivka's story and respond smugly, "Oh, that doesn't apply to us!"

Rivka's story, however, is unfortunately all too common. Many parents raise their yeshiva and Bais Yaakov children today without ever really getting to know them.

All of this may sound to some people like a modern, secular point of view. "Train a youngster in accordance with his ways" (*Mishlei* 22,6), however, would seem to imply that parents are required by the Torah to examine the unique individuality of each child's feelings, attitudes, abilities and aspirations (see *Metzudas Dovid* ibid.)

Preparation for marriage, then, like preparation for *any* of life's goals, involves parental teaching, modeling, guiding, advising, and listening. This preparation process, which must be tailor made to fit each parent and child, should be based on a solid, foundation of parental understanding of their child's individuality and specific needs.

Parents should not shoulder the entire responsibility alone. Teachers, *rabbonim,* and *rebbeim* — the parental surrogates for *limud* Torah — also need to focus more attention on the unique emotional and personality needs and differences among their *talmidim.*

Furthermore, marriage preparation classes and study groups are needed, within the Torah atmosphere of the yeshiva. At best, only the regular *"chassan* and *kalla* classes" are now offered. These accelerated courses often deal only with the laws of *taharas hamishpacha* (family purity). This is certainly necessary, but not sufficient.

Several Torah institutions, however, have taken the initiative of providing their students with a broader-based preparation for marriage. Hopefully, their pioneering efforts will pave the way for others to follow.

The Be'er Yaakov Yeshiva, in Israel, offered a series of *vaadim,* or small group conferences, with the *Mashgiach Ruchani,* Rabbi Shlomo Wolbe זצ״ל, on topics of marital life. In these *vaadim,* Rabbi Wolbe discussed such topics as: the emotional needs of a wife and the husband's responsibility to meet them; the qualitative differences between the close relationship of a *bachur* and his *chavrusa* and the husband-wife relationship; the meaning to a wife of the appearance of the home; the emotional and spiritual differentiation between man and woman, and how this can lead to a harmonious complimentarity or, *chas vesholom,* to frustrating conflict.

Rabbi Wolbe printed a booklet of these discussions which, due to the specific legacy of his late father-in-law, Rabbi Avrohom Grodzensky זצ״ל, is not available to the public.

Rabbi Wolbe had written a second booklet, in consultation with Rebbetzin Jacobson of Jerusalem, designed for young women, which is available to the general public. This booklet, together with a foreword written by Rabbi Yehuda Meisels, has been published by the Beth Jacob Sara Schenirer High School and Teachers Seminary in Brooklyn.

In the second booklet, Rabbi Wolbe discusses such topics as: the impact of life in a yeshiva dormitory on a *bachur,* and the many changes needed for him to adjust to married life; the importance of patience and tolerance from both *chassan* and *kalla* during the first year of marriage; the necessity of avoiding the all-too-common hazard of sharing private, husband-wife matters with others — friends or relatives.

One particular girls' school in the New York area sponsors voluntary marriage-oriented discussion groups for the senior class, led by a married professional who adheres to the same Torah values held by the Yeshiva. In these discussions, the girls have the opportunities to share their expectations for and apprehensions of courtship and marriage, as well as to clarify many of their misconceptions.

(Another girls' school has only had these classes intermittently, because a key ingredient to these classes is the teacher, who must be both knowledgeable and an ideal role model. An appropriate member of the religious studies class has not always been available. — Editor)

Mrs. Shulamis Rogoff, a consultant to one school's discussion groups, remarked, "Some of the girls are very upset by the current attitudes associated with dating and *shidduchim*." Mrs. Rogoff has found that these groups provide the girls with an opportunity to share their concerns openly and learn that they are not alone, out of step or "crazy."

The girls speak for themselves:

"When a *shidduch* will be *redd* (spoken) to me, I know that means that I will be looked over by so many other people that it makes me sick. Sometimes, I feel that I'd rather not go out than to face this 'marriage market' ordeal!"

"Somehow, I find it all so confusing. For 18 years it gets drummed into my head that I'm not supposed to talk to, look at, or even *think* about boys. Then, all of a sudden, literally 'over night,' I'm supposed to be able not only to go out with boys but also to feel *relaxed on the date!*"

"I'd like to know: Why are all decisions about marriage supposed to be made by the fourth or fifth date? Just knowing that I would have that kind of a deadline would make me too nervous to evaluate a situation clearly!"

Ultimately these discussions help the girls to gain a clearer understanding of marriage, in general, and themselves, in particular, all from a Torah perspective and in a Torah environment.

Mrs. Rogoff points out that another one of the goals of these sessions is to help the girls clarify what it is they really want in a *shidduch*. For example, she talks with the girls about where they will place the relationship factor on their list of priorities.

"Even though the girls don't believe me," she adds, "I often remind them that the *boys* are usually worried about some of the same issues."

The examples cited above are, unfortunately, exceptions rather than the rule. It is hoped that more of these kinds of opportunities will be provided to help prepare their *talmidim* for marriage.

Yeshivos and seminaries, however, will follow the lead only after the Torah community as a whole recognizes its responsibility on an individual, family level. The topics addressed in the *vaadim* and the discussion groups mentioned above are those which can be dealt with at home, as well.

❊ *When the Class Could Have Helped*

In the case of Rivka, cited above, her parents were certainly not "responsible" for her divorce. Divorce has many causal factors, only some of which can be avoided. The emotional problems that Chaim brought to the marriage, for example, were clearly beyond the control of Rivka's parents. Nevertheless, had her parents prepared Rivka more thoroughly for marriage, that divorce *might* have been prevented.

It is highly doubtful, however, whether marriage-oriented discussion groups, as described above, would have helped Rivka. If such a group had been available to her, she might have chosen not to attend. Even if she did attend, she would have been quite passive and uninvolved. Her emotional problems were too deeply rooted at home. In other cases, however, in spite of problems originating in the family, a yeshiva or seminary can play a vital role in preparing young people for marriage and thereby prevent divorce.

❧ The Case of Reuven

*R*euven comes from what could be described as a "middle-of-the-road Orthodox" family. Although his father did not have an extensive yeshiva background, Reuven's parents did not object to his decision to continue his full-time yeshiva studies after high school. While they did question him about his future vocational plans and prospects, they never pressured him to leave the yeshiva.

At 26, Reuven was not the oldest bachur in the yeshiva, but all of his friends were already married. Even though his parents did not pressure him to get married, Reuven still felt overwhelmed by the subtle social pressure of his peers.

Reuven had always been a somewhat tense young man. This was due, in part, to the marital conflict between his parents, which he observed at home. Reuven adapted to the unpleasant family environment by ignoring it to the best of his ability. When he couldn't ignore it, he planned elaborate avoidance maneuvers. Reuven learned to use a similar approach in dealing with all of his anxieties. They never went away, nor did his parents' marital conflict disappear; but at least he was able to live with them.

When Reuven's chavrusa (study partner), two years his junior, became engaged, Reuven panicked. He had often felt self-conscious, but now he felt even more so. He was tormented by his bachur status and felt compelled to get married.

Reuven's apprehensions were not unusual, but his way of dealing with them had some very unfortunate consequences.

What were Reuven's worries? First of all, he was afraid that he would make an improper mate selection and thereby condemn himself to repeat his parents' turmoil. In addition, since many of his parents' arguments focused on financial matters, Reuven feared poverty. With no realistic vocational plans, Reuven hesitated taking on the financial responsibility of marriage. Finally, Reuven knew that he had coped with unpleasant feelings in the past by ignoring them and he had handled anxiety-provoking situations by strategically planning to avoid them.

Even while out on a date, Reuven was plagued with these thoughts and was painfully aware of how inadequate his old adaptations were to this *new situation. "How absurd! Here I am going out and at the same time I'm hoping that nothing really comes of it!"*

Characteristically, he did not discuss his fears with any friends although he was most eager to do so. But even Reuven couldn't completely suppress his fears of marriage by the time he turned 26.

He consulted the Mashgiach of his yeshiva. He was so self-conscious, however, that he could not be completely open and failed to present his problem in its fullest proportions. He posed the problem in vague financial terms, and as a result, received an inadequate response. How could the Mashgiach know what was really troubling Reuven?

Reuven finally did become engaged to Chaya, a seminary graduate now working as a secretary. When thinking of his vocational plans, he tried, unsuccessfully, to satisfy himself with vague generalities and abstract prospects. Every time he thought about it, he became more and more anxious. In addition, the slightest, normal disagreement with Chaya aggravated his fears of repeating his parents' mistakes. Furthermore, the multitude of new situations with Chaya, future in-laws, wedding plans, and so on, challenged his avoidance strategies. He had difficulty learning as his uncertainties snowballed, became depressed, feared it was noticeable and tried desperately to hide this, too.

Reuven's marriage to Chaya lasted for an agonizing five months.

Although Chaya certainly could have been much more supportive to Reuven, his apprehensions and anxieties clearly planted the seeds for this divorce. While many of Reuven's worries originated at home, questions about financial responsibilities in marriage, about coping with the future, inevitable strains in the husband-wife relationship, and about avoiding the pitfalls of one's parents are most common. Many young men and women share similar, even identical concerns. Some of them diffuse the time bomb of these concerns with hours of "heart to heart" talks with friends, relatives, and *rabbonim*. A large number of young men and women, however — similar to Reuven — try to cope with these valid questions by ignoring them or suppressing them. In spite of such efforts, these questions often reappear later, in much more frightening and unmanageable dimensions.

Reuven was convinced that his *Mashgiach* would have ridiculed him, had he shared his fears openly. That is most doubtful. Nevertheless, if a marriage-oriented discussion group or *vaad* had been available to him, it is likely that Reuven would have attended. Even if he wouldn't have "opened up" there, hearing the similar concerns of others might have had a positive, cathartic effect in calming his tensions.

Shortly after his divorce, Reuven sought guidance at a local vocational guidance service. The perceptive counselor referred Reuven to a psychotherapist for individual counseling. This counseling, in part, addressed issues of concern for Reuven which could have been effectively handled in a pre-marital discussion group. Had this been the case, it is quite possible that Reuven and Chaya's divorce might have been prevented.

◆ Conclusion

There are no easy answers for difficult questions. Even if parents and *mechanchim* work to get to know their children and students more intimately and work to provide opportunities for marital life education, divorce will not be eliminated entirely from the Torah community. As mentioned earlier, each case of divorce within the community is caused by a unique set of many factors., only some of which may be avoidable. Nevertheless, if even one divorce is prevented, this work will be well worth the effort.

In addition to the *"kol chassan v'kol kalla,"* then, perhaps we will be hearing sounds which will lead to more sustained *simcha* and *sasson*, such as:

"You know, Temmy, there is more to becoming a kalla than just selecting a diamond ring ... "

"Yaakov, there is more to becoming a chassan than simply deciding who should be the eidim under the chupa ..."

Solomon's Nightmare
Custody Disputes That Put Orthodox Children at Risk

Dr. Sylvan Schaffer

This article by Dr. Sylvan Schaffer provides valuable information and insights in regard to matters that must be addressed in marital separation agreements and in court orders dealing with children whose lives are so seriously affected by the dissolution of a marriage. Sadly, with considerable frequency, in the bitterness that often attends divorce, the parties lose sight of the best interests of the children. We have in the past addressed the need for greater civility and less confrontation in the divorce process. Unless we rid divorce of the extreme personal bitterness, the ability to accomplish the laudatory goals that Dr. Schaffer addresses will be hard to achieve. Where war is the first order of the day, children become pawns in the battle and ultimately its first casualties. To minimize collateral damage, religious divorces must also be civil.

Zalman Abraham, father of three sons who attend a yeshiva day school in Chicago, is ordered by a court to send his sons to spend several weeks during the summer with his ex-wife, who, despite attending Bais Yaakov schools from childhood, has aban doned religious observance. To "get back" at her former husband, she takes the boys to non-kosher restaurants, enrolls them in a Catholic day camp, and takes them to a circus on the Seventeenth of Tamuz (a fast day).

- Baruch Isaacs, who still wears a yarmulke and a beard, is awarded custody of Avi, his teenage son, after a protracted court battle. Dena Isaacs' lawyer assumes that Baruch will certainly keep Avi in a yeshiva, and therefore the custody agreement states only that the boy must attend "a Jewish school." Baruch then moves to Connecticut, where he enrolls Avi in a Conservative day school. The mother's legal challenge to this move is rejected by the courts.

- Batsheva Yellin is ordered by a court to drive her children on Shabbos to meet with Mark, their father, who is no longer observant.

- Ahuva Sanders, who became observant sometime after her marriage, files for divorce and is granted custody of her four young children. Her ex-husband, Stanley, then charges that the children are being raised in a cult and persuades a judge to take the children away from their mother and out of yeshiva. The children are now attending public school and Ahuva has very limited contact with them.

* * *

These anecdotes are based on real cases,* some of which were brought to the attention of Agudath Israel of America in search of legal assistance in resolving these dilemmas. Imagine the trauma and shame for children brought up to be strictly observant and *yirei Shamayim*, who are forced to get into a car on *Shabbos*, sometimes in front of their friends and neighbors. Picture the horror of a caring parent, a *shomer mitzvos*, who is watching this occur after pleading in court to prevent this scene!

It is our responsibility to do whatever possible to make certain that these unfortunate situations are either avoided or minimized.

---

* The names and identifying details of these cases have been changed to protect the confidentiality of the parties.

First, however, it is essential to understand how helpless and vulnerable children become trapped in such a state of affairs.

❧ Root Causes of Tragic Situations

These scenarios are the end result when child-custody disputes arise between divorcing spouses who differ in their religious observance and philosophy. This happens in two primary ways: First, both parents were originally observant and one later began to stray from observance; or second, the couple was originally non-observant and one party became more religious and raised the children in this manner with the consent of the non-practicing parent. When these parents decide to divorce, the religious upbringing of the children becomes an issue, and sometimes may be used as a weapon despite the damaging impact it may have on the children.

In addition — this is especially true for families living outside of large Orthodox communities — when the couple begins the divorce process, they may engage attorneys who themselves are not Jewish or observant, and therefore may not be familiar with the religious nuances and requirements that must be put into matrimonial agreements in order to protect the children. For example, the agreement may say that the children must be raised as "Jewish," without defining the specifics of what that means, i.e. Orthodox, Conservative or Reform, or failed to spell out the myriad ramifications of "raising a child as an Orthodox Jew": Shabbos, *Kashrus*, and educational influences. Thus, the critical details of a child's religious upbringing may be left up to a judge to define, and he may have little knowledge about such matters, or may harbor negative myths about Orthodox religious practices.

Such cases may ultimately be dealt with through litigation by attorneys and expert witnesses who are familiar with such issues and the psychological impact they can have on the children, but this method is usually pursued as a last resort. Litigation is generally resorted to only after other methods have been tried and failed, since trials are very costly, and the child may already be in the traumatic situation while the lengthy litigation process grinds on. Also, the outcome of a trial is uncertain, since a judge will make the decision, which is then imposed on the parents.

❧ *An Alternative: Early Prevention*

Far more effective is early prevention. Planning for the religious needs of the children must begin very early, and the rabbinate can play a very important role in making their congregants aware of the need for such planning. The rabbi often has been involved with a couple since the early stages of their relationship, including the premarital period.

A *rav* may detect early warning signs and then speak to the couple about his observations. He may suggest ways to strengthen their marriage before the divorce process even gets under way. Such prevention, aimed at preserving *shalom bayis*, enhances the spiritual and psychological environment of the children, as well.

There may be times, however, when the marriage cannot be saved and the parties begin the divorce process. This stage is not too early to launch the prevention process, aimed at avoiding the tragic scenarios that opened this article. At this point, the parent should seek out an attorney who is not only knowledgeable about family law, but also familiar with the full range of needs of an Orthodox family. If such an attorney is not available, experts may be enlisted with whom the attorney would consult about these issues. One such expert is the rabbi, who can explain the vital religious details to the attorney. Also, the attorney can consult with Orthodox attorneys who can highlight key points that should be included in the separation, custody, or visitation agreement, and indicate time-tested approaches to avoiding unfortunate cases similar to those in the opening anecdotes.

Although the other parent may not cooperate prior to going to court, the Orthodox parent may attempt to bring the other party to a *beis din*, which would certainly be conversant with the religious issues. In addition, the parties may seek mediation with a knowledgeable, neutral party so that these issues may be dealt with in a non-adversarial environment.

⟨ *Some Important Points*

There are several points that are important in formulating separation, custody, and visitation agreements. First, religious issues should be dealt with explicitly. Sometimes, they are actually overlooked. Second, general terms such as "Jewish," "kosher," or "Jewish education" do not in themselves convey enough information. Such terms need modifiers that are more specific. For example, "kosher" should be defined as to the specific types of *hashgacha* (rabbinical supervision) that are acceptable. Examples of the types of schools should be given, or specific schools should be named. If something is too difficult to define or specify at that time, one can name a rabbi whose definitions will resolve ambiguity problems, thus avoiding litigation.

It is also important to include specifics about the future of the children's religious upbringing. These include: the type of *shul* that the children will attend; the distance from *shul* within which they must live; who will pay for the yeshiva education, and until what age; the specific neighborhoods and cities that are acceptable; the living arrangements in the home (especially who else will be living in the home); remarriage; what name the children will call a new spouse; which parent has control of religious standards; standards of religious practice in the non-observant parent's home during visitations, and methods of verification; *bar mitzvas* and weddings (religious, financial, and family issues); travel outside the country (i.e. studying in *Eretz Yisroel*); role of grandparents; arbitration by *beis din*; choice of doctors and therapists; summer camps; visitation schedules (especially as they involve Shabbos and *Yom Tov*); and other similar issues.

It is essential to make the agreement clear enough so that judicial involvement may be avoided or minimized, and the religious definitions are not left open for a judge to interpret. If religious observance issues are spelled out clearly in the visitation and custody agreement, they are usually upheld by the courts. If religious observance issues are not spelled out clearly, the result is quite often the horror stories recounted at the beginning of this article.

Parents need to take these actions as early as possible in the custody process. Courts may question a parent's sincerity if an activity, which is labeled as objectionable, has been allowed to continue for a long period without protest. It should be emphasized to a judge that the child's religious observance is of interest even to a secular court, since its lack of continuity may have negative impact on a child's psychological stability.

❧ A Communal Concern

These religion-based custody cases provide the Orthodox community with an opportunity to assist children who are suffering greatly, and whose lives may be drastically altered by the ordeal. The community should provide emotional, financial, and informational support to the family in a time of personal and spiritual crisis. With proper planning and care, the children can be spared such traumatic experiences.